Wildflower

The Love Song From Heaven

Lesley Ann Richardson

ISBN: 978-1-4866-2520-8
eBook ISBN: 978-1-4866-2521-5

Word Alive Press
119 De Baets Street Winnipeg, MB R2J 3R9
www.wordalivepress.ca

WORD ALIVE
—P R E S S—

Cataloguing in Publication information can be obtained from Library and Archives
Canada.

Dedicated to
All the free and gentle "Wildflowers"
who have loved this song

I dream a shadow fallen on the street,
And the last words he said were written in red
As he handed me his pen and his gun, saying,
"Take one and run;
There are words and there are deeds to be done":
A choice of two lives to be living, with time enough only for one;
The hand that writes the love song also holds the gun,
And strangely enough
It's all out of love ...

CONTENTS

PROLOGUE

THE BEGINNING OF it all was such a simple incident. Yet the events of the next few minutes would alter forever the destiny of David Richardson, and affect the lives of countless others for decades to come. The year was 1970, and Dave was a young Canadian policeman living and working in his hometown of Victoria, British Columbia. As well as his role in law enforcement, Dave was a songwriter, composing perhaps three or four lyrics a night, especially when in the midst of a romance.

As it happened, that was the case at the present. He was head over heels in love with his girlfriend, Jo, who worked as a nurse at the Jubilee Hospital. They were both caught up in their relationship, living on a mixture of youth, excitement and adrenaline, so they often showed up at work a little short on sleep. On this particular occasion, Dave had arrived at Jo's apartment, preparatory to their evening out together.

He knocked, and a few seconds later Jo opened the door. He saw straight away she was upset, so much so that she was trying to hold back tears. She was still wearing a housecoat, and her hair was wrapped in a towel.

"What's the matter?" he asked, alarmed.

"Can I talk to you?–I need to speak to someone," she responded, drawing him inside.

They sat together on the couch, and her words came tumbling out. Two elderly ladies she was caring for in the hospital had died that day while she was at work; Jo had come to know them well over a period of time, had become close to them, and was overcome with sadness. As she spoke, seemingly finding some release in voicing her feelings, Dave listened sympathetically. Finally she seemed calmer.

"Thank you for listening; I feel so much better. I'll go and get ready now," she said, managing a tremulous smile.

She went into the bedroom and closed the door, while Dave sat and watched television. As the minutes kept passing and she still did not return, he eventually rose and tapped gently on her door. There was no response, so he pushed open the door and went in. There she was, fast asleep on the bed, still dressed in her housecoat with the towel wrapped around her head.

Dave realized Jo had been utterly worn out by her emotional day; he placed a blanket over her, being careful not to waken her, and went home. The minute he arrived, he pulled out his notebook and pen. The words began welling into his consciousness like cool water into a fountain, seemingly without his volition; it seemed all he did was hold the pen, and the thoughts came from elsewhere:

> *She's faced the hardest times you could imagine*
> *And many times her eyes fought back the tears*
> *And when her youthful world was about to fall in*
> *Each time her slender shoulders*
> *Bore the weight of all her fears*
> *And a sorrow no one hears*
> *Still rings in midnight silence*
> *In her ears …*
>
> *Let her cry, for she's a lady*
> *Let her dream, for she's a child*
> *Let the rain fall down upon her*
> *She's a free and gentle flower, growing wild.*
> *Be careful how you touch her for she'll awaken*
> *And sleep's the only freedom that she knows*
> *And when you walk into her eyes you won't believe*
> *The way she's always paying for a debt she never owes*
> *And a silent wind still blows, that only she can hear*
> *And so she goes …*
> *And if by chance that I should hold her*
> *Let me hold her for a time*
> *But if allowed just one possession*
> *I would pick her from the garden*
> *To be mine.*

The poem was finished in about fifteen minutes, and following that the story of its recording and release as a hit song was entirely serendipitous. Dave passed the lyrics along to his young friend David Foster, a brilliant pianist who would later become Canada's most famous musical producer. At the time, he was only on the threshold of his career, and together with vocalist B.J. Cook[1] was forming a group called Skylark,[2] after the bird with the dazzling array of notes. He in turn gave the poem to guitarist Doug Edwards, along with a stack of other lyrics, and as Doug leafed through them he was struck by the lines Dave had penned. He knew they had to be recorded, and composed the poignant melody on the organ in about half an hour–just a little longer than it had taken Dave to write the words.

The ballad was recorded for Skylark's first album, and is the only song on which Foster does not play. As the session began, he felt that piano sounded too schmaltzy, so he and organist Robbie King retired to the control room. Doug Edwards was left in the studio with drummer Duris Maxwell and bass player Steve Pugsley, and felt a moment of panicked inspiration. This was the first song he'd written, and he knew he must give it his all. He launched into the guitar solo intro that was to set the bar for rock ballads for decades to come. For four minutes these young master musicians poured their hearts into what they thought was a practice run-through. As the last notes faded, Doug said, "Quick, let's record it before I forget what I played!"

"I've already got it!" Producer Eirik Wangberg was inspired to hit the record button, and without anyone knowing had captured that incomparable performance. This first take became the bed track for the Skylark release, augmented with harp played by Gayle Levant, strings arranged by Jimmie Haskell, and background effects imagined by Bobby Taylor.

Lead vocals were added by singer Donny Gerrard, whose musical range and power of expression seemed tailor-made for the song. His passionate rendition of Dave's lyrics appeared to mesh perfectly with Doug's haunting guitar solo, and when Dave first heard the recording he was amazed at the felicitous marriage of words and music. The composition as a whole seemed to express exactly the emotions which were filling his mind and heart the night he left Jo's place and went home to set down the words of the song.

When the recording was completed, David phoned Dave from California. "Your song is out of the can and onto the album," he told his friend, "but we need a title. What do you want to call it?"

Dave thought for a minute, running through the lyrics in his mind, until he came to the last line of the chorus. "Call it 'Wildflower,'" he said, "but make it one word, not two."

"That's great," agreed David. "By the way," he added, "this means that you're going to make probably two hundred to five hundred dollars in royalties."

"That's nice," said Dave.

Skylark's first album was released in 1972 by Capitol Records. The first two singles didn't make it to the charts, but Rosalie Trombley, an influential hitmaker at CKLW, Windsor/Detroit, listened to the album and said, "You have one hit here and it's called 'Wildflower.' I'll play it for two weeks, and if Capitol doesn't make it a single I'll take it off the playlist." She was as good as her word, but Capitol didn't want to venture a third single from Skylark's album.

Yet—they had reckoned without Rosalee. After two weeks she had fallen in love with the song, and kept playing it for another month. When Capitol still hadn't released a single, she finally had to take it off the air, and immediately received calls from all over Windsor and Detroit asking: *"Where's that song?"* When Capitol got wind of this, they printed 10,000 singles and sent them to the metropolis, where they sold out on the first day.

So the song started as a hit in Detroit, and following that became enormously popular in New York, a success which accompanied it down the eastern seaboard to Miami, and north again to Seattle—"It's like a wave," thought Dave. Skylark released "Wildflower" again as the title track of their second album shortly before the band disbanded. Eventually the song was played throughout the whole of the United States and Canada, and became a huge soul hit before crossing over to the pop charts, where it spent twenty-one weeks and reached Number 9 on the Billboard Top 200. It went on to achieve Number 10 on the RPM Top Singles, and Number 1 on the Adult Contemporary chart in Canada, and eventually sold millions of copies in more than one hundred versions around the world.

Dave's first check for the song was well over seven thousand dollars, a great deal of money in 1973; he thought at first they had the commas and periods in the wrong places! With his first royalties he bought a boat, which of course he named *Wildflower*, and began enjoying some of the fruits of success. Dave counted himself fortunate to live in the beautiful coastal city of Victoria, located on the southern tip of Vancouver Island, where a wealth of waterways entices the boating enthusiast. In those carefree days he would go cruising with his friends over blue-green seas, through islands that dotted the straits like so many jewels. They would fish or call in at various docks, playing pool or offering free drinks to the American tourists, who eventually christened Dave and his companions "the champagne Canadians." Most of all, Dave loved to sit on the deck of the boat in the sunshine, playing his guitar and laughing with his friends.

Yet it was the encounter with fame in the years following the release of "Wildflower" which had an even greater impact on Dave's life. As the song continued to stay on top of the charts, he began receiving various awards and his name was becoming known. Once Dave traveled with David Foster to Los Angeles for an award ceremony, and whilst there they visited Capitol Records where David introduced him to one of the chief executives. Dave expected to see a man wearing a white Panama hat and sunglasses and smoking a cigar; to his surprise, the producer was a young man in his thirties dressed in an expensive jeans outfit. He said to Dave,

"I'm telling you right now that song you've written is forever, it's a standard." (A "standard" is industry parlance for a classic.)

"How can you be so sure?" asked Dave curiously.

"I just know it," he said, "that song is never going away."

Dave was at the same time becoming acquainted with some of the most famous figures in the musical realm. He knew there were many who were writing songs, that success in the entertainment sphere was elusive, and felt that he was exceptionally fortunate; he also felt humbled by the attention. When he first met Lionel Richie, the singer came running up to him, his eyes wide with excitement.

"You're Dave Richardson?" he asked. When Dave nodded an affirmative, Lionel hugged him, saying, "At last I get to meet you."

"Haven't we got our lines backwards?" said Dave, knowing just how famous Richie was.

"When I was with the Commodores, 'Wildflower' was the song that got us going; it was our big number at all the dances," his new acquaintance told him.

There were other accolades, and Dave also received some very tempting offers. One day the office of Quincy Jones called; the hugely successful record producer wanted Dave to sign a contract to write exclusively for him.

"I believe you are absolutely the freshest, best lyricist there is anywhere in the world right now," he told Dave, offering him a five-year contract on generous terms. Dave knew it could be an opening for him into every recording studio in Los Angeles, or anywhere else for that matter, and that he could be writing for some exceedingly famous and talented people. It was a major decision, but Dave already knew the answer. He loved his day job far too much to give it up.

Dave had joined the Calgary Police Force in his early twenties, then shortly thereafter transferred back to his hometown of Victoria, and was working with the Saanich Police Department in that city. There he trained in all areas of the profession, including drug squad and forensics, became involved in undercover work, and eventually participated in some of the highest-level crime cases in the country. It was work he considered himself blessed to undertake; he had grown up with the strongest principles of integrity and courage, and the ideal of protecting the innocent from the depredations of criminal elements that wreaked havoc within society was of greatest importance to him.

For him, it was not the money that mattered, but rather serving people in his chosen calling, and that never changed. So, Dave had no regrets as he turned down the offer. Nevertheless, he continued to get a fair amount of publicity–it was the combination of poet and law officer that stirred the public imagination so much. The story of the songwriting policeman became almost legendary, and a newspaper headline concerning him occurred on a number of occasions: "*This cop walks to a different beat.*"

It had actually been that way from the beginning.

PART I:
A CHOICE OF TWO LIVES TO BE LIVING

CHAPTER 1
A Million Miles of Daydreams

THE FIRST OF the great formative influences in Dave's life emerged just after the end of the Second World War. That was when, in 1946, he came to live on Vancouver Island, on the westernmost edge of Canada.

Dave was born in eastern Canada during the war years, and as a small child traveled overland from Prince Edward Island with his parents and three brothers. His father, Harry, was serving with the Canadian Royal Engineers in England during the war when he found out he had terminal Hodgkin's disease. He returned to Canada, determined that before his death he would give his young family a fresh start in another part of the country, which he believed at the time offered more opportunities. So, he traveled across the vast continent with his wife and four small sons in a 1939 Plymouth four-door sedan, in a courageous and bittersweet journey. He settled his wife and children in their new home in Victoria, on Dysart Road, close to one of the waterways that lent so much beauty to the city, and shortly thereafter passed away.

In that home, as Dave was growing up, was to be found much happiness. His mother Harriet continued after her husband's death to raise her four small boys on her own, and dedicated herself to their welfare. Despite the warmth of personality that gave her so much popularity in her adopted hometown, she never remarried, fearing a new husband might not bring up her sons in a way Harry would have liked. Her steadfastness and unwavering devotion had its reward, for her sons were destined, in different ways, to become remarkable and successful individuals.

Don, the oldest brother, grew up to become a missionary in New Guinea in the 1960s and '70s, living in and preaching the gospel to a village of cannibals and headhunters who had never before glimpsed a white man. He later returned to America and authored some books based on his experiences, including *Peace*

Child, a book which made a dynamic impact upon a whole generation of Christians. Bob, the next brother, was a natural all-rounder, handsome and athletic. Doug, the youngest brother, made his mark as a police officer, rising to the highest ranks of the Victoria Police. As for Dave, from an early age there were two careers he passionately desired to follow—and the first was that of songwriter.

In the early '50s the new popular songs were being played on the radio; it was the commencement of a whole new, incomparable musical era, and the Richardson boys would gather round the brown wooden box in their kitchen and listen to the latest hits as they came over the air. Dave, in particular, was swept away by the romance of the lyrics he heard, and would copy down the words in a notebook. And nothing could stop him singing!

Twice when Dave was very young he came down with a sickness called undulant fever, so badly that at one stage he almost died. He was placed in a ward with other children in the Victoria General Hospital, but would lie awake at night with the melodies he loved running through his head. He was especially fond of "Granada" as performed by Frankie Laine, and would sing this under the bedcovers, then move on to other favorites, such as "The Little White Cloud That Cried" by Johnnie Ray, or "O My Papa" by Eddie Fisher. The nurses would come in. "David, stop singing and go to sleep!" they would say.

After Dave's second stay in hospital, they found a cure for him with an experimental drug, and he never suffered from the disease again. His physician, Dr Dalton, refused to take any money from Harriet, because he knew she was a widow. "I've got patients who can afford to pay, don't worry," he said.

With his health returned, Dave explored his new neighborhood, located in an area of greater Victoria named Saanich. It was filled with young families, with whom he and his brothers soon made connections. The first friend Dave could remember was a boy named Mike Pearce who lived half a block away, whose whole family played important roles in Dave's childhood years. His mother Mickey was a gifted seamstress who worked with the Hudson's Bay Company[3] and made costumes for the local children for their Cowboy and Indian games, while his brother Lanny taught Dave songs from the *Hit Parader*[4] magazine which came out every month with the words of the latest songs. Dave would part with his weekly allowance for this privilege, and counted it worth every nickel.

Yet it was Mike's father Cecil who made the greatest impact on Dave. He was a good-looking man—the boys all thought he looked like Randolph Scott, the movie actor—and had an infectious smile; he was strict, but fair. And he was a sergeant with the Saanich Police. Dave would see him frequently in his Saanich uniform, which became invested in his mind with a kind of halo, and watch him driving past in his police vehicle. One day, Dave went missing; his mother phoned Cecil, and together they combed the neighborhood until finally they found him. He had climbed into the sergeant's car and been so captivated by the scent of old upholstery that he had fallen asleep in the back seat. So it was Cecil, revered by all the kids in the neighborhood, who gave Dave his first attraction to the Saanich Police. He very much wanted to be like him, and not just Cecil, but the other policemen he came to know.

During Dave's childhood, they frequently had visitors staying at their home, relatives and friends, sometimes up to twelve or fourteen people. His mother had a magnetic kindness, and when she came to Victoria several of her brothers and sisters had moved to be close to her. When the house was crowded, it was difficult for Dave to pursue his favorite activity–writing songs and singing. On summer evenings, when the skies remained light until late, he would go out on the streets and walk while singing the lyrics he was composing in his head. In his mind, he could hear these set to music, together with strings and orchestration–electric guitars hadn't yet been invented–and would be lost in the world created by the beauty of words and music. Other times, he would hum the current hit songs which inspired him the most: "Ghost Rider in the Sky," "Cool Water" by the Sons of the Pioneers, or one of Tony Bennett's latest hits.

One evening as he was traversing the neighborhood, a Saanich policeman was going by. "Hello," he said to the young boy.

"Hello," said Dave.

"What are you up to?"

"Just singing, walking and making up songs."

Eventually the policemen came to know him, and would stop and say, "Hi David, what are you doing, making up songs?" Some nights, if it was late, they asked if he would like a ride home, and would drop him off at the house.

After that, he was never afraid of a policeman, and nor were the other children. Every day when they got out of school an officer would be going past and greeting them, checking they were safe; every child knew a number of policemen personally and invariably enjoyed warm and positive relationships with them. In these encounters, Dave was beginning to find his other vocation. Not having a father himself, he saw in these officers an integrity which made a vast impression upon him. When he grew up, he knew he wanted also to dedicate himself to assisting those in need. This aspiration was further strengthened by one relationship with a Saanich policeman, despite the fact it did not have such an auspicious beginning.

One summer evening, Dave was playing baseball down the street with the other boys, when someone hit the ball into the garden of a lady who was notorious for her dislike of children. When Dave darted in to fetch the ball, she emerged on her porch and shouted at him; he retaliated by stamping on her flower bed, at which point she threatened to call the police. Dave was afraid, and ran home. "Mum," he said to his surprised parent, "I'm tired, I'm going to bed." In his room, he heard the doorbell ring, and then his name being called. Downstairs he made his way with reluctant feet, where he found two policemen in uniform standing with his mother. Dave listened as they explained the allegations against him, and felt they were unjust. He turned to his mother and shouted at her.

"That's not fair," he yelled.

At that point, one of the two policemen reached out and gave Dave what they called a "skite," a glancing blow on the side of the head, and knocked Dave on the floor. "You get up, young man, and apologize to your mother–and don't *ever* raise your voice to her again!" he said sternly.

Dave got on his feet. "I'm sorry, Mummy," he said tearfully.

That was how Dave met Ed Anderson, and later he counted that slap Ed gave him as the best thing that ever happened to him. He wasn't resentful, for he knew he had deserved it, and in time Ed became a father figure to him, whom he valued for his help and advice on many occasions. It was through his example that the ideal of becoming a Saanich policeman, one who could offer staunch assistance to the community, finally crystallized in Dave's young mind. In this ambition he was also influenced by the ever-present witness of his mother Harriet that pervaded his early years–it was she who filled their home with needy friends and relatives, who was always ready to help the stranger, and whose warmth overflowed on every occasion.

Yet through it all Dave's desire to be a poet continued unabated. His imagination was stirred by the beauty that surrounded him in his home city, as well as the friendships he made and the rapture that came from his ability to think, wonder, and love. This was expressed in a poem he wrote recalling an event from his childhood, the time he skipped school to spend the day in an apple tree in the grounds of their home:

APPLE TREES AND HEROES

I can still remember the apple tree
That grew on Dysart Street,
It provided my home for one whole day,
Nearer heaven by six feet.
At first I swung, and then I clung
To the branches of my lofty seat,
As trailing leaves, that clasped me close
Made my hiding place complete.
But then came drenching rain,
Another kind of duel,
Which made me feel, if anything,
More like a grown man.
And besides,
Even the rain was better than school.

The hanging apples were green and sour,
They would make me sick, I was told,
I plucked them in my verdant bower
And tasted them like fruits of gold.
The rain, in which all day I bathed
Would make me ill, my mother warned,
But I came through it all unscathed,
Because I was an eight-year-old man
Who dared defy the rain
And green apples and pain.

That tree was lifted up above the earth
Only by six feet or so,
But there I climbed to outer space
To give my fancies birth,
How easy then, my wildest thoughts
To conceive and to embrace,
It seemed the very stars would give me steer …
I had a million miles of daydreams
In the inches between my ears.

CHAPTER 2
Going Out to Find the Earth

AS A TEENAGER, Dave moved with his family to Three Hills in the neighboring province of Alberta; they stayed there for several years as his older brother Don attended Prairie Bible Institute, the organization which would send him as a missionary to the other side of the world. Dave loved that time in the great Canadian hinterland: the sun burning on the plains during long summer days, the freezing winters punctuated by the warm breath of the Chinook[5] wind, and glimpses of the northern lights sweeping through the night sky in impossible glory.

The new experience broadened his world in numerous ways. Gazing at the vastness of the land, a hitherto unknown sense of adventure was awakened in him, that would grow stronger throughout his life. As he encountered many of the stalwart characters who worked the land, in whom a pioneer spirit still dwelt, his nascent sense of idealism also grew:

> *Starting at the end and looking back*
> *I see a child in retrospect*
> *And a star he hoped would fall into his hands;*
> *Too young for coffee's taste to touch his lips,*
> *But with a weeping-willow whip*
> *He'd face the dragons of the land.*
>
> *Imagine this, imagine that,*
> *In his tattered dreaming hat,*
> *A young boy's going out to find the earth …*

(From "The Value and The Worth")

During the school holidays, he worked on one of the prairie farms; it was a whole new, enriching experience. His employer was a local landowner called

George Boles, who managed to enormously impress Dave with his ability to hold the reins with one hand while rolling and lighting a cigarette with the other–a feat Dave had seen accomplished only in the movies. He worked for George ten hours a day for the whole of the season, earned the royal sum of fifty cents *per diem*, and loved every moment.

He was also fortunate to find in his employer another example to follow, for George, in his unassuming way, possessed the traditional Canadian values of integrity and kindness, together with considerable patience. Although he knew Dave was young and inexperienced, and would inevitably make mistakes, he entrusted him with significant responsibility, teaching him to drive cars as well as the larger farm machinery, and showing him how to care for the animals and ride a horse. George was also a practical man, equipped with a good sense of humor. After a few days milking cows, Dave came to his employer, hugely concerned.

"Look at my forearms," he said, rolling up his sleeves. "They're killing me– see how swollen they are!"

George took one look and roared with laughter. "That swelling's called *muscle*, Dave," he said.

During those growing up years, Dave and his younger brother Doug remained close; they both loved sports and excelled at these, especially ice hockey–the great Canadian pastime–and there was also baseball, ten-pin bowling and swimming. Together they joined the town aquatics team, and, as they came from the west coast where swimming and diving were an every-summer-day activity, were the only boys in the prairie town who could swim in Three Hills' brand-new pool. They would put on high diving demonstrations and bask in the admiration of their captive audience, who stood at the shallow end of the pool in awe.

Dave also admired extensively his older sibling Bob, who was so handsome that he always left a string of girlfriends in his wake, which meant Dave himself was never lacking for a date in his teen years. Bob loved dancing and it was from him that Dave learned all the latest steps and rhythms. He also taught Dave how to fight, even while impressing upon him sternly that there were only two reasons one should begin a physical confrontation: to save the honor of one's family, or to protect a woman. It was advice that stayed with Dave after the family moved from the rural area back to Victoria, and settled into a new home in Broadway Road.

He then found himself setting down many more lyrics in his tattered notebooks, and some of the themes that would reappear in his poetry began to emerge. Victoria on the west coast is blessed with some of the mildest temperatures in Canada, and the summer months are especially beautiful. The delight in those halcyon days, as well as the symbolism of the season, would come to feature in many of Dave's lyrics:

GOODBYE FRIEND SUMMER

The midnight mist bids aging Summer
It's time to yield to Autumn's call,
While Night starts stealing light from Day
To mark the invasion of Fall.
And I sense in the dew there's a sadness,
And a grief that Summer's now going,
Withdrawing bright Day to
The warm womb of Spring
While a colder Child is growing.

Autumn, be born, if you must—
Mature into Winter, and die,
For Winter's the seed for Mother April
Who gives birth to a warmer Child.

Now the flowers are closing painted eyes,
Their shaking fingers start to fold
Around their gray, bereft head,
They turn their collars to the cold,
And evening breezes on the beaches
Cry "Farewell!" to the long golden light,
Sending siren songs over shifting sands
Where little feet played in delight.

Are all the beaches now deserted?
Are the seagulls there still calling?
Is anyone still singing summer songs
While the endless rain is falling?
Autumn, be born, and quickly
Bare your throat to Winter's hands,
And you will lie in an unmarked grave
In next Summer's race-track sands.

Goodbye, Friend Summer.

CHAPTER 3
Natural Beauty, Unnatural Evil

DAVE'S DESIRE TO be to be a police officer never diminished from these earliest years, and he eventually applied to join the force when he was in his early twenties. In his hometown at the time they were taking only married men, but he was accepted by the police department in Alberta. So he traveled east through the majestic ranges that stand guard to British Columbia, and as he did so the words of the old folk song, "In the Blue Canadian Rockies," rang in his ears, evoking all the magic of springtime in the foothills.

Imbued with the vigor and enthusiasm of youth, Dave finally reached Calgary, the city where he was to begin his new life. It was located in a region he came to love for many reasons. The town itself, sprawling over the rolling Alberta plains and home to the legendary Calgary Stampede, was a byword for the warmth and friendliness of its citizens. Nearby was the famed Jasper National Park, nestled deep within the Rockies, where mountain trails led through pristine wilderness areas to sparkling pools of water, with snow-crowned peaks soaring on all sides–home to a variety of wildlife, including mountain goats, wolves, elk, and just the occasional Grizzly. South of Jasper was the exquisite Lake Louise, its emerald waters framed against the backdrop of a vast glacier, and nearby the charming small town of Banff, with its chalets and lodges enticing tourists from all over the world.

Despite these drawcards, it was down to work straight away for Dave, and he was plunged into the stark realities of his new world of law enforcement in a dramatic way. While he was still in training school, before he had even donned a uniform, his Warrant Officer, Butch Roberts, spoke to him one day.

"Richardson!" he said.

"Yes, sir?"

"You've been told two or three times to get your hair cut." (At the time Dave had long hair, like Elvis.) "If you don't come back from your lunch hour with your hair cut, you'll be in front of the Deputy Chief."

"Yes, sir!"

The lunch hour came, and Dave was walking out to obey his order when he heard Butch speaking to him again: "Richardson!"

"Yes, sir?"

"What are you doing?"

"I'm going to get my hair cut, sir," said Dave.

"If you get your hair cut, I'll have you up in front of the Deputy Chief," said the officer.

"I beg your pardon?" asked Dave, perplexed.

"You will not get your hair cut! Do you hear me?"

After class that day, Dave found out the reason for the contradictory orders. His senior officers asked him if he would work undercover: as a newcomer to Calgary he would be unknown to the criminal elements in the city, and he agreed. He immediately found himself plunged into a strange twilight existence where, in the words of Shakespeare's arch-villain Macbeth, "nothing is but what is not."[6] It was a surreal world in which the rules of civilized society were in abeyance, the conventions of decency and justice overturned, and a way of life that espoused ruthlessness and violence reigned supreme–a place where every man's hand was against his brother, and the weak were soon vanquished. And now, with hardened criminals, men wanted for armed robbery and homicide, Dave soon found himself sharing jail cells.

Dave's mission was to try to gain the trust of these men, and in this way elicit inside information concerning a particular crime. He soon learned this would involve him in a psychological warfare he needed to wage with utmost skill, either feeding the ego of the criminal, or patronizing and dominating him. It was a tense and dangerous game, and there was the need for constant vigilance. Locked in with a murderer, Dave was often afraid to go to sleep, for he knew that any type of weapon could be made in a prison cell. He would light a cigarette and keep it between his fingers, so that if he drifted off it would burn down and singe his skin and awaken him. In this way he would manage to lie awake all night, until he would be led out of the cell in the morning on some excuse, snatch a few hours sleep and then return to his post.

In Calgary, also, Dave had the experience of being shot at for the first time. He and his partner, Dan, were out on patrol one evening when they received a report concerning a teenager who was trying to murder his family in their home. As they drove down the lane toward the house, they saw that its windows were shattered by bullets, and pulled off to the side of the road. The two men emerged from the car; Dan crouched behind the engine, while Dave moved for cover behind a tree. As he did so, he had the sensation that someone had taken a handful of sand and thrown it in his face; a bullet had hit the tree and the bark sprayed in all directions. Dave would have been more than justified in shooting in return, but he desisted. "After all," he thought later, when it was possible to be more philosophical, "the kid was missing me."

The episode revealed one of the bedrocks of his thinking. Deep in his heart, Dave believed he was invincible–after all, he was one of the "white hats," wasn't he?–and they *never* get killed in the line of duty. It was an outlook which was eventually to come under severe challenge.

Dave had a good sense of humor and was especially adept at one-liners, attributes that would land him in hot water on not a few occasions. Even in his days as a "rookie" in Calgary this propensity could not stay submerged for long. One time, he was walking a beat in McLeod Trail at the south end of the city, which involved doing property checks on businesses in the area, strip malls, car dealers and so on. Calgary is a well-designed city; and all the streets and avenues have alleys or lanes behind them, so the officer would first inspect all the front doors, then move around to the back doors facing the alley. Dave had been out all night on his beat, and faint streaks of light were already showing in the sky when he turned into an alley to complete his check. At that same moment, he saw a man entering the back door of a business in a surreptitious manner. The intruder didn't notice Dave, who came quietly to the entrance and noticed the pry marks which had splintered the lock.

In those days the police did not have walkie-talkies or cell phones, and although each beat had call boxes to request help the nearest could be some blocks away, so they were virtually on their own in a situation like this. Accordingly, Dave stepped inside the door after the man, and found himself in the basement of a café; there were stairs leading upward, and he could see the legs of the intruder from the waist down as he ascended the steps. Dave drew out his gun, a Webley 38, soft-shoed up the staircase behind him and came to the upper level, the main area of the café. The early morning sun was beginning to shine through the large front windows, and Dave saw in the center of the café a long horseshoe-shaped counter. At the top of this counter was the cash register, and his guy was standing in front of it pushing the buttons. Dave tiptoed behind him and raised his gun.

"*Kerching!*" went the cash register as it opened.

It was Dave's cue. "I'm sorry, we're closed," he said firmly, at the same time placing the cold grey muzzle of the gun gently on the man's neck.

The would-be robber leapt about six feet in the air before collapsing in fright.

Yet there was much more for Dave to discover during his stay in Calgary. The scenery of the province, the vastness of the sky and the vista of the heavens he witnessed there each evening, both awed and elated him. He was not wearied by the flatness of the landscape, but rather saw the prairies as having a distinctive beauty of their own, filled with color and splendor. Most especially he loved the flaming sky of dusk, when the sun appeared to set the heavens on fire as a final exertion before it died in the west. Tumultuous thunderstorms often shattered the quiet of a summer evening, and when the calm came afterwards the spectacle of the stars seemed to him almost inconceivable in its luster: "*a treasure chest of innumerable diamonds suspended there in infinity for we minute particles of creation to appreciate and adore.*"[7] And then there was what he called "*the instigator of love,*" the moon, pouring out its silver beams to illuminate the land until it finally paled toward dawn.

So the charm of the landscape made an unforgettable impact upon Dave's imagination, and there was another event, during his first week at work, which also made an impression. He and the other recruits were given a talk by one of the senior officers, who welcomed them to the department and their new careers. Then he held up a gold wristwatch before them, and remarked,

"This might be the most important thing I can tell you. Many years from now, those of you who stay in the job long enough to retire will be given the proverbial gold watch. And it will mean ... precisely nothing." He paused, then continued.

"What *will* matter," he said, "is that you can look back on your life as a police officer and say, 'I did my best and made a difference'—that will long outlive any watch."

And those were the words which stayed with Dave as he traveled back to Vancouver Island after eighteen months at Calgary, and fulfilled his dream of joining the Saanich Police.

CHAPTER 4
The Privilege of Being Young

DAVE WAS TO spend the next three and a half decades working for the Saanich Police Department–a time of tumultuous events both in his personal life, and on the national and international scene.

To his surprise and delight, within a short time after he arrived back in his hometown, Dave found himself working as a partner with Ed Anderson, the same officer who was such a tower of strength to him during his growing years. Ed was then a juvenile detective, and still had that wonderful manner of dealing with young people; Dave never saw him angry, and wondered at his calming influence in situations which were tense or potentially violent. This was even though Ed had a sensitive stomach. If the men were called to a crime scene which involved a dead body, perhaps a suicide or shooting, he would say to his fellow officer, "Go see what it's like, Dave."

Dave would go inside and look at the crime scene, and come back out. "It's pretty messy, Ed," he would say.

"Okay, let's get it over with," his partner would say.

Ed would walk in the house, look at the body, then go outside again and be violently ill; after that he would deal calmly with the situation. Dave realized it was because he cared about people so much.

It was some time later, after Dave had been involved in many different areas of police work, that he experienced a repeat of the lesson he had himself received as a child–but this time he was the one dispensing the advice. Leona was a girl of about twelve when Dave first met her, but she looked like a little boy, very small, and she was constantly in trouble, as was her brother, a tiny squirt who called himself Big Al after Al Capone. One Halloween evening, Dave was out in the police car and heard about a small boy who had just robbed some young people collecting for charity; he knew as soon as he heard the description that it was Leona. A day or two later he was driving down Darwin Street and saw her on the side of the road; he pulled alongside and said, "Leona, I want to talk to you." She started running along the sidewalk; Dave just followed, until finally she got tired and he took her in and charged her with the robbery.

As he was interviewing Leona, she was being cheeky and using profane language, and finally he had enough. "Stop that kind of talk," he commanded.

"Or what, you (expletive) pig?"

At that point, Dave reached across and did exactly to her what Ed had done, gave a glancing blow which clipped the side of her head, so she went down.

"Get up," he said.

"No, you're going to hit me again!"

"That's exactly right, until you stop using that language."

Leona got up. "Are you finished?" Dave asked sternly and she nodded, and he proceeded to deal with the charges against her.

About a week later Dave was at home and off duty when he got a phone call from the police station. "Dave, we picked up this young girl, Leona, she says she won't talk to anyone but you."

"Okay." He went into the station, and there she was, with another young girl. As he walked into the room, Leona turned to her friend.

"See, I told you he was cute," she said, and they both giggled. "How are you doing, Mr. Richardson?" she asked shyly, and they had a constructive talk and got the situation straightened out.

From time to time after that, she would call Dave needing his assistance, and he would talk with and counsel her, until after a while he rarely heard from her. And then, some years later, he stopped in at a pub for a drink on his way home from work. He caught sight of an attractive young woman, part of a group, and thought, "Oh boy, does she look like she could be Leona!" However, he didn't want to say anything which might embarrass her in front of her companions, so he drank his beer and walked out the door to go to his car.

Behind him he heard a soft voice: "Mr. Richardson?"

He turned and looked at the young woman. "Leona?" he said, and she nodded. "I thought that might be you."

"I want to thank you for not coming up to me while I was with my friends," she said and paused, and her eyes became misty. She went on, "I also want to thank you for the day you gave me a smack on the head. I know that I was wrong and deserved it–in fact, you were easy on me. I want to let you know that day changed my life."

Dave knew young people needed warmth and encouragement, and at the same time they also needed boundaries and discipline. Two small episodes from his work with the Juvenile Branch seemed to encapsulate these principles. Sometimes he would drive through Beaver Lake Park, where families gathered in summertime, to check that everything was okay and there were no suspicious persons hanging about. One late afternoon, he saw there a company of seven or eight teenagers in bathing suits, splashing in the water, swimming and laughing together in the golden twilight. Moved by a sudden impulse, he went up to the group. "Excuse me, can I talk with you?"

They turned their attention to the uniformed officer who had suddenly appeared in their midst. "Sure."

"I couldn't help but notice you guys here," said Dave. "It's wonderful to see you enjoying yourselves. Can I give you some advice?"

"By all means," they assured him, their faces filled with interested enquiry.

"Put this day in your mind," he said to them earnestly, "treasure it and remember it, your friendships, how valuable you are to each other. Memories like this are precious, they're a foundation for the rest of your lives."

As Dave talked to them, he could see they were drinking in his words; the understanding that they were receiving advice that was truly worthwhile was written on their faces. Yet he did not always have the same message for the groups of young people he encountered. Now and then he would drive down to the beach in the late evenings, and find teenagers there who were drinking and partying. "Okay," he would say to them, "Who's in charge?"

"No one."

"One of you is the leader," he would repeat, "and I want to know who it is." At this point, someone would volunteer, and Dave would write down his name and details.

"What are you going to do?" he would invariably ask.

"Nothing–if I come back here in the morning and there are no beer bottles, there's no garbage and everything's cleaned up. If there's a mess you'll be hearing from me, and I'll be charging you."

On one such occasion, he witnessed a teen throwing a beer bottle in the sea. "There's a heavy fine for littering," Dave told him, "Five hundred dollars. You've got a choice, you could get a ticket for the maximum, or you go in there and get that bottle–I've seen too many children with cut feet."

The young man went in the water and found the bottle.

Dave was profoundly aware at the time of the importance of youth, and that none of its opportunities should be missed; so many times when he encountered young people he would reiterate his message, urging them to value the wonderful times they were fortunate to have, and their friendships which were full of warmth and happiness, because such memories would one day mean a great deal to them. He even wrote a poem on this subject which he called "On Being Young"; it was published in a local newspaper and he never made a cent from it, yet he wouldn't have sold it for thousands of dollars:

> *I don't have much to do today*
> *I think I'll walk down by the shore*
> *And throw some stones into the wind*
> *And hear the ocean's roar.*
>
> *I don't have much to think today*
> *So I'll take the time to dream*
> *Of wings and kings and other things*
> *Like clouds of soft ice cream.*
>
> *Too soon the years will take from me*
> *These wondrous dreams of fantasy*
> *And replace them with reality.*
>
> *Then all the songs I've ever sung*
> *Will just be words and left undone*
> *In the privilege of being young.*

This sense of the brevity of life and fleetingness of time was reinforced by another event that occurred after Dave had spent a number of years in the force. One quiet Sunday morning he was called to go to the scene of a sudden death, and entered the home near the Gorge Road. There he found the man, who had lived alone, lying cold and naked on the bathroom floor, in all the starkness of mortality. He suddenly saw with shock and horror who it was—none other than his former partner Ed Anderson, who had retired some months previously.

Dave sat down and looked at the body, grieving intensely. All that Ed had done for him came flooding back into his mind, and he could only say, "Thank you, thank you." He still hadn't forgotten what Ed had taught him about helping others, and the ideals of integrity and compassion he had inculcated. They were values that would be invested in Dave's mind with new purity and strength as the years continued to pass.

CHAPTER 5

David and David

DURING DAVE'S FIRST years with the department at Saanich, he was fortunate in being able to maintain a harmonious balance between his work with the police force and his love of songwriting.

Blessed with a warm and outgoing personality, loyal and affirmative in his relationships, Dave had many acquaintances in the worlds of both law enforcement and music. As well as writing songs, he played the guitar in a couple of bands known as The Pacers and The Hustlers. After work he would also often stop in at the Old Forge, a popular nightclub in downtown Victoria, where he grew to know all the musicians well. One evening, as he entered the smoky, cavernous recesses of the venue, he noticed there was a new player at the piano, young and slightly built. The nightclub owner, John Olsen, leaned over the bar and said to him, "Dave, you've got to hear this kid play piano."

Dave watched and listened as the teenager coaxed the amazing notes from the keys. "Wow," he said, "this guy is just in a class by himself."

And that was how Dave became acquainted with the young David Foster, who would later become a famous pianist, as well as a hugely successful musical producer, promoting the careers of some of the most outstanding performers of the following decades. David at that time was only eighteen and completely unknown, and Dave was some years older, but the two men shared a love of music and became firm friends. It was an entirely fortuitous meeting which was destined to transform both their lives.

David had gone to England when he was sixteen, but had now returned and was playing at the nightclub with the house band, the Foundry Brass. Dave got to meet David's fellow musicians, Barry Casson, Rich England and Wes Chambers, as well as the sax player Chris Earthy, who later became manager of David's Canadian business. At the Forge, Dave also met some singers named Judy Ginn and Jim Walchuk, with whom Dave collaborated on a song called "Reaching

Far Too High,"[8] for which he wrote the lyrics. Judy and Jim eventually went to England, where she ended up recording the song; another singer named Shani Wallace also performed it on the Tom Jones show. Yet it was the relationship with David Foster that went from strength to strength.

The musicians in David's band called Dave DTC, short for Dave the Cop. Sometimes David would say, "Anyone like to hear DTC play the piano?" He'd get Dave up on the stage and make him sit down; then take Dave's fingers with one hand and play the melody with them, while with his other hand he would play the rhythm. The Forge stayed open until the early hours, and after it closed the two would go to Paul's restaurant on Douglas Street around three in the morning and have their favorite meal at the time, shrimp cocktail and clam chowder, sharing their musical dreams and planning songs together. Around five o'clock, as the sun was coming up, they would go to the Cedar Hill Golf Course near to David's home–of course neither had much money–and they would pick up on the ninth hole and finish the course, then go home to sleep.

At one point, Dave wrote a poem about the two of them, called "David and David":

> *Constable Richardson, out on patrol*
> *Wearing his haircut and gun,*
> *Looking for bad guys to keep in control*
> *And finds the occasional one.*
> *Drives his police car into the night*
> *Looking at windows and doors,*
> *Spends leisure time writing poems and lines*
> *And found, now and then, at the Forge.*
>
> *What's this I hear, a piano so clear*
> *Over the noise of the crowd?*
> *The boy on the stool? It's Fors'ner, you fool,*
> *Riding his musical cloud.*
>
> *Davey, can you scramble some notes, Davey,*
> *… maybe turn them into a song*
> *I'll write some words*
> *That you've never heard*
> *(And Davey, how'd your hair get so long?)*

As their friendship developed, Dave came to be increasingly in awe of David's musical abilities. Often after a night at the Forge, he would go to sleep over at David's place, where the young performer still lived with his mother Eleanor and three older and three younger sisters–David was the only boy. One morning when Dave woke in the Foster home, he began tinkling on the piano in the basement, playing "Greensleeves." His friend was down the hall. "That's not the right note," he called to Dave, "it's not F, it's F sharp."

"How can you tell from there?"

"I can just tell. Hit any key on the keyboard."

Dave obediently struck a number of keys at random, and David called out each one–his pitch was perfect.

"Now slam both hands down together on the keys and hold them down," commanded the young musician.

"Like this?" Dave struck the keys as directed, and the jangling notes filled the air. With his hands on the keyboard, he waited as David proceeded to reel off every key beneath his fingers.

At another early stage in their acquaintance, Foster was playing keyboard with Tommy Banks' Orchestra, filling in for the band leader who had stayed behind in Edmonton. One evening Dave rode up to Grande Prairie with Jo on his motorcycle to hear his friend playing, and was there when the next night Tommy arrived, came backstage, and spoke to David.

"I miss the road!" he said, "Can you play any other instrument?"

"Well," said David, "I can play guitar, but you already have two."

"Can you play trombone?" pressed the band owner.

"I've never played one in my life," responded David, "but I'll be able to play one by tomorrow night."

And the next night, sure enough, he was playing one on stage.

Meanwhile, despite the frequently grim realities of his day-to-day work, the lyrics continued to flow from Dave's resourceful mind, and he was setting down hundreds of poems and lyrics. Some of these were whimsical creations, in which he indulged his love of wordplay:

DREAMS

Last night I set to dreaming
All sorts of crazy things:
What if we could see the air?
What song a rock would sing?

What thoughts might move a mountain?
And what color would be the sky
If it had a choice? And without a voice
Then would the robin fly?
What if a monarch were never rich?
But a poor and humble thing …
If a pauper good and proper came
Then should we make him king?
If there were never cloudy days,
Pray tell, what would we drink?
And if we never had a thought,
What on earth, then, would we think?
If we had only love, not hate,
Then we just couldn't kill,
And it's just because we never won't
That sometimes, friend, we will.

Yes, last night I set to dreaming
Some crazy things, I know,
But perhaps these astral fancies
Bring down truth to us below …
And crazy people, so it seems,
Might be having clever dreams.

SNAKES AND LADDERS

He offered her a word of love
That never reached her ears,
She gave a moment of her life
When he was asking years,
He offered her a simple gift
Consisting mainly of himself,
And she asked him if he had come
From a bargain-basement shelf.

But please don't call him lonely,
He says that's not his name,
He says no one will see him cry,
That he will take the blame.

At times he wants to be alone
While sadness is in fashion,
To feel the hopeless state he's in
And consider her dispassion,
And though he thought his heart had stopped
He finds that it's still beating,
And so he smiles and tries again
And the game keeps on repeating.

But please don't call him foolish,
He says that's not his name,
It feels like snakes and ladders,
But monopoly's the game,
And oh! she plays so very well,
While he can never buy or sell.

THE END OF LOVE

With the end of love
Comes the end of reason,
Like the summer, it dies,
But God! What a season!

CHAPTER 6
The Hopeless Romantic

WHAT WAS THE source of the songs that welled up so ceaselessly in Dave's heart and mind? As he himself put it, he was a "hopeless romantic." In this way, perhaps he took after his own father.

Dave's parents had met in Prince Edward Island on the eastern coast of Canada in the early 1930s. His mother Harriet was a young woman of nineteen, and working in a restaurant in Charlottetown called Milton's, when his father Harry came in one day, saw Harriet, and started talking with her. When the owner of the restaurant told Harriet there was to be no fraternizing with the customers, she told Harry that she was very sorry, but she was unable to speak with him. Yet Harry was determined to make her acquaintance… and so … he bought the restaurant! Harriet had dark hair and eyes, and he thought she looked Spanish, so he gave the dining room a new name: "The Old Spain Tea Room." Harry and Harriet were married soon after, ran the business together, and began a family.

As for Dave, there was never a time in his young life when he had not been in love–and that same determination his father Harry displayed was evident from his earliest romantic encounters. When he was in kindergarten he fell in love with a little girl named Florence; she had brown ringlets and was completely adorable. One evening he wanted to play with her, but she was in a Brownie meeting at the hall attached to the church of St Martin in the Fields, just down the road from where he lived. And so, he came up with an idea. Although it was late summer it was cold in the hall, and they had a pot-bellied stove going to maintain the warmth. The resourceful small boy found a pillow, soaked it in water, climbed up on the roof, and put it over the chimney, then went back down and waited. After a while, the girls came pouring out of the smoky hall–and Dave got to play with the current love of his life.

Later Florence moved away to Vancouver which to the disconsolate small boy seemed to be on the other side of the world; he never forgot her–until most fortunately when he was eight he met another small girl named Patsy, and became enamored again–and so it continued through primary and high school. There was so much love in his own home, he felt it was always spilling over.

In high school, one of his classmates was a boy who was a little slow and had a speech impediment; however, he was smitten with the most beautiful girl in school and asked Dave to write a poem which he could give to her. As it happened, Dave was also one of her admirers, so it was very easy for him to write the ballad; he gave it to his friend who in turn offered it to the girl as his own composition, and she was totally impressed. After Dave graduated, he found his poem in the high school annual with his friend's name beneath it as the author; it had won the literary award for Greater Victoria.

"Wow, that's great," thought Dave, "it's probably the only time he will ever get something like that … and after all, it was only one poem."

When he was falling in love all the time, he could meet a girl for half an hour, then go home and have a song written about her in fifteen minutes. Many of these were enraptured, idealistic creations:

> *She is to the sunrise, the glow before the sun*
> *And every evening ember before the shadows come,*
> *More radiant than diamonds the dew gives morning green*
> *And more in royal carriage than I have ever seen*
> *In the wildest of my dreams …*
> *For love is really nothing less than I believe*
> *In searching, we achieve,*
> *From the wildest of our dreams …*

(From "The Wildest of My Dreams")

Later in his songs, the understanding of love as a comfort and a bulwark against the tide of circumstances and trials that life produces became more evident:

> *The road is filled with spoils of other burdens*
> *Of those who stumbled, trying to endure,*
> *The time and distance left are so uncertain –*
> *The day behind is all there is for sure,*

But as a star alone, in a vast and barren dark
Finds and shines on those who watch its shining arc,
So like a star alone, from the heaven in her heart
She's finding me, she shines on me.

Light up the sky
To brighten the road,
Light up your eyes
To lighten my load.

The stones beneath my feet becoming feathers,
The wrath of night is humbled by the glow,
The best of life and love is getting better
As the halo of a star shines here below.

She delivers me into the sunrise
To fill my eyes with early morning gold,
Then easily I see how much I was unwise
For a life without love is a story untold.

(From "A Star Alone")

As Dave grew older, a note of cynicism started creeping in on more than one occasion:

THE LADY

And the lady says she loves you
And her beauty fills your mind,
So you tell her that you love her,
You need her,
And so begins the line,
And perfection is the moonlight
When it shines into her hair,
And angels ride her every word
That falls upon your ear,
Then heaven's curtains open
As she lies down at your side,

And you take her with excuses
That someday you really want her
For your bride.

She smiles at you, and rises
And she leaves you all too soon,
And you watch her through the darkness
As she walks across the room.
And perfection is a streetlight
When it wraps in light her figure,
As she combs her dancing hair
And she laughs into the mirror,
And all at once you notice
That the lady's never cried,
And as she leaves, she calmly whispers
That you will never take her
For your bride.

(From "The Easiest Woman to Love")

She cut a hole in my pocket
For the money to fall through,
She picked the change up off the ground,
She said her love was true.
She wanted a convertible,
I said no, and shook my head,
Her eyes looked up, the saddest blue
—the convertible was red—
But she's the easiest woman to love I've ever met,
Although she gives me nothing of anything she gets,
I ask her what my name is and she says that she forgets,
I say that love's a gamble, and she says she'll place a bet …

Yet, during the late Sixties and early Seventies, Dave was also adjusting to a new and unforeseen reality. "Flower power" was sweeping North America and the rest of the western world.

CHAPTER 7
Living through the Love Generation

DAVE HAD JOINED the police force during the Sixties, that turbulent decade which was destined to radically reshape an entire generation. In North America, it was the era of the Kennedys and the Vietnam War, of Martin Luther King's poignant "I Have a Dream" speech, and the musical phenomenon known as Beatlemania. The contours of the Middle East were redrawn after the Six-Day War in Israel; China's Mao Zedong created the Great Leap Forward, and Billy Graham was preaching the gospel to millions in crusades around the world. The decade culminated in July 1969, when for the first time a man set foot on the Moon during the Apollo 11 spaceflight.

It was also an era of social revolution. The post-war "baby boom," together with the emergence of sophisticated new technologies, had created an exceptional number of affluent and politically-conscious young people. Various sociological issues now came to the fore, including racial segregation and the environment, as well as the rights of women and other minorities. Nevertheless, for a decade which claimed to be about civil liberties and human dignity, it was remarkably violent. A number of prominent political figures, including the Kennedy brothers, were assassinated, and the Cold War escalated. Yet it was the conflict in Southeast Asia, resulting in many thousands of American deaths and generating enormous protests across the nation, which was the most potent factor in the rise of the new counterculture.

The hippie movement germinated in San Francisco with the war in Vietnam as the beating heart of its inspiration. In January 1967, some twenty thousand hippies gathered in Golden Gate Park for the "Human Be-In" which helped proclaim their ideals of love and peace throughout the land; later that year as many as one hundred thousand young people from all over the world joined with the flower children of that city in celebrating the "Summer of Love." It was a heady, intoxicating time, when long-haired young men and women, dressed in bellbottomed pants and colorful clothes, handed out flowers to passersby with the firm conviction they could change the world with their beliefs. It was all expressed in the dreamy, flowing lyrics of "San Francisco: Be Sure To Wear Flowers in Your Hair," written by John Phillips of the Mamas & The Papas and sung by Scott Mackenzie.

The movement attracted many other singers, songwriters and poets, who transformed into words what so many of them felt during the rapid social upheaval. Dave himself sensed the epochal nature of the events taking place–nor could he resist their allure. He had some vacation time due, put off his police uniform and traveled to California. Very swiftly he discovered the charming harbor community of Sausalito, across the Golden Gate Bridge from San Francisco. It was a popular destination for day trippers, who would walk or cycle over the bridge or arrive by ferry. Sitting at one of the cafés on the main street of Bridgeway, they could watch the California sunlight flashing on the sapphire waters of the bay, as the fishermen hauled in their nets near the docks and seagulls with white wings soared above. Otis Redding stayed there in a rented houseboat, and was inspired by the idyllic setting to write "(Sittin' on the) Dock of the Bay," then recorded it with the cries of seagulls and waves crashing in the background.

There are many songs about Sausalito, but none of them captured the spirit of the city in the late Sixties quite like American songwriter and poet Rod McKuen. His small volume of poetry, *Stanyan Street & Other Sorrows*, was published in 1966. And Dave too had some experiences in Sausalito, which he set down in a ballad:

THE MILES TO SAUSALITO

Sausalito was a dream, but not in sleep,
Occasionally, people passing brushed my sleeve
To assure me these were waking thoughts,
And San Francisco Bay was not a reverie,
Its beauty came to me unsought
With its blue ocean sweep.
Rod McKuen was right, after all;
Funny, I never really doubted his word
But there is the black, flowing hair I recall
Floating over my face in feathery waves,
And soft notes of a voice that I heard–
He'd not mentioned it in Sausalito at all,

Nor the slender tanned arms that held me
Turning time to infinity.

They sweep down on Sausalito
Every Sunday and Wednesday night,
So I joined the invaders in the fray,
Coming incognito,
While the turtles scuttled back into the Bay;
Standing at the bar, the crowd was tight,
I wondered if the city had been vacated,
But they checked the ages at the door,
And turned away more than a score,
All those over twenty-eight.

You didn't notice me that first time
On Bridgeway
As the drinkers mapped your every move,
Not at all sure
How to come within your sway.
As for me, I often reach for the moon
And take solid hold on a moth,
With nothing left to lose,
While the hours spun their tune
I met your vision,
At Latitude Thirty-Eight and Trident both,
More clearly at Gatsby's, and then at Zack's
As it grew late
And the music began to slow
That night in Sausalito.

I didn't spend much time observing you
(I vowed),
Yet I emptied a book of matches
On cigarettes
While studying you, in Zacks' crowd,
And emptied my mind of every word
With which I've been endowed
And others that I've never heard;
I wanted every memory you could make me

To take back through the miles,
Your movements, sighs and tears
And heart-shaking smiles,
So I could go to my bank of dreams
To withdraw, and find you near.

Had it not been for Stanyan Street
And other Sorrows,
San Francisco may have been just
An acquaintance
Whose time I happened to borrow,
But it's now a friend and lover,
This city I discovered;
And I might have asked if Sausalito
Was something that tasted good,
And how long to cook, do you know,
And why it isn't sold in Canada;
As it was, something sweet
Was blended from a recipe
Called Stanyan Street.

When I came to my home in the north,
A thousand airy miles
From Sausalito,
I thought never again to see you
Or that mesmerizing smile;
I skimmed through the book we wrote
While dreaming of the Blessed Isles,
Hard then, to gauge
That last, sad page
That said we reached The End.

But still I wish I'd met you
On that final desperate day
When I sat in a light-starved bar
In San Francisco's gray,
It should have been Sausalito,
In sunshine or by star,
Shimmering over the curving blue

Of the Bay;
But then you called, and told me
Of a chapter you didn't foresee,
So I think I'll read the book again
And maybe find therein
A different destiny.

If there is such a thing as black starlight
I haven't seen it,
For my eyes are only those of a man,
Yet, I have seen your unbound hair,
And the sheen of its waves in the night;
Sometimes, there shines a blue light
From fallen, forgotten snowflakes
And this also I have caught
Glancing from your eyes at daybreak.

I remember a golden sunset on China Beach[9]
Which set me thinking of your vivid face
Within fingertip reach,
And whitecaps tossing a warning
On a stormy morning
Mimic your eyes when they flash
With sudden bright radiance;
Your expression at the mention of artichokes,
Your restless elegance
In lazy California nights, and at morning rise,
I have seen parables in your face
Even through closed eyes.

CHAPTER 8

Goodbye to All That

THE MOST FAMOUS SLOGAN to come out of the Summer of Love in 1967 was *"Make love, not war,"* and around this time a new culture known as "free love" arose—a sexual revolution made possible by the availability of "The Pill" and other new forms of birth control. The philosophy espoused by the hippies favored peace, love and freedom, just as expressed in the Beatles' song "All You Need is Love," and millions of young people now began to extol the beauty of sex as a natural part of their lives. Traditional codes of behavior were challenged throughout the western world as the new liberation came to include increased acceptance of alternative forms of relationship outside marriage; it was as if the floodgates were opened, and the resulting impact upon society was both immense and long-lasting.

Yet the greatest evidence of the cultural sea change taking place was found in the dynamically evolving forms of music. Rock and roll hits of the 1950s featured a volatile mix of influences from country, rhythm and blues, and gospel; "Rock Around the Clock" by Bill Haley and the Comets marked a seminal moment, and when Elvis Presley came on the scene in 1954 he seemed to epitomize the new and thrilling epoch that had dawned. The music was often raunchy and defiant, echoing the call for rebellion glamorized by movie stars such as James Dean in *Rebel Without a Cause,* but "clean-cut" artists such as Pat Boone and Frankie Avalon were contributing softer, more harmonious melodies.

In 1960 Elvis returned to the music scene from the army, joining other white male vocalists at the top of the charts, including Bobby Darin, Neil Sedaka, and Jerry Lee Lewis. At the same time, a market for soul, reggae and blues music was created by the youthful new audiences springing up in America. The Tamla Motown Company, specializing in black rhythm and blues, aided in the emergence of James Brown, the Temptations, and female groups such as the Supremes, Aretha Franklin, and Gladys Knight and the Pips, while the Righteous Brothers were a popular white duo who used African-American styling to create a distinctive sound. The era of the rock star had been born.

A folk music revival also came about, helped by Bob Dylan, along with Joan Baez, Joni Mitchell, and Peter, Paul & Mary, musicians who were fearless in conveying their anti-war attitudes. Other bands that exemplified the counterculture, including The Mamas & Papas, Jimi Hendrix, and The Doors, were becoming huge mainstream successes. In 1964 the Beatles arrived in the United States, capturing the hearts of teenage girls with their soft rock ballads, Liverpool accents and long hair. The culminating musical sensation of the decade was the Woodstock Music and Art Fair in 1969, a three-day festival that drew four hundred thousand hippies to New York to celebrate peace, love, and happiness–and LSD.

During the 1960s the drug scene began to have a major effect on popular music, when the style known as psychedelic was born around the time of Bob Dylan's decision to play an electric guitar at the 1965 Newport Folk Festival. This form of rock, with exotic instruments, highly amplified and improvisational, bridged the transition from early blues and folk-based rock to hard rock and later heavy metal. It was a style of music which also attempted to replicate and enhance the mind-altering experiences of psychedelic drugs. The hippies used marijuana, considering it pleasurable and benign, and many musicians also began to include drug references in their songs, helping to popularize the use of LSD.

With many band members high on "grass" or LSD, hardcore "acid rock" now became a means of escaping the world–for both the band and audience. By the mid-Sixties, LSD and marijuana had overtaken America, and experimentation with mescaline, sacred mushrooms, or other psychedelics soon followed. Eventually more toxic substances such as cocaine, heroin and amphetamines came to be used for recreation, often disastrously. For, no sooner had 1967's "Summer of Love" passed, than it all started to come undone. In 1969, Charles Manson and his gang committed the infamous Tate-LaBianca murders. By the end of that year, Janis Joplin, Brian Jones of the Rolling Stones, and Jimi Hendrix had all died of drug overdoses.

Meanwhile, the civil rights movement gave up its nonviolence philosophy when it was taken over by extremists, even as opposition to the Vietnam War began reaching a wider audience and became a radical movement on college campuses. In 1964, protests unprecedented in scope took place at the University of Berkeley, California, as students began challenging campus regulations limiting their rights of free speech and political activity. On December 2, thousands of students took part in a two-day sit-in; the demonstration was orderly, and

Joan Baez led the participants in folk songs. It ended when the governor called in the police; hundreds of arrests were made and there were many charges of police brutality. The resulting fallout caused the university faculty to back down and end all restrictions.

The student activists had proved victorious, and given a sense they possessed political and social power, together with a moral responsibility to exercise it. The movement that started there became the younger generation's model for protest throughout the rest of the decade, an activism that reflected broader cultural conflicts surrounding the crucial issues of the time. As American involvement in Vietnam escalated, and the climax of the racial confrontation was reached with the assassination of Martin Luther King, Jr. in 1968, these conflicts grew increasingly divisive. At the same time, the protestors began to adopt more violent methods, such as burning buildings and throwing rocks or bombs.

The campus protests, widely viewed through the new medium of television, caused dismay and horror throughout the nation. In response to what many citizens and government officials regarded as incidents of disorderly conduct, the police began to adopt forceful measures, including the use of tear gas, batons, and fire hoses. The violent confrontations between activists and law enforcement officials taking place at the demonstrations had the unfortunate result of heightening tensions, and many young people began to show a deep distrust of the police, revealed most particularly in derogatory terms such as "fuzz" and "pig." At the same time they came to perceive the dominant culture as a coercive and authoritarian entity, derisively labeled "Big Brother."[10]

These developments in the wider world naturally had a huge impact on the police establishment, and Dave felt this personally and firsthand. In Victoria, attitudes toward the police changed so dramatically that they went, seemingly almost overnight, from being valued members of society to persons viewed with wariness and suspicion. Increasingly, law enforcement officers were forced into a social shell, finding recreation and friendships amongst their own and severing wider relationships within society. As far as Dave was concerned, it was a golden era which had gone forever. Once it was that, if a girl was going out with a police officer, her parents could not have been more delighted. Now all that was changed, and he looked back nostalgically in one of his songs:

A '55 FORD AND ELVIS[11]

A '55 Ford and Elvis
Really moved back in those days,
And Hailey rocked around the clock
'Til someone threw the key away.

The jeans were a little lower,
Only James Dean jacket high,
With a ducktail grown, and a rat-tail comb,
And you'd sleep in the drive-in tonight;
Now that was living, Lord,
Me and a '55 Ford ...

And I'd love to love you tomorrow,
If some time from the past I could borrow,
But me and the Ford, we're stuck in yesterday,
Where there are memories that never get
To go away ...
It's me and a '55 Ford
When every day was play,
That '55 Ford and rock
Really carried me away.

There was also the matter of his relationship with his musical acquaintances, which as a writer of songs he valued highly. Formerly he would get together with his friends at parties, and they would talk and play music, but now a distance was developing. These meetings had frequently become occasions for smoking marijuana or taking harder drugs, and because his friends would not put him in a compromising position he would often no longer be invited. Some time after they had come to know one another, David Foster confessed to Dave, "You know the reason my mother thinks that you hang out with me?"

Dave shook his head.

"She thinks you're working undercover, you think I might be doing dope and you're trying to catch me."

They both laughed, and it became a standing joke between them, even after David's mother Eleanor came to realize the two men simply shared a passion for music, and grew to love Dave dearly. Nevertheless, it remained a painful transition.

During the flower power age, Dave remembered a young man talking with him about "the Establishment."

"How's it feel to be a pig?" he asked contemptuously.

"That's a 'love child' saying that," Dave thought to himself incredulously. Yet he answered calmly. "As a member of 'the Establishment,' I'm here to defend your right to say that. It's the 'pig' that maintains your freedom to express your opinion."

Dave grieved over the societal changes most of all because he knew the integrity and dedication of his fellow officers. He had observed with a steady eye the hard work, the risks incurred, the sheer courage displayed by the men he worked with day by day. The goals of maintaining the law and order which is fundamental to a free society, of preventing and detecting crime and the antisocial behavior which blights the community, of fighting organized crime and making it safe to enjoy great national events–all these were very real to the young policeman. Moreover, he knew firsthand of the perils which abound in the life of an officer; that they were on the frontline, frequently confronted with raw and brutal realities, and ready to intervene in violent situations.

There was no greater act of humanity, he reflected, than to put one's life on the line to defend others, to protect them from evil, and preserve their liberty. Dave knew, in short, that the daily battle to keep people safe in their homes and streets was one which was just and honorable.

At the same time, he was becoming aware of another legacy of the Sixties era–the end result brought about by that time of permissiveness, free love and drug-taking–the young lives that were ravaged and destroyed by substance abuse.

CHAPTER 9
Casper the Friendly Ghost

IT WAS NOT long before the forces unleashed during that tumultuous decade started to impact Victoria with all the swiftness, suddenness and devastation of a tsunami. In early 1967, Dave was with another officer, named Bob, when they received a call concerning some teenagers and a developing situation in the Ten Mile Point area of Saanich. They drove out to the address they were given, and found a low-set dwelling located on a narrow lot leading down toward the ocean; it was open to the sky, with gaping holes for doors and windows, and the abandoned air of a derelict house. The two men climbed over a stone wall and approached the building; they soon saw four or five young people inside, who, as the policemen drew near, began a frantic and futile attempt to hide plastic bags filled with some kind of plant material.

"What are you doing here?" the officers enquired.

Shrugs and averted eyes. "Nothing, we're just hanging out," one mumbled.

Dave bent down and picked up one of the green "baggies" from beneath a chair and held it out to them. "What is this stuff?" he asked.

One of the teenagers ventured an answer. "Well, it looks like marijuana," he said.

"Yeah, sure," said Dave sarcastically, and Bob laughed. This was Victoria, not New York City, where everyone knew that "reefers" were widely available. Nevertheless, because the teenagers had boxes of packaging material as well as scales, and were clearly preparing to market the plants, the men called Headquarters and asked for detectives to be sent. In due course they showed up, yet couldn't identify the mysterious substance. So they decided to call the Royal Canadian Mounted Police, the RCMP.

"They're Federal," said one of the detectives. "They're sure to know what it is."

Shortly after, the Mounties arrived on the scene, but were also nonplused. "We'll have to take it in to analyze it," they determined.

So they seized everything and took it back to the police station along with the young men. Within a day or two the results came back: it was indeed marijuana, a whole thirteen ounces. The case made headline news in the *Victoria Times Colonist*, and eventually the story was broadcast across the nation: "*Saanich Police Break Drug Ring.*"

The five young men were duly charged with possession of drugs, and each hired lawyers for their court appearance, to no avail. All were sentenced to a considerable time in prison–for an activity which is at the present time no longer considered illegal. And that was how little known marijuana was in Victoria, indeed in the whole of Canada, in the mid-Sixties.

Yet, within a short space of time, the drug scene exploded, and the problems within the British Columbia capital were particularly acute. Victoria's proximity to the United States, and the many islands and waterways which surround her, made the city a natural gateway for the entry of drugs into the vast hinterland of the country. Further west, on the other side of the Pacific, lay the shores of Asia with seemingly limitless supplies of mind-altering substances, many of which were carried in by navy vessels and then peddled by dealers in Victoria. And Vancouver Island itself was a goldmine when it came to the cultivation of marijuana, being large enough and isolated enough in areas to make the growing of the drug almost impossible to detect.

At one time, when he was working with the Drug Squad, Dave was given a lead which informed him that an area of marijuana was being cultivated on Saltspring Island, lying in the strait between Victoria and the mainland. The island had only a small population, quite a few areas were still uninhabited, and the climate was perfect for growing the drug. Together with a group of fellow officers he traveled to Saltspring, and almost straightaway they discovered a huge plot of land with close to a thousand marijuana plants, healthy and flourishing; a length of chicken wire was stretched around the perimeter to keep out the deer. The officers now had to make some decisions. The field was unattended, because the rainfall was so abundant the plants could thrive on their own; they also had no way of knowing when the cultivator would return to gather his crop.

Eventually they pulled out the plants and tore up the wire fence, then in the middle of the erstwhile plantation left a bottle with a note inside:

Dear Sir,

Thank you for the chicken wire and the marijuana plants. If you would care to retrieve them, please call in at:

RCMP Drug Squad,
999 Fort Street,
Victoria.

Strangely enough, they never did hear from the owner.

It did not take long before marijuana became a popular street drug in Victoria, and also started appearing in high schools, but the problem was not confined to young people. One evening, Dave got a call concerning a disturbance taking place in the front yard of a Saanich home. He drove to the address he was given; it was a wealthy area and the house was large and imposing. In the front garden was a teenager who, although not violent, was obviously "stoned," gazing up into the large trees that were spread over the manicured lawn, and occasionally flailing his arms in fruitless gestures towards the boughs. Dave addressed him.

"What are you doing?" he asked.

"We gotta get those gorillas out of the trees," the teen responded, still gazing up at the branches.

Dave produced a flashlight and played it among the foliage, although it was clear the young man was hallucinating. He thought he should find the boy's parents, and went to the front door and knocked. A man of about forty answered the door.

"Yes?" he said, peering into the dark at the police officer who had suddenly appeared on his doorstep.

"Sir, we have your son out there; he says he's trying to get primates out of your trees."

"Yes, I know," came the response. "I've seen them too … do you think you can help us get rid of them?"

Dave realized with a shock that the father was stoned as well.

In the 1970s, the Drug Squad of the Saanich Police had two main spheres of operation. The first of these focused on sending a number of police officers to patrol the streets and beer parlors of downtown Victoria, which were rife with drugs and dealers. The second area, that of intelligence, was considered far more crucial, for it was concerned with targeting the importers and suppliers who sold for profit, rather than the hapless victims of their trade. It was after Dave became involved in this latter sphere of operation that he first began working with informants, a collaboration with an element of danger about it which he nevertheless relished. The intelligence they provided often proved invaluable, especially in investigations related to organized crime, homicide and narcotics.

Some of the informants he dealt with were members of the public who would divulge their inside knowledge in order to gain some kind of protection–perhaps a prominent figure in the community who is afraid that word of his habit will emerge, or a teenager terrified his parents will discover his addiction. Usually, however, Dave's informants were criminals themselves, who provided the intelligence either for financial reward or to gain leniency for their own misdeeds, either immunity from prosecution, or a reduced charge or sentence. Sometimes, however, those in this second group were operating from a genuine desire to help the police in their quest to solve a crime. These were usually men who dabbled on the fringes of illegal activity, but who had, reluctantly and against their will, become caught up in murder.

Indeed, drug-related homicides accelerated after the Sixties as the availability of new, stronger–and more expensive–drugs accelerated, and the major drug cartels began emerging on the scene. The first cocaine "bust" in Victoria was in 1973; yet Dave, like the other officers, came to prefer to arrest someone for heroin rather than marijuana. The heroin addicts didn't argue or justify themselves; they knew without being told that their habit was wrong. However, when the "potheads" were apprehended, they could actually be violent because they believed so passionately what they were doing was right, and felt they were taking a moral stand against an oppressive establishment. Dave knew, however, that marijuana was dangerous in the sense that it led to other dependencies; he almost never met a heroin or cocaine addict who hadn't first started experimenting with pot. There was always that desire to look for an even greater high; as the Doors song said, to "set the night on fire."

It was during his time with the Drug Squad that Dave also acquired his reputation as someone who could seemingly be invisible at will. He had started the practice of giving his fellow officers nicknames, some of them drawn from his own compositions. For example, there was Feathertoes, who was short but powerfully built and lightning quick in his reflexes. Dave had named him from his song about a little girl:

> *Feathertoes been dancing since the cradle threw her out,*
> *Landed lightly on her feet and started shufflin' about ...*

Then there was Walter the Altar Boy, whose innocent features belied his tough nature, and Crowbar, who excelled at breaking in doors. Dave's own nickname, Casper the Ghost, was bestowed on him by his colleagues, who were amazed at the number of times he should have been seen by the criminals he was chasing, yet somehow evaded detection.

In one such incident, he and his fellow drug squad members were undertaking surveillance on a suspected dealer who owned a property near the beach. It was a dark evening and Dave was kneeling outside the house, almost in a fetal position, when two men emerged from the front door. They drew near to where he was crouching, then paused, and sat down exactly beside him. They had come out to smoke a joint, and passed the smoking stub between them as they conversed together in low tones. Dave knelt there within touching distance, barely daring to breathe; one of the dealers actually leaned back against him as they talked. After five or six minutes, when the joint was finished, they returned to the house completely unaware that a police officer was in the vicinity–and were successfully apprehended.

At that time the Churchill Hotel was a major drug outlet in Victoria, and Dave went in one evening with a fellow officer; they were both in plain clothes and sat in different parts of the bar. It so happened that Dave found himself seated next to a young woman, and they fell into a casual conversation. After a while, his new acquaintance nodded her head toward the other officer. She leaned forward and spoke in Dave's ear.

"Watch yourself," she breathed, "that guy's a narc."

"You're kidding," he said in surprised tones, and they continued their conversation; when he finally got up and left they were on the best of terms.

And when in time the addicts came to know Dave in the course of his duties, they also came to recognize him as a person who would always treat them well. One of them summed up the general verdict. "He's the friendliest ghost I've ever seen," he said.

CHAPTER 10

Summer Is the House Where We Will Live

DESPITE THESE SOCIETAL problems, Dave was continuing to lead his double life as both a lawman and a writer of ballads. Some of his songs gave voice to the playful, fanciful side of his nature; other of his love poems began expressing a yearning for something more than the immediate thrill of romance:

IT'S BEEN A JOURNEY

It's been a journey all my life –
Never changed a lady to a wife,
But sometimes, I'm so alone,
Yes, sometimes – the blues come home.

I've seen the birds fly in my time
And I have followed close behind,
But it has been just sound and foam,
'Cause sometimes—the blues come home.

I sleep on unfamiliar floors—
I follow footsteps, nothing more,
The other dogs all got a bone,
Me, I get to see the blues come home.

I recall the times I've seen
As I have run this crazy race,
While the mirror keeps reminding me
Of the stranger in my face.

Ain't been to heaven, but just about—
Time wasn't right, they threw me out,

I guess I'll make it on my own
In time to see the blues come home.

I guess the way I live my life
Was in the rolling of the dice,
But how alone can one heart be—
As lonely as the blues and me.

LOVE'S WISDOM

At any end, I'd love to find me
Locked within the vision of your eyes,
In every breath, as time unwinds me
To borrow from you wisdom, to be wise,
And if a dream should catch you sleeping,
Let it leave at least half a thought of me,
And in every word that finds you speaking,
For tomorrow only knows where we will be.

And all these things that make you wonder
How solid is the ground on which we stand
Well, every season isn't summer,
And answered dreams aren't always close at hand,
It's not as if it proved convenient
The choice of time that gave us to each other,
For lasting love is not that lenient,
But rules with wisdom magic realms
We are hoping to discover.

JUST WHEN YOU THINK I'M GONE

Just when you think love is over,
That you've forgotten.
And you're learning how to live with yourself;
When the memories you thought would last forever
Don't come as often,
And you think you'll share yourself with someone else.

When your heart doesn't pound at the sound of the phone,
And you don't think of me when you're sleeping alone,
And just when you think I'm gone,
If you still care,
I'll always be there …
Just when you think I'm gone.

And though it has changed, you'll still remember the place
I used to take you to,
And though it has aged, you'll still remember the face
That can't stop loving you.

If I could, I'd wish it was over,
Forget it, if I may,
But the time of chasing dreams goes on and on,
And it never changes from day to day
Or year to year,
And I'll always be right here …
Just when you think I'm gone.

And when your heart doesn't pound at the sound of the phone,
And you don't think of me when you're sleeping alone,
And just when you think I'm gone,
If you still care,
I'll always be there …
Just when you think I'm gone,
Just when you think I'm gone.

All the time, Dave's relationship with his girlfriend Jo, who had inspired his song "Wildflower," was becoming more serious:

Dirty times and grinding in my brain
Sunshine days reclining in the rain
Passed away and won't find me again
For I've got Jo to go to now.

Eventually they decided to marry, and it seemed to Dave they were fair set to live happily ever after:

SUMMER HOUSE
(Or anything else you like)

Hear the summer's song
As it floats by on the wind,
Calling out to everyone:
I have returned
To sing again,
And we've got so much to do,
In love with me, in love with you.

And summer is the house where we shall live,
Giving to love
And loving to give,
And sunshine is the suitcase that we came here with,
We might as well stay here a while,
A while …

Happy is our song
As we run through greener fields,
Winter's come and gone
And now we know how loving feels,
And we can live each summer through,
In love with me, in love with you.

Feel the summer breathe
A warmer breeze into our lives,
All the rainy days,
They fade away before our eyes,
Leaving us so much to do,
In love with me, in love with you.

And summer is the house …

Hear the summer song
Floating through the trees,
Winter would be wrong
To bring us to our knees,
We've got so much to do,
In love with me, in love with you.

And summer is the house …

CHAPTER 11

The Poet Cop of Saanich

IT WAS NOT just Dave's personal life which was providing a new source of equilibrium and happiness. His song "Wildflower" continued to go from strength to strength and eventually was played all around the world. Dave's brother Don, who was working as a missionary in the jungles of New Guinea, wrote to say he had heard the song on short-wave radio from Australia. Back on Vancouver Island the status of "The Poet Cop of Saanich," as he came to be known, was also notably enhanced. He would find some of the younger police officers coming to him to shyly ask his opinion on their own compositions.

Above all, Dave was learning that "Wildflower" seemed to have a special power to minister to women suffering from the aftermath of traumatic emotional experiences. In the decades that followed the release of the song, Dave many received letters from around the globe that testified to its power to change lives. The most momentous of these was from his hometown of Victoria, years after the song was a hit. A local woman sent him a letter addressed to the police station, saying that when she was a girl of eighteen her life had become more than she could bear, and she had decided to end it all. She went to a beach near Mount Douglas Park, and waited for the sun to go down and everyone to leave so she could commit suicide by drowning herself.

When it got dark, and the scene had become deserted, she slowly stood up, walked to the water's edge, and moved forward. Behind her, on a blanket in the sand, she had left her purse and belongings, as well as a transistor radio that was still playing. She continued wading into the water until it reached her shoulders, and at that point she heard the lyrics of a song come floating over the waves from the transistor. They were words she had never heard before: "*She's faced the hardest times you could imagine.*" She stopped and listened to the entire song as it played, and when it was over she turned and walked out of the water. At the time she wrote to Dave to thank him for the song which had saved her life, she was happily married and a mother of children.

When Dave read those words, he knew he would gladly have traded every cent he had made from the song for that one letter. And there were other surprising encounters as well, that revealed to him just how great had been the impact of the ballad.

One sunny day around noon, Dave was pulling on to Douglas Street out by Saanich Police Station when he looked to the left and saw a car speeding toward him, clearly over the limit. As the vehicle passed, he saw it was a girl who was driving, and he could also see that her face was distorted and she was crying. He pulled out behind her and turned on the "toys"–his lights and siren–and she slowed down, came to a halt at the side of the road, and wound down her window. As he walked up to speak to her, Dave saw that she was young–about nineteen or twenty–and pretty, and was now drying her eyes.

"Can I have your license, please?" he asked her, and she gave it to him; he noted that she was an American from California. "Did you know that you were really speeding?" he continued.

"I'm so sorry," she said in a distressed tone of voice, "I just had a fight with my boyfriend." It was a good line, but Dave believed her because he had seen her tears before he pulled her over.

"Driving like that is very dangerous," he began saying to her sternly, still standing beside her car, when suddenly she interrupted him.

"Would you excuse me?" she asked. She reached over and turned up the volume of the radio. "This song, I just love it."

And then, to his utmost surprise, Dave heard words floating out, words that he knew, oh, so well: "*Let her cry, for she's a lady …* "

And now the girl was crying again into her handkerchief as she listened to his song. "I'm really sorry; it's just that I'm so upset," she managed to say after she calmed down.

Dave was completely taken aback! "Should I tell her I wrote that song?" he wondered–yet even as the thought crossed his mind he dismissed it. She would never have believed him, and he could visualize her expression as he did so. "Yeah, right," he could picture her saying scornfully, while thinking at the same time, "What kind of move is this!"

"Well, I understand," he finally said to her, "but maybe in future you shouldn't drive when you're feeling emotional."

She nodded obediently and drove away, clearly relieved he had been so lenient. Still, in those circumstances he certainly could not have given her a ticket!

That for Dave was a time when life was magical. As "Wildflower" was becoming more famous, he would find girls and women coming up to him and asking: "What was the situation you were writing about in the song?"

He could see they were really looking for an answer, and found it hard not to have compassion for them, so he would say, "How do you interpret it, what do *you* think it's saying?"

Invariably some memory would emerge of a relationship that was important to them, and they would explain, very emotionally, what the ballad meant to them in terms of their own experience. And he loved what it had done for people. As long as he lived, he wanted to have women come up to him, perhaps even in their seventies and eighties, and say to him, "When I was a teenager that was the song we were listening to when I fell in love with my husband."

This was what he desired for all his songs: that they would bring encouragement to those who longed for the intimacy of a deep love relationship, and to experience the enchantment that can only be found in affairs of the heart:

SOMEONE'S OPEN HAND

Save your happy heart until tomorrow,
Someone's open hand is waiting there,
Take it out of storage,
Someone is looking for it,
Just around the corner someone cares.

You held out your hand, and it was empty,
The love that you were holding slipped away,
But love can sing a minor song,
Have you been lonely so very long
That you'll forsake tomorrow for today?

So find yourself a happy thought,
Everything your tears have taught,
Hold it fast till it is caught
And do not fail to think it,
Pour some love into your cup,
Then lift your glass and – bottoms up!
It will taste ambrosial
When you try to drink it.

Take a longer look into your future,
Wait until the sunshine comes again,
Turn your eyes toward the sky
And soon your tears will dry,
And someone's open hand will halt the rain.

Everyone who searches is a finder,
And everything you give you will receive,
And you will keep on living
To get the love you're giving,
In someone's open hand you will believe.

So find yourself a happy thought,
Joy is what your tears have wrought,
Hold it fast till it is caught
And do not fail to think it,
Pour some love into your cup,
Then lift your glass and – bottoms up!
It will taste ambrosial
When finally you drink it.

CHAPTER 12
Meeting Valley

WHEN "WILDFLOWER" WAS first released, Dave knew nothing about the intricacies of promoting his music or handling royalties. Fairly soon he was contacted by a man named Roger Paradiso, who was in the business of supporting Canadian recording artists, and who brought international theater and concerts to Canada. He suggested he would like to meet Dave, and proposed to travel over from Vancouver and take him to lunch at a restaurant in Victoria's Inner Harbor. The two men agreed on a place and time, and eventually Dave found himself seated with the entrepreneur at a table that provided them with stunning views of the waterfront. After they had ordered and been served their meals, Roger turned to the business for which he had come.

"I want you to know you've written a fantastic song there, Dave," he said.

"Thank you."

"It's beautiful–but it's never going to go anywhere."

"Why not?" asked Dave.

"You called the song 'Wildflower,' but nowhere in the song is the word 'wildflower' mentioned. That means it's going to bomb."

"Maybe so," said Dave, "but I like it. I didn't write it to make money."

"Well," remarked Roger thoughtfully, "I hate to see a budding young songwriter like yourself with so much talent come out of this without any money. So I'll give you ten thousand dollars for the total rights to the song."

"Mr. Paradiso," said Dave, "if the song is going to be such a bomb, why do you want to blow so much money on it?"

"Just because I want to see you get something out of all this."

Dave leaned back in his chair, and laid down his knife and fork. "Personally, sir," he said, "I don't care if this song makes only ten cents. I wrote it, I like it, and so does Doug."

The meal ended amicably. And Dave's first royalty check, when it came, was almost as much as Paradiso had offered.

Dave's years of police work continually gave him insights into human nature which were sometimes reassuring, but all too often dismaying. Similarly, his encounters with personalities operating in the realm of show business brought him glimpses into the human heart which could leave him either elated or depressed. Another whimsical poem he wrote around that time reflected some of his thoughts:

TOAD'S SONG

Well, I've just arrived in town, sir,
On a crazy errand bound,
I've come here searching for a friend,
But no one's noticed I'm around.

The barber in the pool hall
At the bowling alley's end
Said that he would cut my hair
For a dollar-and-a-half a pound.
And then he laughed
From the bottom of his pot,
And then he says that it's a joke,
But we both know that it's not.

So the barber laughed his merry laugh
As he waves me on my way,
And he says that he's a busy man;
Well, be that as it may,
I'd gladly stay and talk of love
'Till there's nothing left to say,
And stars are shining up above ...
Isn't that what friends are all about?

Well, I can't remember home, sir,
So I don't know where I'm from,
I'm in between twelve and twenty-two,
You'd have to ask my Mom,
And though I'm small in stature

My heart is six-foot-four,
And for a friend of mine
There's nothing I won't do.

Well, it seems a pleasant town, sir,
And I'm still hoping for a friend,
A fortune is burning in my pocket
That you can help me spend;
So won't you step inside, son,
And rest your weary bones,
I'll be the finest friend to you
That you have ever known.

And so my turn has come to laugh
As I look at him and say,
I know that all is just a joke,
But then to my dismay,
With a shiny eye and a broken nose
He sends me on my way,
And I'm left wondering, pray tell,
What friends are all about?

But still I'll give
To the person who ain't got,
 Only got one life to live …
Isn't that what friends are all about?

On the edge of the city limits
There's another boy like me,
Making his way into the town
Just as I start to leave;
What's waiting here for me? he asked,
And I slowly shook my head,
He smiled, and said, but it's just the same
Where you go, I believe.

And so we shake our hands
For we walk a common road,
And on our backs—O Lord,
We share a common load;

His name is Frog, he tells me,
And I laugh with a freer air;
That's fine, I said, and mine is Toad …
And I think that now I know
What friends are all about.

In the early days after "Wildflower" was released, Dave was making what he thought was pretty good money, but as he didn't know what lyricists made he had nothing with which to compare it; he also felt a concern for royalties detracted from the creativity of his writing. He and Doug Edwards continued receiving checks as "Wildflower" began selling around the world, yet they never knew if these funds were fair and equitable. Fortunately, a remarkable woman named Valley came into their lives.

Valerie (Valley) Hennell was a pioneer in the arts world of British Columbia. As she grew up, her two main desires were to become a lawyer and a poet, and somehow she managed a career that combined both roles. Her adventure began in 1966, when at the age of seventeen she enrolled in the newly established Creative Writing Department at the University of British Columbia, and gained a master's degree. It was a vibrant time on the UBC campus, and Valley's instructors encouraged the students to take film production classes and collaborate with the theater department. While garnering an array of skills, she became friends with many of the artists who went on to forge careers on radio, stage and in the recording studios that began springing up in Vancouver. They provided a major creative force that would shape the arts scene in B.C. for decades to come.

One of these friendships was with emerging folk singer Ann Mortifee, whom she met while working at the Musical Theatre Society. The two women began composing songs together, and Valley soon produced her first concert and earliest recordings. When she overheard Ann speaking on the phone making arrangements for a show, and asking for only a pittance in return, Valley became galvanized. In the world of art and performance, it was the creative work issuing from a person's imagination that was crucial and irreplaceable–yet it became glaringly clear to her that many talented artists lacked the business acumen to promote and protect their work.

Valley, however, was gifted both creatively and with the ability to handle the commercial aspects of "showbiz." And so, imbued with a fierce determination to champion artists and their rights, she launched another career as Artist Manager.

As it happened, around that time she became connected with another female music business pioneer in Vancouver named Lynne Reusch, who established a West Coast office for the Performing Rights Organization BMI Canada. Lynne quickly became a friend and mentor to Valley, and taught her, along with countless others in the emerging music industry in Vancouver, the basics of music publishing and the value of copyrights.

In 1973 Ann Mortifee introduced Valley to Doug Edwards, the same year "Wildflower" had become a major hit for Skylark. It was not long before she discovered Doug had signed away the copyright and publishing rights to the song, and became concerned that a major injustice was taking place. With Doug's blessing, she set out to take back control of the copyright and retrieve any missing royalties; it was a challenge that took several years, but Valley was determined and persevering, and her efforts finally yielded success. Dave and Doug began receiving a just recompense for the sales of "Wildflower," and eventually the two men formalized their business arrangement with Valley. A half century later, she is still managing the royalties as administrator of a classic soul standard which has impacted audiences around the world.

During that same period, Valley has combined her creative and business skills in every aspect of the arts in Canada: she has written for stage, page, media and television, and produced countless arts and educational events both nationally and internationally. She has continued to manage the careers of several well-known B.C. artists, and is recognized in the music industry as a force for integrity and fair dealing. Her numerous awards are a testament to her talent and dedication, and in 2021 she was inducted Star Meritus in the B.C. Entertainment Hall of Fame.

Over the years that she managed the ballad, Valley and Dave also became firm friends; their connection was never primarily a matter of business, but one filled with warmth and mutual admiration. "I don't care if you get to be the biggest in the world," he told her earnestly, "the most important thing is honesty and that alone will last the distance." He was indescribably grateful to her for her role in safeguarding the royalties for "Wildflower," and turned to her for wise counsel on many occasions, not just those related to music.

As their relationship endured through the decades, Valley also came to understand and appreciate the inner essence of the man with whom she worked. She wondered how it was that this songwriting cop had created a ballad with such a universal and timeless appeal, and eventually felt she had found the key. It was the union of fragility and resilience Dave had managed to capture and portray in "the free and gentle flower growing wild" that enabled the song to reach so many hearts. How had Dave done that, she also wondered, and finally came to realize.

"He is a true romantic," was her summing up.

CHAPTER 13

The Secret of Success

THE SUCCESS OF Dave's song "Wildflower" as a single from Skylark's first album had cemented and deepened his friendship with David Foster, and the relationship continued even after David moved to Los Angeles with the other band members. Yet Dave was not surprised when he learned the band had broken up. He knew the real reason: David was a driven man. The other members of Skylark had returned to Canada because they preferred a less frenetic lifestyle–but David had elected to remain in Los Angeles.

Dave knew also that his friend had both the talent and the personality that destined him for greatness. While David was still touring with Skylark, he called Dave one night from a payphone in Fort Lauderdale, very upset and despondent. He shared with Dave he had become entangled in a disastrous contract, and the party on the other side was threatening to break his fingers. "David, don't give up," Dave encouraged his young friend, "You're the king, you're going to be successful, but if you come back here you'll just end up being a nightclub player, and you're better than that. You're better than anybody."

Soon David had moved permanently to California, where his career started its spectacular rise, and Dave visited him down there a number of times. On one occasion when he was staying at his friend's apartment in Los Angeles he got up early in the morning and came into the living room. David was there, seated at the piano; he had his back to Dave and didn't know he was there. His daughter Amy, only a baby at the time, was seated on his lap, and he was talking to her as he played.

"What would you like to hear, Amy?" he was saying, "a little Frank Sinatra?," and he played one or two of Frankie's songs. "But maybe you're still too young for that," he mused, "How about we listen to the Beatles instead?," and he swung into one of their latest hits. "Or maybe some Chuck Berry?" he suggested, launching into an entirely different rhythm, then asking, "Now a little Bach? Or Rachmaninoff?," and the beautiful classical notes filled the air.

Amy never made a sound; Dave was sure she was sitting entranced on her father's knee. He himself sat quietly listening and never said a word to let David know he was there; it was an impromptu performance he would not have interrupted for the world, and he was astonished by the display of such musical virtuosity. He always felt when watching David play that it was like watching Michelangelo at work, and indeed in all the years he knew his friend he never tired of seeing those fingers go over the keys.

As time went by, when Dave phoned David it would be to discover he was in New York or some other destination; he was always on the go. Dave still managed to fly down to Los Angeles to see him on regular occasions, and continued making new acquaintances there. Many more artists were recording cover versions of "Wildflower," including Hank Crawford, Johnny Mathis and the O'Jays. Kenny Rogers told Dave that, of all the ballads he had written and recorded, he couldn't compose one that compared to "Wildflower." "Nothing I've written has come close to it, Dave," he said. It was the favorite song of his wife, Marianne.

Dave was also introduced by David to Olivia Newton John at a recording studio in Los Angeles; she was in town to make a movie called *Two of a Kind* with John Travolta. Dave had just begun to engage her in conversation when her co-star arrived, and David introduced him as well. Dave said, "Hi, John," and turned straight back to Olivia. She was gorgeous, not wearing a scrap of makeup, and he was almost tongue-tied in her presence.

Over the years, Dave's respect for David as a man, apart from his musical genius, also grew deeper. "Foz," as he was called, had a well-attested gift for recognizing and promoting talent in others. He discovered Celine Dion in Quebec when she could not even speak English, and transformed her career, as well as setting Andrea Boccelli, Michael Bublé and Josh Groban on their skyward trajectories. In addition, he reinvigorated the careers of a number of formerly famous entertainers.

Less well known was the entirely unobtrusive way in which David would go about helping others. At one time, he heard an unknown singer named Warren Wiebe performing in a mall and hired him; Warren had the voice of an angel and never realized his own giftedness, but David ended up taking Warren with him wherever he traveled. Dave especially had a soft spot for Warren, who put his heart and soul into singing "Wildflower" in a manner which would do it justice. He grieved when he heard the performer had died while still a young man.

Dave didn't care how famous a person was, what mattered to him was integrity. He had found, especially in the United States, that the true superstars were the genuine ones, who would stop and talk to people in the streets and never say no to an autograph–David himself, Kenny Rogers, Wayne Gretzky. The "wannabe superstars" were the ones who looked down their noses at other people; the ones who were truly great remained humble and maintained a respect for others. He remembered someone who once remarked to David Foster, "Perhaps you shouldn't do this gig with Lionel Richie, because he's black."

David was infuriated. "Don't you ever speak to me again about race," he said.

More than all, Dave admired the phenomenal generosity of his friend, who after his success in the world of entertainment turned his attention to promoting various charitable causes, and eventually established the David Foster Foundation. This was created to provide financial support to Canadian families with children in need of life-saving organ transplants, and over the years the Foundation has helped more than 1400 families through the millions of dollars David raised by staging spectacular concerts in cities across the nation.

Of all the new acquaintances he made through David, Dave enjoyed meeting none more than Wayne Gretzky, the superlative hockey player who was also a true son of Canada. As Dave grew to know the sporting star better, he came to admire him enormously for his modesty and down-to-earth nature–as well as his incomparable athletic abilities. In one stellar year, 1982, Wayne had scored 92 goals for his team, the Edmonton Oilers, and Dave asked him curiously,

"Wayne, do you think it's possible for someone to score a hundred goals in a year?"

Wayne looked at him directly. "Dave, why do you say a hundred?" he asked. "Why not two hundred–or five hundred?"

And it came to Dave, in the nature of a revelation, that this was the secret of success–for Wayne, for David, for himself, and all those who desired to use their gifts–this sense of reaching for the sky, and of boundless possibility.

CHAPTER 14
Writing Angels' Words

DAVE'S POLICE CAREER was thriving, he was making new friends in the world of law enforcement, and continuing to write many lyrics. In fact, it was a marvelous creative period for both Doug Edwards and himself; the two men felt caught up into a realm of inspiration that astonished them, so much so that Dave wrote a song about it:

There were days when we would write the words of angels …

The fundamental truth about Dave was that he was a lover of life and of beauty–in women, yes, but also in the characters of the men and women he met who became role models for him–and also in nature. The beauty of the seasons in Victoria was a perennial source of inspiration, and he loved watching them "*turn, turn, turn*" throughout the year.

As spring came nudging its way back into western Canada, and the sun made an appearance after long months of gray, he delighted in seeing its rays glinting on the ocean waters that surrounded the city. The light would caress the waves dancing on the narrow strait that separated Vancouver Island from the coast of the United States, where Port Angeles sheltered beneath the lofty ranges of the Olympic Mountains, still snow blanketed. To the north the dense woods of Malahat Drive, leading to the interior of the Island, were clothed in new mantles of green, while in the streets of the city itself the maple trees put forth soft masses of leaves.

In the evenings, he would watch the moon, that "*instigator of love*" as he called it, riding high in the heavens, together with the other celestial bodies in their differing splendors. During the summer months, the clouds that floated over the Victorian skyscape lent their own enchantment to the scene, and then, tinted with the pastel shades of evening, adorned the setting sun with consummate artistry. The gentle waves that lapped the beaches were suffused with ever-changing hues of blue, and a wondrous sheen lay on the numerous ocean inlets that penetrated the city, over which the seagulls floated on warmer currents of air. All these things were never-ending providers of delight to him.

As the autumn drew on apace, the maple leaves in their burnished red and gold would fall to the ground in great drifts; then, as the first cold fingers of frost stretched over the countryside, the trees and bushes became transfigured with delicate patterns of ice. On some occasions also the large powdery flakes of snow came softly descending, spreading a white veil across the landscape, and evoking a magical hush. As the waterways around the city became frozen, the young men would emerge onto the transformed surroundings for winter sports, baseball and ice hockey, taking deep breaths of the exhilarating air, and reveling in the joy of vigorous exercise. Dave also loved to watch the incomparable grace of the girls floating on their skates over the ice-covered waterways, who appeared to him as figures from a dream of beauty.

VICTORIA'S SELDOM SNOW

Victoria's seldom snow has fallen again
That sometimes stranger of the north,
Spread over us a pure white blanket
That's been resting on some icy porch;
And still we call him inconvenient
And blame him for the mishaps
Complaining of his ill intent
To catch us in old winter's trap.

He must be frightened by our greeting
As we score with sand his silver flakes
Pierce him with our studded tires
And lash him with our metal stakes;
To this bequest from heaven's vault
We don't care to aspire,
And then we paint those wounds with salt,
No wonder then his visit's fleeting.

It falls so quietly, his gentle freight,
I think it's love that he emulates,
And wonder if he becomes discouraged
That we his snow-white gems disparage;
Or if he is saddened by our fears

When we rip right through his frozen tears,
As if we thought his malign intent
Was to bury forever the flowers' scent.

But I think he may be grateful to those
Who respond to his rare descent,
Artists, athletes and children who love
The treasure they have been sent.
I also doubt that he then worries
When we attack his stormy flurries
He knows we can't destroy him
Though we try;
Little wonder then, that he only visits
By and by.

For Dave, the very ideal of perfect loveliness crystallized in his mind when he ventured out in his boat *Wildflower*, often with his friend Pete Schibli, who was also passionate about sailing. The men loved to explore hidden reaches of the Georgia Strait, the narrow body of water that separates Vancouver Island from the mainland. There they discovered a place known as Chatterbox Falls, locked away in a mountain fastness at the head of one of the deep inlets penetrating the mainland, accessible only by boat or seaplane. Dave would first guide the boat into Jervis Inlet, and from there approach the entrance to Princess Louisa Inlet, guarded by the Malibu Rapids, running at seven to ten knots and dropping three feet as they rush out. These he would slowly negotiate, and once past they would find themselves afloat on a tranquil body of water, smooth as glass and reflecting the surrounding vista high up into heaven.

The glaciation of millennia past has carved a magnificent granite-walled gorge through snow-tipped mountains which rise sharply from the water's edge to heights in excess of seven thousand feet. The deep calm of the enclosed space is broken only as the warm sun melting the mountain snow creates more than sixty waterfalls that cascade down the precipitous walls to mingle with the waters of the fjord; Chatterbox Falls itself at the head of the inlet tumbles 120 feet. The white wall of rushing water in contrast to the lush green rainforest and the shiny gray of the polished granite mountains added to the spectacular scenery, and for Dave this place had a beauty which was beyond imagination. The water in the inlet had a silky warmth; when he would go swimming the seals would come up to look at him and dive down again; fish such as perch would also come, and he and his friends would feed them like little pets.

Dave never forgot one evening he was there, when a breathtaking full moon was shedding a radiant light over the landscape. His boat was moored at the dock, and he took an oar and ran it through the water, stirring up the phosphorus, which flashed with a myriad of tiny points of light. Meanwhile, down the cliffs of rock which surrounded the inlet the waterfalls were streaming from the melting snow, and in the moonlight they looked like silver ribbons. When the fresh water hit the salt water, stirring up the mineral content, the inlet seemed ablaze with diamonds, millions of sparkling green gems.

All these scenes and many others were recorded indelibly in his memory, so that even though Dave was involved on a daily basis in work which showed the darkest side of human nature, he could continue to draw on the wealth of images he had committed to that inner storehouse. He would find that at the end of a twelve-hour night shift, when he was drained of energy, the ideas and melodies would often spring into his consciousness unbidden, and he would sing these into the little tape recorder he always carried. Or, in the evenings after work, he would enter a kind of creative "bubble" in which he would be immersed, and the lyrics would seemingly emanate from elsewhere and captivate his imagination completely.

THE SILVER ROAD OF LOVE

Like a child on the edge of a dream
I never could understand,
How you touch my heart as easily
As the way you touch my hand.

The silver road of love
Is a road that never ends,
And a single journey is not enough,
For here I travel again.

Just yesterday I told myself
That dreaming never pays,
Such thoughts are meant for wishing wells,
But that was yesterday.

The silver road of love,
Oh, I've been there before,
The losing's not enough,
And so I try once more.

The morning comes when I'll awake
As the dream continues on,
And into love we'll fall away
To find the search is gone.

The silver road of love
As the moon shines o'er the sea,
Begins somewhere above
And ends with you and me.

Yet this idyllic period in his life was about to be shattered.

PART II:
I DREAM A SHADOW FALLEN ON THE STREET

CHAPTER 15
Summerless

DAVE'S MARRIAGE TO Jo began to unravel as they both realized they were too young and wild for a lifelong commitment. Dave knew, as well, that his involvement in police and songwriting activities consumed so much of his time and energy he had little left to devote to the relationship. A new, darker mood began to suffuse many of his poems, as mixed feelings of regret and loneliness began to emerge.

NIGHT TRAVELER

I still travel the night,
But things have changed
Since I knew you,
I still know nocturnal shades
Of deepening blue,
And hidden creatures roving
From a world that's far too bright,
Moving only in the sequence
Of flashing neon light.

I guess I'm a little older,
For I'm beginning to feel
The chill of darkness
And sundry qualms,
Even if only slightly,
And most of the familiar faces I knew,
Have gone to the day lightly
From a woman's arms.

They pass sometimes across my sight,
When they are on their way
Home from the day,
And I am traveling in dusk's last light
To the night,
They look back at me, their glances lengthy,
And we exchange some envies.

I still travel the night
And you are on the other side of the world
In a place called
Nine-to-Five,
I must have been out of my mind,
And giving naught its proper due,
When I thought the night was
More beautiful than you.

A small incident occurred in the late Seventies, which ended in having a major impact on his life. He was taking a two-week police course on the navy base at Naden, and at the finish of one of the evening classes spent some time talking, then went back to his car. He found the gate to the parking lot closed, and to save walking all around the base to find another entrance decided to climb over the gate. It was dark, and when he landed on the other side he hit the edge of a pothole and his right ankle twisted over. It was extremely painful, but he got in his car and was able to drive home.

At that point, having separated from Jo, Dave was living with two other police officers, and when he got home one of them took Dave to the hospital where the emergency room physician x-rayed his ankle. He thought Dave had stretched some ligaments, so he bent the foot straight, and put a cast on it. In the morning Dave woke in agony; he could see his toes were turning black, and his friends took him back to the hospital. The orthopedic surgeon in the emergency ward cut the cast off, and he immediately felt relief as the circulation returned.

The doctor then phoned the radiology department and asked them to look up the x-ray; they came back on the line and repeated it looked like stretched ligaments, so he bent back the foot, put another cast on it, and Dave left on crutches. After several weeks, he cut the cast off and Dave started going to physiotherapy, but it was still painful to walk. His physiotherapist suggested he have another x-ray taken; accordingly, he returned to the same surgeon. When the new x-rays arrived, the doctor looked at them, his face went white, and he swore aloud.

"Your foot is f ... ed," he said.

"What are you talking about?" asked Dave. He could see the doctor was panic-stricken.

"When did I look at the x-rays?"

"You didn't look, you phoned radiology, and they told you it was ligaments."

"I never saw them?"

"No, not that day."

The doctor said, "You've got five fractures and a total dislocation of your foot. We've got to get you into hospital *now*."

"But I've got a dinner engagement ..." began Dave.

"*No!*–this has to be done immediately, you've got a *hospital* engagement."

The doctor operated on Dave's foot the next day, drilled holes in the bones, and put rods through them. Every so often Dave would be taken back to the operating room; they would put him under and adjust the rods, until finally they took these out and allowed him to go home–but the pain worsened. Another surgeon was called in, who examined the foot minutely.

"You need to have a triple arthrodesis," he informed Dave.

"A triple what?"

"Arthrodesis–it's a surgical fusion of the joints of your foot; we use bone which we take from your hip."

The operation went ahead in the Jubilee Hospital, and Dave woke there in the middle of the night in agony. He was lying in a pool of blood coming from his hip, and when he called a nurse pleaded she should either stop the pain or get him to a mental ward. The emergency room physician gave him morphine, and almost immediately the pain vanished; he felt he had never been so grateful to any human being. Four days later they took him off morphine, back to a regular painkiller.

Two other men were sharing the hospital room with him. "You're sure a barrel of laughs under morphine," they told him.

"Why is that?"

"The nurses brought you a bowl of cherries with your supper, and you'd put your spoon in the bowl and bring it to your mouth, but you kept missing the cherries. Then you'd chew slowly with an expression of great enjoyment. And when the nurse came to take the tray, and asked why you didn't want your cherries, you told her you were full, you had eaten so many!"

Dave was in hospital for a while, waiting for his foot to heal and the joints to fuse; no sooner had he got out, his foot still in a cast, than it started hurting again. A plastic surgeon was called, who cut a window in the plaster, and insisted he go back into hospital. A cut made across the old incision had become infected and the flesh was dying; they grafted skin from Dave's thigh over the wound, and three times a week debrided it, as Dave gripped the bars of the hospital bed. At this stage, there was a real danger that an amputation would be needed, until finally the surgeon gave Dave a word of hope.

"Right in the bottom of that wound in your foot," he said, "there's a piece of skin the size of a pinhead, it's pink and it's sticking, and eventually it will grow and fill up the wound. But," he paused and looked at Dave severely over the rim of his glasses, "I cannot make this clear enough–you are going to have to keep your foot elevated above your heart for quite some time."

It was a lonely and difficult time while Dave lay immobile waiting to heal, and, although he continued writing, his creations were often infused with a dark and somber element. At one stage he remembered a certain girl and a lake they used to visit, and this inspired a poem he called "Summerless." It expressed completely his present state of mind, without a ray of light or cheer:

> *Someone walking in the shadows*
> *Of a distant memory's place,*
> *Summer love can be forgotten,*
> *Yes–but how long does it take?*
> *Sad eyes gazing into water*
> *Of a lake once danced upon*
> *By the sun when it was younger,*
> *And less inclined to moving on.*
> *Offering love to an acquaintance*
> *That was never yours to give,*
> *An aging story with an ending*
> *Of how short a love can live,*
> *As you discover what it is*
> *To be alone and summerless.*
>
> *Summer lives at the far end of a street*
> *Beyond the edge of town–*
> *But now no one's ever home,*
> *The shades are always drawn,*

And the light of the sun is never on—
As if God Himself had gone.

April slipped right into August,
Instant summer filled your hands,
Sunshine stripped the sky of color,
Turning sunburns into tans;
Are you sure there was a river
Where you think you thought it was—
As you walk upon the water,
Leaving footprints in the dust.
Words once whispered under green trees
Now are whistled through their bones,
And their leafless, groping fingers
Seem to wave to something gone—
As you discover what it is
To be alone and summerless.

However, even while Dave was in hospital his informants did not forget him, and they would call and provide him with details about various crimes. One evening toward midnight, as he lay half dozing, he heard footsteps tiptoeing to the side of his bed and came awake instantly, all his senses alert.

"Dave!" a feminine voice whispered.

"What!"

"It's Jean." It was the wife of an informant; she continued speaking hurriedly in hushed tones. "Lonny says I have to tell you about this murder."

"How on earth did you manage to get in here?" he asked, astonished. And, to this day, he doesn't know how she evaded security to bring him the message.

Altogether, Dave stayed in the hospital bed for six months, from January to June; during the whole time since his accident he had seven operations and thirteen casts. Finally, though, to his vast thankfulness, he was well enough to end his hospital sojourn, and take up his life and police career once again.

CHAPTER 16
Bearing Witness to the Truth

THE SAANICH POLICE Department was very considerate in helping Dave find work he could undertake while still regaining complete mobility. At first they offered him a place in the fraud section, but when he found this a little dull they asked if he would like to go into forensics. He agreed immediately, and was sent to Ottawa to train with the RCMP in Identification Techniques, a highly professional course renowned as one of the finest in the world.

The class of sixteen included police officers from several different countries; it lasted two months, was very demanding, and included three subjects: Photography, Fingerprints, and Crime Scene Identification. Dave returned to Saanich, having excelled in the course, and spent the next three years in "Ident," during which time he returned to full health and strength.

One of the things impressed upon him during the course was the fact that it was impossible for a person to walk into a room and not leave evidence that he or she had been there. Dave had always enjoyed matching his mind against that of a criminal, and now appreciated the new techniques which could help him demonstrate a suspect's involvement in a crime. He was made of a mettle which reveled in the danger of his profession, in matching his wits against those on the wrong side of the law and in catching the "bad guys." His spirit rose to the challenge of going to work each day not knowing what was going to happen, working as an undercover agent, spending time in jail with prisoners, and praying he wouldn't get spotted by some criminal he had "busted" already down the line.

He was continuing to gain for himself a reputation as a truthful and reliable police officer, which stood him in good stead with his own department, as well as the legal world with which he came to be involved. Dave took a certain amount of pleasure in the cut and thrust of court appearances; they were challenging exercises, and for him on these occasions only two people could be present to his consciousness. These were the judge, and the lawyer asking the questions, whether for prosecution or defense; the interchanges in the courtroom were intense, and paramount for him was bearing witness to the truth of what he had discovered. He could not afford to get distracted by members of the public, by other witnesses–or by the demeanor of the accused toward him.

One court case in which Dave gave evidence involved an East Canadian who had contacted a bank employee in Victoria, threatening to detonate a bomb unless a certain amount of cash was placed in a bag and left in a locker at the bus station. Despite the fact the message specified the police were not to be informed, the bank manager had contacted the law enforcement officials, who staked out the bus station and caught the perpetrator as he came to collect the money. Unfortunately, however, they did not have enough evidence to convict him, and Dave was asked if he would join the man in jail as an undercover agent.

Dave spent two or three days with this man, Gregory P., in the cell; the accused man never admitted his involvement with the crime, but he did make one mistake. No one knew how much money was demanded by the robbers because this information had never been made public, and the amount of one hundred thousand dollars specified in the newspaper reports was simply a round figure. However, when telling Dave about what he was charged with, Gregory mentioned the figure involved. It was an unusual amount, and the only person who could have known this, apart from the bank officials and the police who were immediately concerned with the case, was the criminal himself.

Some time elapsed before the case went to court, but eventually Dave came to give evidence. He took the stand and counsel for the prosecution questioned him concerning the time he spent in the cell with Gregory.

"During this period," he asked, "did the accused mention to you the reason for his incarceration?"

"Yes, he did. He told me he was accused of threatening a bank with a bomb in order to extort money."

"And did the accused admit to you at any time that he was responsible for this threat?"

"No, he did not."

The prosecutor now asked the crucial question. "Did the accused mention to you the figure involved in this extortion threat for which he was being charged?"

"Yes, he did," replied Dave.

"And what was that amount?" asked the prosecutor. It was the make-or-break moment.

"He told me that the amount being extorted was 110,000 dollars," answered Dave.

"And were you aware beforehand that this was the amount involved?"

"No, I had no knowledge of this whatsoever."

Counsel for the prosecution had now established his most important point, but before dismissing Dave from the witness stand he asked a further question.

"Were you able to engage in other conversations with the accused while you were together in the cell?" he enquired.

"Yes, we had a number of discussions," replied Dave. "Of course, at the time I was being friendly in order to get him talking."

"And can you recount for the court any of those conversations?"

A dialogue flashed back into Dave's mind. "Well, at one stage we had a conversation about winemaking; Gregory asked me if I had ever tasted home-made wine, and explained to me how he produced his own vintage."

"Can you remember any of the details he explained to you about this process?"

Under the skilled questioning of the prosecutor, Dave was able to relate many of the finer points Gregory had imparted to him concerning winemaking, and he was then released from the stand.

It was now the turn of the defense counsel, one of Victoria's leading attorneys, to take the floor, and he attempted vigorously to refute the evidence Dave had given. He alleged that it was impossible Dave should have remembered the amount of extortion money Gregory had mentioned: "Far too much time has elapsed since the two were in jail together," he averred.

This objection was finally answered in the summing up of the judge, who commented concerning Dave's evidence: "If this constable can remember such minor details as those concerning the winemaking, details that have nothing to do with the crime, then I'm convinced that what he does remember of the crime must be fact."

And he pronounced a verdict of guilty.

When the convicted man realized how he had been taken in by Dave he was incensed, and began to swear aloud in tones of unmitigated hatred, "I'll get you, Richardson!" On quite a few occasions Dave testified in court against other such defendants, whose association with a crime he had managed to elicit through working as an undercover agent, and often their rage would know no bounds when they learned how they were deceived. They would be led away uttering the direst of threats against him.

Yet Dave would also without hesitation say something in a person's defense if he felt that was warranted. One evening a young man and his girlfriend, both teenagers, got drinking and smashed the windshields of some cars on a lot in Saanich. Dave apprehended them, and somehow knew that this kind of behavior was contrary to their natures, it was completely alcohol-related, and they felt genuine remorse. The young couple agreed that they would plead guilty, and Dave told their lawyer he wanted to give evidence. He got up before the court and judge, and said, "Your Honor, I don't think these two will offend again; I'd like to ask that you give them a break."

An article then appeared in the *Victoria Times Colonist* with the headline: "First He Arrests Them, Then He Testifies on Their Behalf." Still, he never regretted he did that, and never did hear about them again, so felt that his judgment of character was vindicated.

CHAPTER 17
Maybe You're in There

DAVE'S INVOLVEMENT WITH the music scene continued hand in hand with his police career, and around this time he became acquainted with another gifted musician. This was a man named Jim Vining, who would end up becoming a close friend, with whom Dave collaborated on a number of songs.

The connection originally came through David Foster. Jim was another Victorian who was living in Los Angeles during the '70s, writing and recording his own "demos," and hanging out with David in his studio at night. Foster listened to some of his music, mostly instrumentals, then asked if he knew Dave Richardson.

"I know of him," replied Jim, "but we've never met."

"You should get in touch with him when you're back in Victoria," said David. "I believe you should write together!"

As it happened, Jim's uncle, Bob Vining, was with the Esquimalt Police Department, so when he returned to Victoria Jim asked if he could connect him with Dave Richardson. Bob called back shortly with Dave's phone number.

Jim immediately contacted Dave, and their first conversation lasted over an hour; they both felt at ease with each other, as if they were old friends. Jim was living "Up-Island" in Shawnigan Lake at the time, and Dave invited him to Victoria. He arrived with his cassette demos and the two men sat on the living room floor to listen. Jim confessed later that he was nervous, but then hugely encouraged by Dave's first response.

"I can write to that!" he said.

He gave Jim a couple of his poems to set to music, and soon a fruitful partnership sprang into being. Jim was especially inspired by "Summerless," and a couple of weeks later had something put together. This time Dave went up to visit him at Shawnigan, where Jim explained that the melody he had created didn't really fit the words, but he felt it might work as an underscore to the poem.

"You could just read the lyrics," he suggested. "You've got that deep Leonard Cohen kind of voice."

He then played another of his compositions, as Dave listened intently. "I can write to that!" he said again, and recorded the melody on a pocket-sized cassette recorder as Jim played it through once more. A couple of weeks later he returned, bringing some lyrics that fitted the music perfectly. He had called this new song "Maybe You're in There," and the words were pensive and intriguing:

> *There are secrets about you*
> *Hiding in your eyes,*
> *Something I can't see through,*
> *You keep it all inside.*
>
> *You're still looking for faces,*
> *The smiles they wore for you,*
> *Hoping they will come back,*
> *And yet they never do.*
>
> *Slip into daydreams*
> *To a place out of long ago,*
> *Maybe you're in there,*
> *I don't know.*
>
> *When it rains on the sidewalk*
> *That carries me away,*
> *Maybe you'll remember*
> *Just one more yesterday.*
>
> *And maybe you'll love me*
> *When it's too late to tell me so,*
> *And maybe I'll come back,*
> *I don't know.*
>
> *You draw the blind*
> *So I can't see,*
> *You draw the line,*
> *It stops at me,*
> *Keeping your distance,*
> *Calling it innocence.*

I've waited so long
And I don't think you'll ever show,
Maybe you're in there,
I don't know.

There are secrets about you
Hiding in your eyes,
Something I can't see through,
You keep it all inside.

But maybe you'll love me
When it's too late to tell me so,
And maybe I'll come back,
I don't know.
Maybe I'll come back,
I don't know.

Over the next months the two men wrote four or five more songs together. Jim had a contact with Summit Sound Studio in Los Angeles, and they decided to go there in the summer of '83 and record a demo. "Maybe You're in There" was sung by Karen LaFlair,[12] a psychology student at UCLA, and when it was completed Dave took the demo over to David Foster's house for him to listen to the songs. He loved all of them, especially "Maybe You're in There" with its evocative melding of lyrics and melody, and wanted to record it himself when he was back in Victoria for Christmas.

Jim booked the Legacy Studio in Victoria, and in December 1983 he and Foster were sitting at a Fender Rhodes piano while David began working on the basic tracks. After some time he looked up.

"I think it needs another verse," he said.

Just at that moment Dave Richardson walked through the door, and Foz repeated his words. "We definitely should have some more lyrics," he said.

Dave disappeared into a back room, and about ten minutes later returned with a piece of paper that he handed to David—the new verse. Foster read it, then looked at him quizzically.

"How do you do that!" he said.

"Maybe You're in There" was recorded by Foster with local singer April Gislason doing the vocals. Neither Dave nor Jim had met her before, but they soon discovered she had a wonderful singing voice, and were carried away by her powerful rendition. They later became good friends with both April and her husband Grant.

Meanwhile, Dave's career with Saanich Police was going from strength to strength. He undertook a course with CLEU–Coordinated Law Enforcement Unit–also known as "Secret Squirrel." Here he learned more about background investigations, including surveillance, wire taps and other "behind the scenes" techniques, and eventually worked with the Detective branch.

It was a time of personal and professional consolidation for him; he married again to Debbie, a young woman originally from the north of Vancouver Island who was employed by the police station in Victoria. They bought a house in the outer suburb of Metchosin, a beautiful, wooded area with distant glimpses of blue water through tall pine trees, and settled down to family life together.

CHAPTER 18
The "Man's Man" Officer

WHEN DAVE FIRST joined the Saanich Police Department, his propensity for taking risks and finding himself in scrapes had accompanied him. There were a number of episodes he remembered from those early years with a wry smile. On one occasion he and another officer were sent to stake out a community recreation center where several break-ins had occurred. The men took up their positions in the large swimming pool area, and whiled away the night, waiting for any action which might occur. Eventually the dawn began to break, and it seemed there was now no possibility that a criminal might enter the premises.

It was warm and sticky in the confined area, and the men looked longingly at the swimming pool. Finally, unable to resist, they climbed out of their uniforms, dived into the water and began swimming, enjoying the refreshing sensation of coolness and buoyancy. Suddenly, they heard a loud crash coming from the rear of the building, and were instantly out of the water and seizing their guns. Silently, they made their way to the room where the safe was located. Someone was there, with his back to the officers, intent upon twiddling the knob.

Dave barked a command: "Hands up!"

The robber turned, and found himself confronted by two naked men pointing guns at him. He almost fainted with fright.

The officers took the man in and charged him for the offence … yet Dave was always glad the robber had pleaded guilty, and there was no need for any elaborate rehearsal in court of the circumstances of the arrest!

Over the years, Dave's considerable abilities developed; he was dedicated to the work of the force, and the warmth and charm of his personality helped him make friends within the department and the wider world. He continued to rise through the ranks and eventually was appointed as Staff Sergeant, but even then would sometimes leave his desk job, put on his blue jeans, attach his shoulder holster, and join his men on the road. "Come on, boys," he would say, "Let's go out to play!" That was his attitude all the way; it was never work, but always pure enjoyment.

Dave certainly had the essential skills that would have enabled him to achieve the highest ranks in his police career, and later some wondered why this had not taken place. The reason is best explained by one of his former "rookie" cops, who had worked closely with him.

Geordon Rendle was originally from Victoria, and had traveled with his family to Colombia, South America, during the Narco-Pablo Escobar years. His father and mother were missionaries, which meant that almost every weekend Geordon found himself behind bars, together with his parents! They were visiting the inmates of some of the most destitute, hopeless prisons on earth, endeavoring to show them compassion and bring them hope.

It was during these years that Geordon learned about God's grace: that there was no one so far gone, so unreachable, that His love was not able to find and redeem them. It was during this time, also, that he felt he was called not simply to minister to men and women languishing in jails, but to keep them from going there in the first place. Most especially, he wanted to help young people build meaningful lives and stay out of trouble; he wanted to be about *prevention*.

That was where policing came in. Geordon applied for a summer intern job with the Saanich Police Department while he was still in his third year of Criminology at Simon Fraser University. There were hundreds of applicants for the four vacancies, but his application made it, and he was chosen to become a full-time officer at only twenty years of age. He believed this was partly because he was one of the only police officers on Vancouver Island, and in Vancouver itself, who was completely fluent in Spanish, and especially Medellin Cartel Spanish. This also meant that, as it happened, he came to serve on Dave's platoon for a number of years.

Dave, according to Geordon, was "a man's man" police sergeant. He was tough when he needed to be tough, yet could also be compassionate when the situation called for that as well. This psychological insight and wisdom enabled Dave to be a phenomenal investigator, who could elicit amazing confessions from perpetrators who needn't have told him what they had done. He was not coercive, but his questions were penetrating, and he understood the importance of really listening.

Although Dave was not living as a committed Christian during his police years, he had a respect for those who lived out their faith that never diminished. During Geordon's early years with the department, he was often harassed by some of the older officers about his religion, and the fact that he wouldn't go out "drunking" with the guys. Dave would step in and say to them, "Give him a break. He believes in something more important than drink!" This made a material difference to Geordon's time there, and he was always grateful for Dave's advocacy.

Dave had a good understanding of his fellow officers, a keen eye for detecting their gifts and selecting areas where they could work most effectively. Geordon himself was given the opportunity to take a number of special courses and some of the men baulked at this fact. "Why does Rendle get all the perks?" they asked. Dave had an instant response: "Because he doesn't just learn from the sessions, he brings them back to us, and offers to pass them on!" He appreciated a strong work ethic and the camaraderie of his men as they helped each other out.

In fact, Dave's "sweet spot," according to Geordon, was with his troops. He understood street cop realities, and cared about the officers under his command as well as the municipality he served. Rather than having to deal with bureaucracy and the headaches of political leadership at the top, he desired to interact with the public, relate to those in trouble on the streets, and confront the issues of Saanich head on.

Geordon therefore understood Dave's work with the force as what he called an "incarnational ministry"; that is, even before Dave had committed his life to Christ, he was modelling His character in strength and compassion. And so, although Dave abounded in leadership skills and administrative ability, it was his by own preference that his career was put on hold, to allow room for his own personal set of skills and gifting.

Geordon loved his work with the police, and always said that he never left for something better, but seven years into his service at Saanich he felt called by God to go and help teenagers beyond Vancouver Island,[13] in Latin America, and then all over the world. Throughout his time at Saanich, however, he had attended Central Baptist Church in downtown Victoria, and every Sunday Mrs. Richardson, Dave's mother, was there. Invariably, she would ask Geordon, "Are you praying for Dave?" Geordon would assure her that he was, and let her know that Dave was looking out for him as well.

Much later, when he returned to Victoria from one of his overseas missions, Geordon would find out how those prayers were answered.

CHAPTER 19
The Knight and The Sheriff

AS A LAWMAN, it might be said that Dave had two exemplars. The first of these was Sir Galahad, a knight of the Round Table, who had devoted his life to the search for the Holy Grail, and along the way had helped so many "damsels in distress." It was he of whom Tennyson had famously written:

> *My strength is as the strength of ten*
> *Because my heart is pure.*[14]

In Galahad's dedication to duty, the nobility of his aims, and his aid for the helpless, Dave saw delineated the qualities he himself wished to emulate. Dave's other hero was more contemporary, one who exemplified the western ideal of the lone warrior who stands up for truth and justice, and who would fight to the end to "get his man"—Gary Cooper in *High Noon*.[15]

Dave had grown up in an era when western movies, with their romanticized view of the pioneer days in America, dominated the screen. They were fast-paced narratives that usually focused on an archetypal conflict—good versus evil, white hat versus black hat—set against a panoramic backdrop. The heroes were often sheriffs or ranchers, reserved and laconic, but also principled and courageous, able to stand alone against the forces of lawlessness in a rugged frontier outpost. Such protagonists were literary descendants of the medieval knights in shining armor: they too embodied the ideals of virtue and honor, and went riding out to rescue the weak, protect the fairer sex, and resolve the moral dilemmas arising in this elemental framework.

High Noon, released in 1952, is possibly the best western ever made—an austere drama shot in black and white, the plot of which revolved around a simple story line: the wedding of a retired marshal, named Kane, is interrupted when he learns a killer he had sent to jail will return to town on the noon train to seek revenge. He takes up his badge and gun again–but in doing so alienates his new bride, played by Grace Kelly. Thereafter, the suspense of the movie is built around the tense anticipation of the arrival of the nefarious Frank Miller and his gang of outlaws. Due to the townspeople's cowardice, Kane is refused help at every turn against the killer. Despite the mortal danger he faces, he cannot shrink from the path that duty and honor hold out before him.

The battle which develops between Kane and Miller's group of desperadoes forms the outward, ostensible struggle of the movie, and provides the standard action and spectacle of the western genre, complete with gun battles, saloon scenes and horse-riding stunts. And, as is right and usual, goodness triumphs in the end, and Kane eventually vanquishes the enemy, thereby sparing the town the barbaric justice brought by the deadly gang. However, it is the internal conflict in the hero which is the real driving force of the movie, indicated also by the theme song, which imparts its haunting refrain throughout the action.

In this song, the "fair-haired beauty" the hero has taken as his bride is invoked as a figure of strength, one upon whom he is desperately reliant–and yet, when it comes to choosing between the love of a woman and the role of valor, he will inevitably choose the latter. It was this complexity which helped make "The Ballad of High Noon" so widely known, and open the floodgates for the pervasive use of theme songs in movies. Dave loved both the song and the movie itself; undoubtedly this film and others like it had a subliminal effect upon his psyche, his development as a person and as a police officer, an influence which displayed itself in countless incidents over the course of his career.

This might be illustrated by one occasion when Dave was working as a Saanich detective; the date was December 20, and he was out in the early evening with his wife Debbie doing some Christmas shopping. It happened also that Debbie was pregnant with their first child, and due to give birth at any moment. They were in Hillside Mall in downtown Victoria with their purchases, and planning to have something to eat, when Dave's eye fell upon a man whose face he recognized. The adrenaline immediately started pumping, for it was a man he knew as Al McCormack, and there was a warrant out for his arrest. As he watched, he saw McCormack send his girlfriend into a pharmacy with a piece of paper in her hand, and knew it would be a forged prescription for drugs.

"Stay here," he said to Debbie, pointing to a payphone. "I'm going to arrest that guy." With that, he dashed after the man, who had entered a restaurant inside the mall. He caught up to McCormack at the counter and produced his police badge. "You're under arrest," he said. Without taking his eyes off McCormack, he spoke to the proprietor behind the counter, and instructed him to call the Victoria Police and have them send a car.

"What has he done?" the man behind the counter enquired, and Dave turned to look at him. At the same moment, McCormack made a break for it. He ran, threading his way between the tables, cannoning into people, and Dave began to pursue him, also running fast. McCormack leapt on the tables and thundered across them, sending china and glass flying, and Dave followed hard. McCormack made it out of the restaurant and to the mall entrance, then tore across the car park to the street intersection outside. Dave was pounding after him, but hampered by the fact he was wearing heavy Dayton boots to protect his reconstructed ankle; this meant McCormack was steadily drawing away from him.

The traffic light on Hillside Avenue had just turned red, and at the stop light, waiting to go, was a bus with several cars behind it. McCormack ran to the first car behind the bus, opened the driver's door, punched the woman driver in the face, and forced her to the passenger side. He then leapt in the driver's seat, and began twisting the wheel preparatory to coming out from between the bus and the car behind; as he began moving the car back and forward Dave reached the passenger door and tried to open it, but it was locked.

Dave could see the woman inside looking at him with large, panic-stricken eyes, and the dawning realization that the man banging on the passenger door was probably wanting to help her, and she started scrabbling at the lock, trying to open it. He also caught a glimpse of the offender's face; his eyes were hard and filled with determination. At that moment, McCormack floored the accelerator and was about to tear past the bus; Dave could see he would be jammed against its side, and dropped off the door. The car ran over his ankle, and was away.

Dave gave no thought to any injury he might have sustained. He ran to the service station located at the corner and explained to the proprietor what had happened, asking him to call the police. He then sent one of the employees back to the mall to find his wife. "You'll know her," he said, "She's blonde, with a lot of parcels, standing by the payphone. Oh, and she's nine months pregnant." Soon Debbie joined him and they went to have a meal, then headed back to their home in Metchosin. On the way, however, Dave became uneasy about his ankle, and they decided to drop in to the hospital and have it X-rayed. The doctor came to tell them what he had found.

"The car ran over the ankle where you had the surgery," he said "and because the bone there is reinforced by the steel rods there's no damage at all, just a few bruises. But if it had been your other ankle, you would have major problems!"

Reassured, Dave and Debbie drove home and went to bed. At three o'clock in the morning, Debbie woke her husband. "Dave, the baby's coming!"

"Go back to sleep," he said, "It's false labor!" Their little girl was born later that afternoon.

Dave learned the same day that the criminal was apprehended successfully; he had "got his man." Yet the whole incident was another subtle reminder that he himself had frequently been "torn betwixt love and duty"—and this was bound to place a strain on any relationship, but especially that of marriage.

CHAPTER 20
Master of Deceit

OVER THE YEARS, the songwriter and the lawman had appeared to coexist comfortably within Dave's psyche, yet just as the placid surface of a lake may hide the turbulence beneath, so deep within him the tensions were brewing. After the release of "Wildflower," he found himself thrust into a world composed in equal measures of genius and ambition, glamour and ruthlessness; when his lyrical skills were sought after by some of the greatest talents on the musical scene it was a heady success.

However, the fact he had written such a famous song placed Dave under a great deal of pressure. All the lyrics he had formerly written were born out of that urge to expression which welled up in him as sheer gift. Now he found himself constantly fighting the tendency to compose his ballads to please others, and wondering whether he might have another hit record on his hands. Various individuals would come to him and ask, "Could you write me a song?", but he knew they wanted another "Wildflower," and that was a unique creation–"I'm not crazy about sequel movies," he would say. Moreover, this subtle obligation to write for others seemed to hinder his own natural talent–so there were more complex reasons for Dave's refusal to sign to any of the offers he received. Perhaps, most of all, he knew in his heart he would never survive the all-consuming demands of stardom.

His other career, as a lawman, brought its own stresses to bear. The police work involved a constant adrenaline rush, and even though Dave thoroughly enjoyed living life on the edge this could often exact a cruel price. After he became involved with one of the longest and most expensive trials in Canada's history, the infamous Cumberland murders, he became painfully aware of this truth. The investigation, which sought to bring four men to justice for an execution-style killing in a drug-related matter, lasted ten years, and Dave worked on and off this assignment for the whole of that time.

For Dave, the case was both an adventure and also a massive strain; his own life was threatened on several occasions during this period. And, like other policemen, during the course of his career he saw so many gruesome sights, especially when working with forensics, that he would often wake with nightmares.

These things were hard on a marriage. Dave's second marriage lasted longer than his first, and produced two daughters whom he loved, but also eventually collapsed. Both his wives found certain elements of his work difficult to cope with. Most especially, when Dave was involved with the Cumberland case, he worried that the powerful criminal figures they were battling might find out where he lived with his wife and children. He would wear a gun in a shoulder holster even on such innocent outings as a trip to the movies, would constantly glance behind him when driving the car home at night. If he saw a headlight that stayed too long, he would turn off the road.

Like many policemen, Dave would drink after work, and over the years this habit grew more insidious. With two failed marriages behind him, and after he had semi-retired from police work, the grip of this addiction grew stronger. He entered a detox unit on two occasions, to no avail. And then, although born with a gift to embrace all the good life had to offer, he began to withdraw from the company of others, and to forsake the activities he formerly loved so much. He could never stop writing poetry, but now the elements of doubt and disillusion became far more pronounced:

MASTER OF DECEIT

And Love steals its way through the darkness of night
Down satin-wreathed stairs falling soft from the moon,
To reach a heart waiting, unsuspecting its plight,
As it dreams of a love that has gone far too soon.
And the moonlight is glinting like a sword or spear
That pierces its way to the lament of his heart
As he remembers his love, when it drowned in his tears,
This love that should never have arrowed his dart.
But Love still comes stealing like a thief on his path,
Enwrapped with the Moon, like a faithful confrere
And guiding his steps, sure and sinister as death,
To the lover lamenting, in his lonely despair.

O Love, you Samaritan, you seem such a friend!
You seek out each heart as you travel your path,
All of whom, then, to your desires must bend
Before you unleash the sharp darts of your wrath!
O Love, then deceive, for that one is blinded
From the light your abetting accomplice bestows
Upon the pure heart that seeks only to find
The love that he yearns for, that he lost long ago.
But you do not care, you slithering thing,
You entice saddened hearts and then turn them about,
As warmly, easily, as you steal your way in …
Then, Judas, betray, and tear your way out!

THE THRILL OF IT ALL

You know me,
I could never hold a dollar in my hand,
I'd blow it on a weekend
Or some other stupid plan;
I guess I've always known
That love and money were easy come and go,
And I've never missed a thing.
But it doesn't pay to steal the show
There on that old wooden dance hall,
Emulating Buddy and the King;
It was just for the thrill of it all,
It was just for the thrill of it all.

And there's something I will never understand,
How easily you slipped into my heart
And through my hands;
I should have guessed, and didn't someone say,
It isn't if you win, it's how you play.
But with all my hip and groove
I couldn't make a move,
And my days of being cool are fading fast,

The best times of my life have nearly passed,
And all the things that once held me in thrall;
It was just for the thrill of it all,
It was just for the thrill of it all.

There were telephone numbers on bus station walls,
There were those who write them and those who would call,
And in desperate times, yes, I have spent a few dimes
For a voice on the line who would listen to mine,
When there was no more saving grace in being proud,
And nines looked more like sixes on my floating cloud;
And the only reason I'd call
Was just for the thrill of it all,
It was just for the thrill of it all.

THEN YOU KNOW

When the links of the chain that you welded with care
Start corroding, eroding, and breaking and falling
To the earth as it lies 'way down there at your feet,
When the ties are untied and she's drifting away
In excuses and lies that you know by her eyes,
And the way that she just has less time to meet.

Then you'll recognize the pain the poets talk about
In all the songs and stories that they wrote,
And you'll know it when it comes, intruding doubt,
As her gaze becomes still more and more remote;
And you sense that all the times you've spent together
Don't seem so much to matter any more,
And memories that once you so much treasured
Are just like copies made of paste
On the back shelf of a dime store …

Then doesn't it feel funny,
Doesn't it feel new,
But doesn't it feel lonely
Too?

LOVE IN HELLO AND GOOD-BYE

It's a thought that's been lost in the thinking,
And an inch that's been hidden in a mile,
It's a drowning man's prayer as he's sinking
And the journey to a man from a child.

It's a dream that is almost remembered
And the answer on the tip of a tongue,
Or the light from a star, ten years embered
When the plan for creation was young.

That's how gentle love is in hello,
And how cruel it can be in good-bye,
When the only thing left is a memory
Of the birth of a love born to die.

There must be a love I've not tasted,
And an ocean I can William in the deep,
There must be a dream I've not wasted,
There must be a night filled with sleep.

If you follow my footprints on the highway
You can whisper my name to the wind,
Try to chase me right into forever—
Where I'm going, love has always just been.

CHAPTER 21

Nowhere Place

THE CRISIS WAS not long in coming. Closeted alone in his apartment, Dave began to drink large amounts of alcohol, usually whiskey or vodka, at any hour of day or night. If there were occasions when he tried to free himself from this dependency, he would then turn to tranquilizers in an effort to calm his fractured nervous system; he was to say later he had "a love affair with every Pam in town": diazepam, lorazepam, oxazepam, as well as lithium, prozac and the other anti-depressants.

Dave was thankful that he was a lawman, and chosen to stick to drugs that were legal. Nevertheless, the despair and loneliness he felt in the depths of his psyche were poignantly expressed in one of his poems, "Month of A Thousand Days," a title which referred to the seemingly endless passage of time spent in detox. Yet the closing lines of the song held out a radiant glimmer of hope.

> *Beware the road of yellow bricks*
> *That seems to lead you on,*
> *There are tortured bones in every ditch*
> *Of the users, dead and gone.*
>
> *There's not much worth remembering*
> *In a dark and dismal past,*
> *When the mirror of your only friend*
> *Is in the bottom of a glass.*
>
> *When the needles seem to fill your arms*
> *Through the cracks in leathered veins,*
> *And you scream for mercy in the night,*
> *But no one hears your pain.*

But the Higher Power never hides
From those who bare their souls,
Who sacrifice their very pride
When their blood runs icy cold.

There is nothing left for us to lose
When we've thrown our lives away,
So in one final desperate move
We finally learn to pray.

Then all at once a Silent Strength
Begins to hold us fast—
For the Eyes of God have followed us
From the shadows of our past.

Dave did not understand it at the time, but his real problem was a spiritual one. There was a compelling cry in the depths of his soul that he could never silence, even with copious amounts of liquor. Dimly he comprehended, in the recesses of heart and mind, that there was a life to which he was called, that was greater and richer than anything he had so far experienced, but it seemed as far away as the stars in heaven. Still, he was to experience what so many had discovered before him: the power of God to enter and work in a situation which seemed utterly hopeless.

Although Dave's family did not realize the depth of addiction into which he had plunged, they were greatly concerned on his behalf. His mother Harriet never ceased to pray for him, and to those prayers Dave's brothers added their pleas. And mercy came …

Early one spring morning, Dave's younger brother Doug woke with a start. In his still-drowsy mind, there formed a distinct impression: "Get your brother into detox."

He got out of bed and went immediately to the phone to call the detox unit on Pemberton Street, which specialized in the treatment of alcoholism and drug addictions of all kinds. Dave had already been through their program twice, but Doug obeyed that early morning prompting, and asked if they might take his brother at such short notice. Their answer was brief and to the point.

"Sorry," they said, "We only take those who call every day and are really showing interest. Tell your brother to start phoning in," they advised.

Doug hung the phone up slowly. "What was all that about?" he wondered, as he headed back to bed.

Within minutes the phone rang again; it was the clinic. "We just had a cancellation. If you can get your brother in this morning, we can take him!"

Doug dressed quickly, his mind on the immediate problem confronting him: that of getting Dave to agree to go to the unit.

Now, no two human beings had ever been closer than these two brothers, the two youngest of the four siblings. From their earliest years they were playmates and best friends and when, later, the time had come for them to choose their professions, Doug had followed Dave into police work. Both brothers during their long careers had exhibited the highest degree of professionalism and integrity in their work, a legacy of the values their mother had instilled in them, as well as the secure moral codes of the Canadian society in which they had grown up. The brothers achieved a fair degree of renown for their roles in the force, and at one time featured in an article in the *Victoria Times Colonist*. They each divulged what they admired about the other:

> *It's Doug's presence which can always make me feel on top of the world,* said Dave, while of his brother Doug confided, *There were times when I worried about him—he's absolutely fearless!*

They were as close as blood ties and natural affection could make them, and until now had never had an argument, let alone a fight. Yet Doug, worried that Dave would be reluctant to enter the program and expecting him to resist, was now prepared to take a strong stand. He arrived at Dave's front door, took a deep breath, and knocked.

To his surprise, the door opened almost immediately. And then he stopped still in utter amazement. For there in front of him stood his brother. He was freshly showered, shaved and dressed. In his right hand he held a small attaché case. "I'm ready!' he said.

Dave, much later, could not recall the scene, nor what prompted him to be prepared and waiting for Doug–but he did remember walking through the front door of the clinic. It was his third time there in a period of twenty years, and the manager, Jan, was shocked when she saw him.

"Dave," she exclaimed involuntarily, "I've never seen you in such bad shape!"

"Oh, I'm not so bad," he articulated.

"Oh, really," she said skeptically, and then put him to the test. "Can you tell me where you are and what city you are in?"

"I'm in Port Alberni," he replied firmly (naming a town in the north of Vancouver Island).

Jan sighed. "And what are you doing here?"

Dave glanced around, and his eye fell upon a First Nations man sitting in the waiting area. He said, "I came up to meet my friend here, he's going to teach me how to carve totem poles."

Thus began for Dave a period of sixteen days in the detox unit, where the usual period required to overcome the effects of alcohol abuse was six. One of his poems caught something of the introspective, hallucinatory, claustrophobic, fear-filled and bewildering thoughts that afflict a person suffering the pangs of withdrawal:

NOWHERE PLACE

The voices that call my name
Come from every door of day,
Every window of night;
I answer them quickly
And run to them
One at a time,
Sometimes two,
With a rapid heart.

Finally, like any bird that must fly
I tire, fold my wings
And drop to my knees,
Exhausted,
In some strange place that has walls
Against voices
I stretch out in some new grass,
Greener than before,
Softer than I've known
And—I look up to find that the sky
Is really blue
And has birds that walk its ceiling
Upside down.

My outstretched hands clutch the grass
As if to tether me, to that one place,
My chest rises, falls
From the labor of answering voices;
I've never noticed—Lord!
I've breathed this side of twenty-seven years
And never noticed the vital taste
Of air.

People step over me and say hello,
They don't know me, or call me,
They just say hello;
I find myself screaming
"What place is this!"
Someone says a word that I will forget
By the time I get up.

I think I knew a place like this once,
If I remember correctly,
It died.

CHAPTER 22
Where Is the River?

DURING HIS TIME in detox, the pain Dave endured as his body went through withdrawal was close to unbearable. He experienced a number of seizures, and on at least one occasion was rushed by ambulance to hospital. Yet the most extraordinary knowledge was beginning to dawn on him: he knew that he was never drinking again, never taking another tablet–it was *over*, and he was liberated completely. He had said this before–but this time, he understood, it was only because Someone had come with him into the depths of hell, and was lifting him out, irresistibly, with undreamt-of grace.

At the same time, his trials were not finished, not by any means. After the sixteen days, Doug returned to the clinic, picked up his brother, and took him back to the apartment. There Dave continued to have more seizures and some major panic attacks, as well as shattering headaches. Nevertheless, he wanted to try something radical. Dave had been told by the doctors that he had a chemical imbalance, and because of this would be on anti-depressants for the rest of his life. Now he wanted to challenge that, and to give up completely all forms of medication. He went to his doctor, Brock, a dedicated individual who had previously helped Dave when he was with the police force, coping with some horrific experiences including the threats to his life. Brock arranged to see Dave once a week as his final patient for the day, and they would sometimes talk until midnight.

"I want to try and deal with these panic attacks on my own, Brock," Dave told the doctor. "No more pills–I've been through that deadly cycle, and I don't want to go back."

Brock shook his head. "You'll go through hell if you try it that way, Dave," he said.

"I'm ready for whatever happens," he replied. "This is something I just have to do."

"Well, on one condition," his doctor replied cautiously, "that if you can't handle it, you'll resume medication. And you have to be completely honest with me!"

Dave agreed. After all (he told himself cynically) no addict is ever completely honest with his doctor. He knew in himself that he would rather lose his life than go back to drugs and alcohol; and an extraordinary peace took hold of him with the knowledge that, if he died, he would at least die trying.

For now, just as the doctor had warned, the physical misery seemed to increase. He would be at home, perhaps cooking a meal, when a seizure would come upon him like a ravening wolf. Immediately he would panic and freeze in one position, immovable as a statue, and would shout out loud: "I will not give up!" Other times, he would awaken covered in hives as a result of his ravaged nervous system. He would lie on his bed and sweat, curled in a fetal position, repeating fiercely: "I refuse to give in!"

Strangely, while Dave knew that it would take only one small tablet and the pain would vanish away, like smoke into ether, at no time did the thought cross his mind. And as he gradually came through the worst of the physical reactions, it was as if his eyes were opened to see a fathomless beauty in things he had never seen before, in the clouds that floated high above the Victorian skyline, in the wind moving through the fir trees, the roseate colors of the sunset limned with gold, in the faces of the men, women and children who moved through the city streets. It was a kind of euphoria, and he wondered if it might be the "pink cloud" which recovering alcoholics sometimes experience.

As Dave continued to improve physically, he began going to AA (Alcoholics Anonymous) daily, and trading experiences with others who had similar challenges. At the same time, however, he was becoming aware that the true answer to addiction was not to be found there. A new light seemed to be dawning in his consciousness, assuring him that whatever was taking place in his psyche was supernatural. Even the commonplace events of his life seemed to be filled with a kind of preternatural significance: it seemed to him that, each day, his thoughts were being given to him, and all he had to do was listen to their guidance, and this inner prompting would tell him where to go, or about someone he would be meeting. Along with this prescient knowledge, Dave was experiencing what he called "eyelid movies," when he would close his eyes and seemingly find himself in another world.

On one of these occasions, he found himself seemingly in outer space, in a vast, star-sprinkled realm, its infinite dimensions stretching away on all sides.

Suddenly he found himself caught up in a kind of nanocone, and could see that, far in front of him, the ether narrowed to a single point. Then he, together with everything else around him, began rushing toward this distant goal at an impossible speed, and finally he found himself shooting through a tiny microscopic portal, and knew he had left behind time as we know it on earth. On the other side was another wondrous vista, startling in its crystal transparency, where somehow he had become so small that small now became huge and huge became small. He realized he was in the dimension opposite to that in which we presently exist.

In another startling vision, like an opaque dream, Dave found himself standing in a mysterious land filled with a wild beauty, as if he were in a forest full of richness and strangeness such as he had never seen: there were creeks and rivers and mountains, trees were growing and decomposing at an astonishing rate, volcanoes were erupting, animals were eating other animals, and a constant osmosis was occurring. With part of his mind, he understood he was watching life in an accelerated state.

"Where am I?" he wondered.

A voice said, "Don't you know where you are?"

"No."

"You're standing on human skin."

Of course: the salt water, the creeks, the earthquakes, the organisms eating foliage–and all this was a microcosm of the universe itself.

One particular "eyelid movie" seemed to stand out for its beauty and clarity, and was repeated on a number of occasions. In it, Dave was walking across a desert filled with sand dunes, without a single blade of grass or sign of life; it was blazing hot and he was making his way westwards, straight toward the sun. As he slowly continued walking, he saw on the horizon a small cloud, and even as he noticed this it started to come toward him in a straight line, until it was directly above him. Looking up at the cloud, Dave saw raindrops beginning to fall; they landed on him, and the sensation was incredibly cool and refreshing. And then it started to rain quite heavily from the little cloud, and he opened his mouth and drank, a delicious benison which seemed to bring a soothing balm to his entire overheated body.

As Dave stood there, time lost its meaning; then he looked down at his feet and saw the sand beneath them start to fill up with water from the rain. Soon he found himself standing in a puddle of water, and as it continued to rain a tiny rivulet started to flow out from this puddle in a westerly direction. Then, while he watched in wonder, the rivulet became a small creek, moving away through the dunes, and as it did so little sprigs of grass appeared on either side amidst the sand, a beautiful emerald green. Following the grass, a myriad of small plants covered with buds began springing up, and in their midst emerged the supple trunks of young trees. And what had been a lifeless desert was now an Edenic garden, with a profusion of richly flowering shrubs and trees of variegated hues, almost surreal in its splendor.

Much earlier, Dave had composed a poem, in which he expressed his longing to discover truth and meaning in life, as well as his despair at ever finding it:

WHERE IS THE RIVER?

They say there's happiness flowing
Deep and evermore,
They say the waves are golden
Once you find the shore;
They say the water's cool,
And soothes a thirsty mind
It makes a wise man from the fool,
And turns a cruel man kind.

But where is the river,
Where is the river
If it's really true;
Where is the river
With its silver hue,
If I only knew!

They say wild flowers are growing
High above the reeds,
They say true wisdom is knowing
How to fill all mankind's needs.
But where is the river
That takes our cares away,
Where is the river,
Who can show the way?

Without a map in hand
The search will be forever,

To find that gleaming strand
An endless endeavor,
Through a riverless land,
Through a riverless land.

The poem Dave had written seemed to have a prophetic element, and he understood that this new vision he was seeing, which came to him time and again, was related to it in some way. He knew it had a deeper symbolism, and it was beckoning him on his journey. However, he was not yet ready to discern its meaning–that was for the future.

CHAPTER 23
Heroes

AT THIS POINT in his life, when he reflected over his career, Dave also felt that any kind of excellence he had displayed paled in comparison with that of his brothers.

His brother Don, some six years older than Dave, had become the "man" of the family when their father had died at an early age, and took his responsibilities seriously. Even while still a child, he had known the direction his life would be taking. He pointed to a far-distant land on a map and said to his mother: "When I grow up, I'm going to be a missionary in that country." Dave had composed a poem about this strong sense of purpose in Don's life, as well as its sacrificial aspect; it was called "Raise the Child," and the chorus went as follows:

> *So mother, sweet mother, raise the child,*
> *For he is more than an offspring of birth*
> *Mother, sweet mother, raise the child*
> *For he will be an offering to the earth.*

Don was gifted in many areas: he could paint, play the guitar, and was a superb runner; later in his life he would become a Grand Master in chess. He also had an intensely enquiring intellect, and Dave's poem focused on this aspect of his personality:

> *Out of his mouth there are questions*
> *That we'll never answer,*
> *The things that perplex him*
> *We've taken for granted,*
> *He's seeking direction*
> *For knowledge just planted,*

To be spent between
Somewhere and here.

With striking single-mindedness, Don never swerved from his original vision. In his teens he studied at Prairie Bible Institute[16] at Three Hills in Alberta, and all the family packed up and joined him there. After completing his course he married Carol, who had also attended PBI and trained as a nurse, and in 1962 they were sent out by the Regions Beyond Missionary Union, together with their seven-month-old baby, Stephen. Their destination was a remote area in the steamy jungles of Netherlands New Guinea, on the far side of the Pacific Ocean, which "remains the most breath-taking, dangerous, unpredictable, mysterious and rugged graveyard of missionaries on the face of our planet."[17]

To reach their own heart of darkness, the young couple paddled in a wooden dugout canoe twenty miles up a winding river into the heart of a crocodile-infested swamp, where the Sawi tribe dwelt in thatched tree houses perched above the canopy of the rain forest. In this distant part of the world, far from the nearest outpost of civilization, the Richardson clan established the home in which they were to live for the next fifteen years. The contrast between this life and the one which Don had known while growing up was subtly evoked by another verse of Dave's poem:

For the child on his way to a dream
There are marvels of marbles and cream,
And in the meadows of brown turning green
There are treasures that he will redeem,
Does he still see the man on the moon
Smiling back into windows of rooms,
Painted wallpaper petals and blooms,
Is he still growing up much too soon …

Don and Carol had stepped into a primitive world, far removed from twentieth century western culture, and were dwelling in the midst of a stone-age group who practiced cannibalism and headhunting as a way of life. In this environment, various tribes warred against one another constantly, explosive rivalries and horrific practices were everyday events, and one's life could hang on a knife's edge in a fraction of a second. Apart from the ever-present threat of violence, the newcomers were faced with the hazards of contracting tropical diseases such as malaria and dysentery, as well as the task of learning the Sawi language, which was altogether daunting in its complexity—nineteen tenses for every verb.

The newcomers were soon highly regarded by the Sawi as "magical people," with medicine that could treat diseases and tools that could make work easier, and it was not long before three different Sawi tribes moved to live near the missionaries. They, meanwhile, set about acquiring fluency in the language, and, after some months of eight-to-ten-hour daily learning sessions, Don achieved a level of proficiency which could allow him to tell the Sawi people the gospel. Yet, as he learned the language and lived with the people, he became increasingly aware of the gulf that separated his Christian worldview from theirs; the cultural barriers to understanding and accepting his teaching seemed insurmountable.

Close to despair, the Richardsons were considering leaving the area—but the Sawi peoples did not want them to go! The tribes in the embattled villages came together and decided they would bring an end to their warring; however, to secure peace between the tribes there was only one way, a way which was very costly. It required that a father from one of the tribes must give his son, one who moreover was an only son, as a "Peace Child" to an enemy tribe. And as he watched this ceremony unfold, Don knew he had found the key to reaching the hearts of the Sawi people. He saw the giving up of a cherished child as an exact replica of God's sacrificial gift of His own Son, and was now able to point to the perfect Peace Child, the Son of God and Prince of Peace, to bring the tribal groups to a knowledge of Jesus Christ.

Following this event many villagers converted to Christianity, a translation of the New Testament in Sawi was published, and peace and progress began to come to the native villages and spread to surrounding areas. In 1977 Don and Carol returned to North America, where Don wrote his book *Peace Child*, telling of his experiences in New Guinea and outlining his concept of redemptive analogy: that in every tribe and people group throughout the earth God has deposited a key to revealing the ultimate salvation provided through His Son. He continued to travel widely, speaking about communicating the gospel message amongst other cultures, and his best-selling books have had a significant impact on ongoing Christian missionary work. And so Dave's poem concludes:

> *For the child, in his part of the plan*
> *To continue the ages of man*
> *In creations he won't understand*
> *Will abide in the faith of I Am,*

Then his legend the futures will tell
Of a life so completely fulfilled
That he gave such as others would sell,
Showing blind men the roads out of hell.

So mother, sweet mother, raise the child
To be strong beyond strengths of a man;
Mother, sweet mother, raise the child,
For the day of the Dawn is at hand.

Dave's younger brother Doug had also played a large role in his life, and the closeness the two siblings had enjoyed during their growing-up years continued throughout their careers. However, while Dave had elected to join the municipal police, Doug took a different course.

It was during the Fifties that Dave's mother Harriet opened a restaurant in downtown Victoria, just near the busy waterfront area. It was not long before "Betty's Café" became famed, not only for its excellent meals, but also for the warmth and friendliness of its owner and employees. During his school summer holidays, Doug worked there to earn extra pocket money, and it was during these times that a major future direction of his life became apparent. It just so happened that the Headquarters of the Royal Canadian Mounted Police was located in the same block as his mother's café, and many of these renowned policemen frequented the restaurant. This meant that countless of their stories and adventures were related to him—for the Mounties have played a leading role in Canada's history and their legacy, like that of Canada itself, is one of great events, sweeping backdrops and exceptional individuals.

Canada had become a confederation in 1867 when only four of the provinces as they are known today were part of the new nation: Nova Scotia, New Brunswick, Quebec and Ontario, while British Columbia on the west coast was still a separate colony. The three prairie provinces, Manitoba, Saskatchewan and Alberta, were largely owned by Hudson's Bay Company, the fur trading empire; at the time there were few European settlers in the area, and together with far northern parts they were known as the North-West Territories. The fur traders and First Nations peoples maintained a relationship of cooperation and mutual respect, especially as the latter were needed by the newcomers as guides, interpreters, trappers, and instructors in wilderness survival skills.

In 1873 the North West Mounted Police was formed in Ottawa, Canada's capital; their mission was to maintain a national presence, and to ensure good order in this huge jurisdiction. The Mounties, as they came to be known, were organized along the lines of a cavalry regiment, and adopted a uniform comprised of a scarlet tunic and blue trousers. In July 1874, the first detachment of red-coated young men set off from eastern parts on a nine-hundred-mile trek toward the Rocky Mountains; their destination was the notorious Fort Whoop Up, hub of an illegal whiskey trade. Within a few years the barter was put to an end and they had earned their reputation as fair enforcers of the law; the network of posts was then extended year by year until it covered all the territories.

The Mounties thus laid the ground for European settlement, and prepared the way for a vast influx of settlers as the result of the Canadian Pacific Railway construction–but a new challenge was ahead.

In the 1890s, word of gold discoveries in the Yukon near to Alaska brought hordes of fortune hunters to the region, as tens of thousands, many from the United States, traveled to the area to pan for gold. The task of maintaining peace and security fell to the NWMP, and their presence ensured the Klondike gold rush would be the most orderly in history. In 1903 King Edward VII conferred the prefix "Royal" in recognition of their outstanding service, and in 1920 their title changed to Royal Canadian Mounted Police as the organization was charged with enforcing federal legislation through the entire land.

This impressive history had contributed to give the Mounties a certain mystique, which only increased during the twentieth century. American newspapers had carried pictures of the Mounties in their distinctive scarlet coats and Stetson hats, and this image was later romanticized by Hollywood. The cinema portrait of the Mounties is that of a stoic and polite lawman, who nevertheless possesses a steely determination and a physical toughness that sometimes appears superhuman. The image of these invincible yet gentle champions of the law has been celebrated in hundreds of novels and films over the last century–in all of which the Mountie "fetches his man." This has caused them to retain their popularity to the present day as the most recognizable symbol of Canada.

The magical tales of adventure in an untamed land that he heard in his mother's café fired Doug's imagination; as he grew older he was attracted as well by the diversity of assignments available in the force. Another major influence on his decision to join the RCMP was their reputation for rigorous training at the Depot division in Regina, Saskatchewan, which he saw as a personal challenge. This required high academic standards in the legal field, and also tough physical preparation, including equitation or horsemanship.

The training proved every bit as demanding as Doug had anticipated, but he persevered and graduated in 1965, being assigned to southern Alberta, which suited him especially as it was close to Dave in Calgary. Over a period of two years he had four postings to rural towns in the area; and being young and single at the time worked long hours with no extra pay. Nevertheless, he loved the work because of the experience he gained. In this kind of small-town policing, he was personally responsible for everything related to law enforcement: crime investigation, jail duties, even prosecuting his own cases in court. He also loved the warmth of the prairie folk, for in these small communities there was no end to dinner invitations and other socializing as well.

Doug's decision to leave the RCMP for city policing was a difficult one, but the allure of his fiancée Marlene in Victoria proved too great. The two were married shortly after he returned, and settled down together in the city; Marlene was a warm and gracious hostess, and Dave spent many happy hours in their home over the years. Meanwhile, Doug adjusted well to city policing and progressed through the ranks in various assignments. Over the course of his career, he came to be highly respected for his outstanding abilities, and eventually was appointed Victoria Chief of Police. He was known for his steadiness and common sense, as well as his exceptional way of dealing with all kinds of people because of his courtesy and ability to take a stand without being insulting.

As Dave reflected on Doug's career, he found the words of an old hit song, concerning a man who was fearless, true and kind, were coming into his mind: "True Grit," sung by Glen Campbell. More than ever, he was beginning to realize that all the things he admired about his brother–his humility, his selfless devotion to duty, and his quiet strength of character–were undergirded by a deep faith. It was this, he was coming to understand, which more than all else could create in a man–and a woman too–a character which was steadfast, immovable and rock solid as the mountains.

HEROES

I've seen them come,
I've seen them go,
I've seen them die too young
Or live to be too old;
I've seen them stand,
I've seen them fall—
But every woman, every man,
They're heroes all.

Why do they choose
The lives they live?
They never take as much
As they can give.
May I stand proud,
May I stand tall,
And may my name be there—
With the heroes all.

CHAPTER 24
Mothersong

AT THIS EARLY stage in his recovery, Dave was still reveling in the wonder of his new life, which was handed back to him as a gift. Even his physical appearance had altered. Like many addicts, he had worn a great deal of black, a color symbolizing the darkness in their souls. Now he donned blue jeans, no longer walked with head down or eyes averted, and as his life of hiding ended his natural extrovert tendencies reasserted themselves. He volunteered for a local radio station which invited people to come in and do their own programs, and his show proved so popular that he was invited to host a weekly broadcast. In short order, he learned to manage the microphones, play commercials and conduct interviews. Yet, at the same time, he was aware he would not be doing this for long.

Dave was six feet two inches tall. His height gave him many advantages when he was growing up, playing sports, and throughout his police career. Nevertheless, he would say that, up until that time the possibilities in his life were limited to six feet two. Suddenly, now, life had become exciting, the opportunities seemed endless, as if he were gazing into boundless space. The conviction his life was going in a new direction began to grow strongly in him.

"But this time," he averred, "I'm not making any declarations."

"What sort of declarations?" asked his mother, Harriet.

"That I will never drink again ... it's time to let my actions speak louder than my words. And I know it's time to make up to my family for the pain I've caused you all."

His mother looked at him affectionately out of her warm countenance. "What are you planning on doing?"

"I think you know, don't you?"

"I think I do."

It was the last week of May, almost three months after Dave's experience at the detox clinic, and he was sitting with his mother at a waterfront café in downtown Victoria. He had just taken her to see the annual May Parade, a festive event with a carnival-like atmosphere which she had always loved, and they were now drinking coffee, talking together and reminiscing. Dave tried to spend time with his mother whenever he could; he was determined to make up in any way possible the time he had lost in their relationship. This was only the ostensible reason; the truth was that Dave's mother was the most selfless human being he had ever known, and he loved being with her.

After their father had died, his mother was a tower of strength to her young family. In order to support her boys, she began working as a waitress at Betty's Café in Government Street for thirty-five cents an hour, and ended up owning the business—in fact, everything she touched turned to gold. Yet Dave knew she never stopped missing her husband, and he dedicated one of his poems to her, calling it "Mothersong":

> Another time too often
> She waits between the midnight and the dawn,
> In an endless chain of days ,
> But her pillows never soften
> The stones between what is and what has gone
> In a thousand different ways.
> There's a man she still thinks about
> With a candle and a cat she's putting out,
> And some unexpected letters
> That are due here from the war,
> And she wonders still, what all the waiting's for:
> She prays for love she had, and nothing more.

As the boys grew up, their home in Dysart Road became a haven for many—members of Harriet's own family who followed her from Prince Edward Island, and numerous others experienced her kindness and generosity. Once during Dave's police career, he even took home a couple of German tourists he found sleeping in the park and his mother gave them shelter for the night. In every way, Harriet was an exceptional person, adored by her sons and grandchildren, and Dave knew that, whatever he had learned of love, it was from her:

> And so the Mothersong lives on
> Until her final breath is gone …

And I will love her till then and far beyond,
And my father will be waiting for her song,
The way she sang it then.

And in the truest love that I have ever known,
I thank God that in her love I've grown
To see my dreams come true,
In Mothersong, as long as I have you,
Then what else could I do ...
Without my loving you,
And here is where we belong
In Mothersong, oh yes,
Sweet Mothersong ...

Dave knew also that she was unspeakably happy his life was turned around. As they sat on the open terrace a gentle breeze played about them, full of the warmth and promise of summer. Although they had seen it countless times, they were both charmed by the scene before them.

Victoria's Inner Harbor is only small, but must be one of the loveliest in the world. It is filled with boats and other craft–private yachts, sightseeing ferries and whale-watching boats, water-taxis to Seattle and other destinations–and is the only harbor designated an airport in the world, with numerous float planes taking off and landing each day. Two large buildings dominate the curving waterfront. In the central location the Empress Hotel, with its massive ivy-clad façade, presides majestically, while to the south stands the Parliament Building, its graceful neogothic contours illuminated each evening with over three thousand strings of lights, evoking a fairytale scene. The terraces and quays surrounding the harbor are always at that time of year filled with tourists, many enjoying the spectacle from one of the horse-drawn carriages that ply the waterfront. At sunset, street entertainers gather behind the statue of James Cook, the English captain who first landed on British Columbia.

Dave and Harriet watched a seaplane soaring into an ethereal sky, then resumed their conversation.

"So what is it you think I'm going to do?" he challenged his mother.

"Well," replied Harriet, "you've always liked helping people."

"Right."

"I suppose now you're free yourself, you'll be doing what you can for the addicts?"

"That's absolutely true," he declared. "First of all, that I've been set free, liberated completely, and I believe others can experience this as well." He leaned forward, his blue eyes intense. "I don't know one hundred percent where this assurance has come from, but I do know one thing–it's too good not to share. And so I feel this overriding purpose, which is to enable others to achieve the same freedom."

His mother nodded; she understood him perfectly. "When will you start?"

"I've contacted the clinic, and they tell me ninety days need to elapse before I can come back and help others with the same problems that I had. That means I can return at the beginning of June–and I intend to be there."

"It's interesting, Dave," said Harriet thoughtfully, "that right from the start of your career you were involved with the drug scene. I'm so glad you're going to do this new work; I have a feeling it's the right thing for you."

Dave became pensive again.

"You know," he said, "in our family, it was always pretty clear to me what each of my brothers had. Don got the brains, Bob got the looks, Doug got the common sense ..." he paused dramatically, "but I'm still not sure what I've got ..."

His mother smiled "I know what it is you have," she said, her eyes soft.

"What is it?"

"I promise I'll tell you one day."

And Dave had to be content with that. He drove his mother home, and returned to the downtown area in which his apartment was located. Evening was drawing on and he was restless; he decided to walk down to a local coffee shop. This café, although a battered sign proclaimed its name as "Café Fantastico," was better known to locals as "The Hole"; the coffee, however, was excellent. Driven by some inner impulse, Dave took some diversionary turns on the way, making his way through the darkened back streets near his home.

It was a world far removed from the waterfront with its glittering store fronts, the pretty lamps that winked on at nightfall, the flowering baskets and horse-drawn carriages. The area in which Dave lived was known to have a high rate of drug use. In these streets were found denizens of the Victorian underworld: the drug addicts, alcoholics and homeless, enduring a lonely and danger-filled existence, which alternated between desperate craving and elusive moments of euphoria. His eye fell on a young woman who stood under one of the streetlamps; her skirt was short, her heels high, and her makeup exaggerated. "She's out too early," thought Dave to himself–prostitutes were not permitted to ply their trade in Victoria until after ten in the evening for fear of offending the tourists. He took another glance at her; she was hardly more than a teenager, and her face under its mask of paint was set and vacant.

Dave knew exactly how her story would have started–it was a tale he had heard a thousand times. As a young runaway, she would have been taken under the wing of a drug dealer and begin a relationship with him. He would give her a little dope, later a tiny snort of cocaine. After a while he would add heroin, a fraction at a time, and soon the girl would be hooked. Before long she would be on the streets under the direction of the drug dealer, now turned pimp, earning money to pursue her habit.

It was not just heroin, there were a myriad of other drugs available with which to bewitch the bodies and imaginations of the young people of Victoria–highly addictive substances, promising an immediate high, but carrying all the attendant risks: dementia, premature aging and early death. The lethal list included, as well as marijuana and heroin, crack cocaine, and–the latest in the slew of mind-altering substances–crystal methamphetamine, which was cheap to make but horrific in its side-effects, causing its users to literally "burn up."

Dave's years with the Drug Squad had made him aware of the extreme toll exacted by illicit substances, on both society and the individual. As he noted the inert figures on the sidewalks, the furtive bargaining on the street corners, the averted faces, his heart was filled with pity. He was reminded of the words of the poet William Blake, who witnessed comparable scenes in another large city:

> I wander through each charter'd street,
> Near where the charter'd Thames does flow,
> And mark in every face I meet
> Marks of weakness, marks of woe.[18]

Dave noted the "marks of weakness and of woe," the lineaments of shame and despair he discerned upon the countenances of those who passed, and was aware that occasionally a frenetic glance would be directed toward himself. "Drugs and fear," he thought to himself, "they are the same word." The resolve he had spoken of to his mother crystallized into complete firmness of purpose.

Baby Dave with brother Don, mother Harriet Richardson (nee Stewart), father Henry (Harry) George McNaughton Richardson, and brother Bob. Pembroke, Ontario, 1942.

Young David, newly arrived in Victoria, British Columbia:
I had a million miles of daydreams
In the inches between my ears
(from "Apples Trees and Heroes," Chapter 1).

Dave riding "Redwing" on George Boles' farm in Alberta:
A young boy's going out to find the earth ...
(from "The Value and The Worth", Chapter 2).

A teenage Dave striding the streets of Victoria in the late Fifties:
The jeans were a little lower
Only James Dean jacket high
(from "A '55 Ford and Elvis," Chapter 8).

The idealistic young police officer, who wanted to "do his best and make a difference" (see Chapter 3).

Dave, the young rock star, with Vancouver singer Judy Ginn.

DTC (Dave the Cop) with his mother Harriet and a young David Foster:
And Davey, how'd your hair get so long?
(from "David and David," Chapter 5).

The band Skylark, photographed in Vancouver in 1971.
Top left: Doug Edwards, top right: David Foster.
Bottom left to right: Steve Pugsley, Duris Maxwell, Carolyn Cook, B.J. Cook, Donny Gerrard.
(Credit: Heather Aston)

Dave, second from right, with the "boys in blue" at Saanich Police Station, Victoria, B.C.

At the 1988 PROCAN Crystal Awards, which honored "Wildflower" as one of the all time most performed songs on Canadian Radio. Dave in the center, with Gordon F. Henderson, Chairman of the Board of PROCAN (now SOCAN), and.Valerie Hennell. (Credit: Franz F Linder Photos)

Some of the biggest names in Canadian music were present at the 1988 PROCAN Awards.
Front row, left to right: Ken Tobias, Dave Richardson;
Middle row: Randy Bachman, Frank Mills, Valerie Hennell, Gene MacLellan, Hagood Hardy;
Back Row: Eric Kagna, Terry Jacks, Burton Cummings.
(Credit: Franz F Linder Photos)

Dave and Lesley at their June 2009 wedding in Christ Church, Jerusalem, Israel.

Dave with Lesley at the spectacular Butchart Gardens in Victoria, fall 2009.

```
      She's faced the hardest times you could imagine
      and many times her eyes fought back the tears
      until(it seemed)her youthful world was about to fall in,
      each time her slender shoulders bore the weight of all her fears
      and the sorrow no one hears
      still rings in midnight silence in her ears

***   Let her cry, for she's a lady
      Let her dream, for she's a child
      Let the rain fall down upon her -
      XXX she's a free and gentle flower, growing wild
      And if chance holds that I should hold her
      let me hold her for a time,
      that if allowed but one possession
      I could pick her from the forest to be mine

      Be careful how you touch her, she'll awaken
      and sleep's the only freedom that she knows
      and when you walk into her eyes, you won't believe it -
      the way she's always paying for a debt she never owes
      and a silent wind still blows
      that only she can hear, and so she goes.

         Let her cry, etc........
```

The original typewritten copy of "Wildflower."

PART III:
THERE ARE WORDS AND
THERE ARE DEEDS TO BE DONE

CHAPTER 25
Meeting Lara

PROMPTLY ON THE first morning in June, Dave returned to the clinic on Pemberton Street, where he met two young men named Andre and Murdo who were cocaine addicts and alcoholics. Dave warmed to them immediately, and the three soon became friends. As the days went by he met many others as well, and to all he would speak of the hope of freedom from drugs, saying, "If you want help, here's my number." He had an authority and ease of manner about him that could not be resisted. Soon his cellphone was ringing twenty-four hours a day.

Dave now looked forward to every waking moment, for he never knew who would be calling. He took under his wing all those who came to him, counseled and encouraged them day and night, and brought them to the AA meetings he himself was still attending. His whole attitude toward these individuals had changed. Three decades as a policeman had bred a certain amount of cynicism; but now, because he had learned there was nothing in his own life which was beyond redemption, he was looking for positive qualities in everyone he encountered. He knew he would be devoting himself unreservedly to ministering to these vulnerable people ... yet didn't realize that this commitment to helping others was about to be tested–to the limit.

At this early stage Dave was counseling–or, as he put it, "talking with"–about fifty or sixty addicts; his primary message to them was: "Let me show you how not to drink." This, of course, had the same goal as that of AA, of achieving and maintaining sobriety. However, there remained with him one nagging thought, that he was teaching people something at which he himself had failed more than twice before. From personal experience he knew most addicts were willing to listen to anything that could help them break their habit; consequently, they taught in AA of a "higher power," represented by an object such as a flower, or even a light bulb. This could generate a certain amount of success; nevertheless, Dave found himself deeply questioning the AA philosophy. He felt he knew what

Higher Power was truly giving him this freedom, and the confidence he would never drink again.

Dave's older brother, Don, had led him to faith in God when he was still a child, and somehow he had veered away from that early commitment. Many years later, in a mood of self-disillusion, he had penned the following lines:

IN THE DAYS WHEN I WAS TWELVE

Jesus did me a favor once
In the days when I was twelve,
He said He'd do His best
To keep me out of hell;
I swore to change my ways, nor be
The way I was before–
And that's the only swearing
To the time I'd ever sworn.

But I had time to change my mind,
And Jesus, are You sad
To see a good boy turning bad
And changing for the worse?
A Sunday morning search
Will find, upon a velvet bed,
An empty, foolish, drowsy head
Instead of bowed in church.

The vulture waits for someone
Who has a soul to sell,
And when that person dies,
To carry him to hell;
The shadow of a claw now lies
Upon my window sill.

Lord, I am much older now
And not too well preserved,
Soon to be the carrion
Of the life that I have served;
So if You still remember,
Release me from my shell,

And leave it for the vulture
As all Your mercies tell;
Then take me to the days
And the ways when I was twelve.

Now, as Dave remembered embracing a belief in Jesus all those years ago, a question arose in his mind with such urgency that he knew he must find an answer. "Has He really been waiting for me all these years?" he wondered.

The realization was dawning upon him that this Higher Power of which they spoke in AA was no flower or light bulb, but rather the One who had created the flowers and everything else, the whole cosmos. And as Dave spoke of liberty and wholeness to the addicts he counseled, he was frequently astonished at the words that emanated from his lips. Whereas his own wisdom or confidence had often let him down, now he found he was relying on that of Another; he also discovered himself naturally gravitating toward this Person, speaking with Him about the challenges he was facing, calling on His help.

However, at this stage Dave was adamant there was something for which he was not ready. He didn't want to read the Bible: all the "thou shalt nots" had too many bad associations for him. Yet even as he mused on these things, a distinct impression came to him which took the wind out of his sails. "You don't have to, for a while," he sensed a Voice saying to him. "Just now I am filling your life with My love."

A day or two after this experience came the summer solstice, June 22. It was a beautiful day of sunshine, and during the morning Dave had been speaking with a woman about her problems with alcohol; this talk had gone well, and he was feeling lighthearted. He made his way down to "The Hole." Outside were a couple of little sidewalk tables with plastic chairs; Dave got his coffee and sat down at one of them. Then he prayed a silent prayer, thanking God for a good morning, and saying,

"If You have anyone else You want me to help, I'm here."

Within seconds a young girl came walking around the corner; she seemed about twenty-one or twenty-two, and was petite, blonde and pretty. She looked at the coffee shop, walked past him into the interior, stayed inside a couple of minutes, then came back out with her coffee and sat down on the opposite side of the table. She nodded a "hello" to Dave.

"Hi," he said, "you're new here?"

"Yeah," she replied, "I just moved here from the interior of B.C. Do you live here?"

"Just round the corner."

"What do you do?" she asked.

"I'm a retired policeman."

"And what do you do now that you're retired?"

"I try to help people," he answered simply.

"Can you help me?" she asked. "I'm a heroin addict." And with that she clapped her hands over her mouth, as if gasping in horror that the words had escaped her.

Dave, meanwhile, was also surprised, for this girl didn't look like an addict. Most gave themselves away clearly, were emaciated or unkempt, but this young woman seemed far too attractive and well dressed. Nevertheless, he replied calmly, "I'll be glad to help you … what is your name?"

"My name is Lara."

Dave took out paper and pencil, and they exchanged names and phone numbers. Just at that moment, before they could talk any further, another young woman arrived on the scene; she had come to keep an appointment with Dave's new acquaintance. As soon as Dave saw this person, he became alert; all his police training and the sixth sense he had honed over so many years told him something was wrong.

Some time later, Dave learned what had led to Lara's appearance at The Hole on that fateful June morning; it was an extraordinary sequence of events. Lara was new to Victoria and did not really know her way about town; still, she had an appointment with her dealer she was determined to keep, and with this intention caught a bus from the outskirts of the city. On the way she began reading a pocketbook and became completely engrossed in the story. When she finally looked up from the pages, she realized she had passed her stop and panicked, not knowing where she was. She grabbed the cord to stop the bus and got off, then had to find a telephone to call her dealer. At that moment she saw the café and came in and ordered coffee. The woman who arrived on the scene just after Dave began speaking with her turned out to be her heroin dealer.

Lara and the woman presently left together, while Dave mused over the encounter. "Will she call or not?" he wondered.

CHAPTER 26
The Third Kind of Love

A WEEK WENT by. Dave's cellphone was as usual ringing day and night, but from time to time he wondered about the pretty young girl in the café: would she call him for help with her problems? Usually he would wait for an addict to contact him first, because that would show him that person was serious. Yet something kept telling him to call her, and finally he picked up the phone.

"Oh!" she said when he called, "It's the strangest thing! I had the feeling that I should call you too."

"Are you interested in getting together then? I'd love to help you if I can."

"I'd like that," she replied, and they made a date to meet for coffee.

At their first meeting, Dave began to probe a little more deeply into her background. "How did you get into drugs?" he asked.

It was a long and unhappy story, revealed gradually over the weeks ahead as Lara learned to trust Dave and unfold her heart. She was from a town named Vernon in the interior of British Columbia, and had a regular enough upbringing, quick and bright at school, and enjoying an active social life. When she was still a young girl, even before her teens, she had an exceptionally strange experience. One quiet afternoon, she was playing in the front yard of her home when a boy, a few years older than she, appeared. Lara stared at him in surprise, because he was dressed in a bumble bee costume. Then the boy spoke to her, and the words he said made a powerful impact:

> You're going to have trouble in your life. Your mother and father
> will split up, and you will think it's your fault. Things will get really
> bad, but someone will be sent to help you.

Lara ran in to tell her mother about the boy's sudden appearance, but when she looked out again he had vanished. And then, as she grew up, in due course her mother and father did split up and she continued living with her father. In her teens she became a bit of a party girl, even then smoking a little dope or taking some ecstasy. After leaving high school she was given a grant of money to undertake a hairdressing course; at around the same time she met a young man named Jason, and they fell in love and became engaged.

Jason, however, had a driving record, and when he bought a new car he asked if he could put it in Lara's name to save on the insurance costs, and she agreed. One evening after leaving her place in the new vehicle he stopped at a friend's place and began drinking. When he left to drive home, he had an accident, and killed himself and another woman. As alcohol was involved, the insurance company would not pay out any money. And now, because the car was registered in her name, Lara was liable for an amount of over a million dollars. The death of her fiancé and the appalling situation it left her in placed Lara in a highly fragile emotional state, and the slide into excessive drug use was just around the corner. It was at this time she first began using heroin and gradually became more dependent on it.

One day toward the end of summer, while she was staying with her father in their oceanside cabin, he was taking apart the outdoor furniture to pack it away for the winter. Suddenly, as he was removing the sections of a folding table, a used syringe fell out of the hollow interior. He picked it up and angrily accused Lara of having placed it there. She protested her innocence with tears, but he told her he would no longer have her in his home; her mother and brother also said they wanted nothing to do with her. Sad and disconsolate, she left her hometown and came to Victoria to stay with her uncle; she was working for his small company, and using her wages to buy drugs. It was at this point she met Dave.

Dave was a little skeptical of Lara's version of the story of the syringe, knowing that addicts frequently lied about their behavior. As he came to know her better, he saw she never tried to hide from him anything about her habits or addiction, so he began to trust in her basic truthfulness. Much later, Lara was telling the story of the discovery of the syringe to her sister and relating how it had led to her alienation from her father. Her sister cried out in dismay, because she remembered what had actually taken place. She and a group of friends were staying at the cabin and partying; they had taken the syringe and used it to inject vodka into a watermelon, then stuffed it into the furniture, and although she meant to remove it later, she had forgotten all about it.

Still, there was something that struck Dave with far greater effect about Lara's story. Each time she related some new detail of her family's rejection, the tears would well up in her eyes and she would be overcome with sadness, yet she never uttered a word of judgment against them. Instead, she spoke only of how precious they were to her, recalling them with expressions of deepest fondness and yearning.

Dave was amazed at the enormous devotion the young woman continued to demonstrate for all the members of her family, even though they had treated her so harshly and cast her out. He knew there was a word for this kind of love. It was not the natural tie of affection that a parent would have toward a child, nor the attraction shared between a man and a woman. Rather, it was a love he himself was feeling toward Lara, which gave him the desire to see her made whole and set free. Later he would be able to give a name to this kind of love–*agape*–but, as he did not know it at the present, he called it "the third love."

There was something else that Dave knew about Lara. Dave was still himself attending AA, and Lara was going to NA (Narcotics Anonymous, the drug-user's equivalent of AA), yet he was certain that the concept of a "higher power" had no capacity to minister to the depth of her spiritual need. Something told Dave that Lara needed God–but he also knew she was a confirmed atheist. One day as they sat over coffee at Alzu's restaurant, a block away from the "Hole," he decided to broach the subject.

"Lara, I think that you need God," he announced straightforwardly.

She looked at him scornfully. "And *what* is God?" she asked.

Dave was struck with sudden inspiration. "I remember reading that He said, '*I Am.*'" Even though he had not read a Bible for many years, somehow that majestic title dropped into his mind.

"And what's *that* supposed to mean?" She was skeptical, but also a little intrigued.

"I'm pretty sure that's the name God told Moses in the desert–'*I Am Who I Am.*' He's always been God, and He always will be–but He lives in a kind of eternal present."

"I don't get it."

"It means His existence comes from Himself alone. And He is the source of all life: yours and mine, and everything that lives. He knows everything, the past as well as the future." Dave added gently, "And it means He knows everything about you, and He'll always be there for you."

She shook her head, and once again tears came into her eyes and ran down her cheeks.

"Everyone I've ever loved has gone away," she said sadly.

"I'll never go away," Dave assured her. He knew it was not just a sentimental statement; he meant it with every fiber of his being, and it came from outside him.

"You'll go away–they all do," she said stubbornly.

"I won't leave you," Dave reiterated. Something made him add, "I have a special kind of love for you, and I believe it's something God gave to me. I care about your wellbeing–not because you're my child, or even because we're friends. I call it 'the third love.'"

Lara leaned forward, her face suddenly alight with interest. "What kind of love is that?"

Again Dave was visited with a memory from the past. "I remember this definition: '*Love suffers long and is kind.*'"

"Where's that from?"

"The Bible–I can't believe I remembered that from all my years ago at Three Hills. Come on," he added suddenly. "I've got a Bible at home. Let's go find it."

Back at Dave's place, they searched for and found the old NIV Bible his brother Don gave him many years earlier, back in the Seventies when this version was first printed. It was on a back shelf, and dusty from its long neglect. Dave set it on a table, and he and Lara sat down together. He flipped the Bible open. The heading at the top of the page read "1 Corinthians 13," and as he gazed at the text he could hardly believe his eyes. There was the exact passage he had quoted to Lara in the restaurant!

> *Love suffers long and is kind; love does not envy;*
> *love does not parade itself, is not puffed up;*
> *does not behave rudely, does not seek its own,*
> *is not provoked, thinks no evil;*
> *does not rejoice in iniquity, but rejoices in the truth;*
> *bears all things, believes all things, hopes all things,*
> *endures all things.*
> *Love never fails* (1 Corinthians 13:4-8).[19]

Together they read through St Paul's incomparable passage in its entirety, moved by the simplicity and beauty of its expressions. Somehow they sensed there was a challenge here for them both, and they were embarking on a new journey together. Lara was a young woman who had already been shattered emotionally and spiritually by life. Her wounds were raw and deep, and her spiritual need an abyss which only the boundless love of God could fill. But, for Dave, this young woman was to prove the catalyst that propelled him further on his long quest for God, and drew him back to the scriptures which contained the words of eternal life.

CHAPTER 27
When I Consider Your Heavens

DAVE WAS NOW aware that he was dealing with God Himself, who had irrupted into his life bringing peace and freedom, and was revealing to him the purposes of His heart. Late in the evenings, when he was free from his ministry, he would find himself walking about his neighborhood, gazing at the stars. Never had they seemed to him to shine with such luminosity; they mirrored a longing in his soul. He knew he did not want to be the way he had been; there was a great yearning in him to be made completely new, to make up for the years he had gone his own way and been lost in self-seeking. "Lord," he said as he walked, "I want to be genuine; I want to be a real person." It was a cry from the depths of his heart.

At the same time, his work of counseling continued with ever more demands upon his time and energy. His condominium apartment had two bedrooms, and now he seemed always to have one drug addict after another, homeless and penniless, staying in the spare room so he could look after and feed them. There was a group of addicts including Murdo and Andre with whom he met regularly; Lara now also became a part of that circle. Her aunt and uncle had told her she had to leave because of her lifestyle, but Dave felt this development would bring her into a more intense counseling situation.

A girl he knew named Alicia, an addict whom he had met in detox, had taken a two-bedroom apartment across the street from his condo, and Lara now moved in with Alicia. Dave would meet these young people in local cafés, or sometimes in a park across the way. He knew it was important to take them out of the depressing confines of that drug-infested neighborhood, so he would frequently drive with one or other of them to the beach. It seemed to him that there, surrounded with the vista of sky and sea, God could begin to move with new power and grace in their lives.

Dave was still astonished at the wisdom he seemed to access as he ministered to these young people; at the same time he continued to possess a prescient knowledge that manifested itself when needed. He assumed that this was part of the normal Christian experience, that God had given him special gifts to help those enslaved by their addictions. He was quite aware that part of the reason Lara continued with his counseling sessions was that she was entertained by the unusual events that would happen around him. It might be that his phone would ring, and he would hand it to Lara, saying, "It's for you," and it would prove to be so. Or he would announce that a parking place would open up for them at a particular location, and this too would happen. Dave knew also that he would be encountering certain people in advance.

"Lara," he said one day, "I'm going to be meeting someone, a young man, not tall, with blond hair; he'll be an addict. And I'll know it's him because his right foot will drag noticeably behind him. It won't be a limp; he'll have hurt it in some way."

The next day he and Lara drove to the naval base at Naden; Dave was asked there to meet a troubled individual named Nolan. They walked into the reception area, and Nolan was pointed out to them, a young man, not tall, with blond hair. He raised a hand in greeting to them. "I'll just get my coat," he said, and turned and walked away. His right foot dragged behind him, and Lara froze.

"It's him!" she said in an electric whisper.

"Yes," said Dave, "and he's going to come to Christ."

"How can you be so sure?" she asked wonderingly.

"I don't know," he replied, "I just know he will."

Nolan, like Lara, was "a hard sell" as Dave put it, because they were both determined atheists. Dave spent many hours counseling and encouraging the young man, and yet, although their conversations frequently touched upon spiritual matters, he adamantly refused to believe in the possibility of a Creator.

One evening Dave drove with him to Willows Beach, where they could talk quietly and without interruption. It was a dark night, but clear, and the lights on the boats in the Juan de Fuca Strait could be seen twinkling through the blackness. The little waves crisped softly on the shore, and above them the immense vault of the sky was adorned with a myriad of shining lights. As Dave gazed up at the Milky Way, filling the night with beauty, his heart was filled with a great wonder. The words from one of the psalms he had recently read filled his mind, lyrical statements that expressed both awe and humility:

O Lord our Lord,
How excellent is Your name in all the earth …
When I consider Your heavens, the work of Your fingers,
The moon and the stars, which You have ordained,
What is man that You are mindful of him,
And the son of man that You visit him? (Psalm 8:1a,3-4).

Psalm 8 was one of many written by King David, the great leader of Israel, perhaps in memory of the days when he was still a shepherd boy and tending his flocks on the hills outside Bethlehem. Dave was beginning to discover his own affinity with this other David, who displayed that unusual combination in his personality, both a songwriter and a warrior. But, for now, he pointed at the star-studded sky and said to Nolan:

"Just look at the incredible intricacy and regularity of the universe. Don't you think something is holding all this together?"

"Yeah, sure," Nolan agreed, "there is some kind of cosmic energy out there. I just don't believe it's God."

"Is it okay with you then if I talk about this 'cosmic energy'?" asked Dave.

"Yeah, okay, just so long as you don't call it 'God.'"

"Is it okay if we give this cosmic energy a name, then?"

"You can give it a name so long as it's not God," said Nolan firmly.

"Okay, how about Charlie?" Dave suggested.

"Charlie!"

"Yes, Charlie. Does that name bother you?"

"No, well, all right, I guess we can call it Charlie," Nolan agreed grudgingly.

So from then on Dave's conversations with Nolan were sprinkled with references to Charlie, and Nolan gradually began to be compelled by what he was saying.

Yet the major part of Dave's focus at this time was upon Lara. Time seemed to them to become condensed at this stage, even irrelevant, as they each had a sense of being caught up in a drama not of their own making. Dave continued to have repeats of his earlier vision of the desert wilderness which was transformed into a paradise, but a new element came to be added to the picture.

One day, much to his surprise, as he was watching the "rerun" and standing in the little pool formed by the water falling from above, he saw a second rivulet flowing out from between his feet. It reached a distance about thirty feet away from him, then stopped and began sinking into the ground, and formed a pool similar to the one in which he was standing. From that pool a tiny green shoot started to grow, which turned into a shrub, then a sapling, and finally a most beautiful thing happened. At the top of the small tree, two branches started to spread out, and as they did they turned into arms–Lara's arms–as if she was growing out of the ground, out of the former desert.

Around the same time, however, Dave had another vision which was not at all pleasant, but instead terrifying. As it commenced, he found himself standing in the public square of a large city; the buildings were so tall he didn't think he was in Canada. Everything about the cityscape seemed an unrelieved dark grey, and his position was somewhat elevated, so it seemed he was looking down at a stage from above. At the back of the scene were two buildings which were much taller than the others, and from their tops smoke and fire were pouring out profusely. Ashes were falling like snow, causing the surreal darkness, and people were running and screaming below him in a scene of indescribable pandemonium. A number of office chairs, desks and business machines were overturned, smashed and broken as if after an earthquake, and he also saw a Green Machine on its side.

And now Dave knew what this vision was about. In Canada, one of the first banks to have an ATM was Toronto Dominion Bank, which had green ATMs called Green Machines; Dave understood with sudden clarity that this was all about money–and death.

As Dave continued looking into the center of this horror, the stage below him gradually drew all his attention, for in the middle of the stage was Someone he knew to be Jesus. And this part of the vision, at least, was beautiful. Jesus was glowing, shining with light; His robe seemed to flow down and become part of the stage, the floor of which appeared white and gold, as if lit from beneath. Dave couldn't see His face, because it was too brilliant, but he knew that in the midst of this chaos He was absolutely calm, the embodiment of peace. His arms were held open in front of him with His palms down, and instantly Dave knew why: in the midst of the panic-stricken crowd, fleeing in fear, every once in a while he could see a person standing still with eyes fixed on Jesus; and meanwhile His hands were like umbrellas, shielding everyone looking at Him from the ashes and fire falling from the sky.

The vision was like a dark intruder into Dave's new world, disturbing him deeply, nor was that the end of the matter: Dave knew by now that the prescient knowledge he possessed was not part of the usual Christian life. Was this something mental, physical, or spiritual? And, if it was spiritual, *where was it coming from?*

CHAPTER 28
Doing the Moonwalk

DAVE WAS DETERMINED to discover the source of his newfound mental abilities. The first thing was to check out his bodily health; accordingly, he had a complete physical examination including an MRI and a CAT scan. After this, his doctor declared he had never seen Dave in better shape. Next he made an appointment with a psychologist, who told him his faculties were in perfect working order.

That left only the spiritual realm, and here Dave was faced with a disturbing possibility. He remembered hearing earlier in his life that Satan was a counterfeiter, and could emulate God as the magicians in Egypt copied Moses by throwing down their staffs and turning them into snakes. Dave thought his new gifts were there to help people–but what if their source was satanic? He knew he had to speak to someone about God, and it was urgent.

One Saturday evening, with these thoughts pressing heavily upon him, he walked uptown looking for a church and found himself simply banging on closed doors. It dismayed him there seemed to be no one available to "minister to a mind diseased."[20] He ventured forth again the next evening, Sunday, by this stage truly desperate to speak to someone who could give him sound Christian advice. Upon reaching Pandora Street in the center of town, it was as if a light switched on in his head. Pandora Street! That was where Central Baptist was located, the church he had attended as a boy. Dave walked on and discovered the church where he remembered it, entered the vestibule and found several people standing around as if a service had just ended. He approached an elderly man, and said abruptly:

"I've got to talk to someone who knows about God!" He mentioned the name of a pastor he had known there many years before. "Is he still here?"

"Oh, no," the man replied. "He hasn't been with us for some time. We have a Pastor Holmes now."

"Well, anyone will do, so long as they know about God."

"He certainly does. Come with me; I'll introduce you."

The two men threaded their way through the crowd until they reached a gentleman seated in a wheelchair on the far side of the room. Dave felt a rush of relief. He had known already he was going to meet an older, bald-headed man, that he would have two canes and ride an electric scooter—and there was that very person in front of him!

The other man left, and without any preliminaries Dave spoke to the pastor. "I need your help," he said.

The man in the wheelchair looked up at him with eyes that were both keen and compassionate. "What is troubling you?" he asked.

"I'm experiencing really strange occurrences, and they're accelerating; I have knowledge of things I've never known before, and visions I see when I'm awake. I know I'm working for somebody, and am worried it might not be God."

"What is your name?"

"Dave Richardson."

The pastor scrutinized him again. "Are you any relation to Don Richardson?" he asked.

"He's my brother."

"I married your brother and his wife in this church forty years ago."

"Well, that's nice. Do you want to help me or not?" Dave didn't mean to be rude; he was just so anxious to find out what was happening to him.

"So you're seeing visions?" asked the pastor.

"Yes, I see them whether my eyes are open or closed; they're unbelievably clear, and I can't make them go away."

"Well, the church is closed on Mondays. Can you come in and see me on Tuesday at, say, two o'clock?"

"Yes, that's good."

As he walked home, Dave felt as though a weight were lifted from his shoulders, but he was still uncertain: how could this man, experienced in spiritual matters as he undoubtedly was, be able to determine if Dave's gifts were inspired by God—or by demonic powers? He was soon to find out, and in a way that surprised him completely.

Dave arrived at the church on Tuesday promptly at two. He noticed the main doors were closed, but the side door which led into the office area had a buzzer for visitors. As he walked to the door, an older gentleman arrived simultaneously; out of courtesy, Dave stood aside to let him go in first. The two men walked in and stood side by side at the desk where the receptionist, Jackie, was seated. Dave introduced himself.

"Oh yes," said Jackie, "You have an appointment to see Pastor Holmes."

Dave and the girl were both astonished when an interjection came from the man on Dave's left. "No! I have to talk to Pastor Holmes *now*," he said. His tone was almost violent.

"But I'm afraid this man has an appointment," said Jackie quickly, gesturing at Dave.

"I don't care, I've come from out of town," replied the other visitor.

He was so clearly determined to have his way that Dave said to Jackie, "It's okay, I'm happy to wait."

"Well," she said reluctantly, "I'll just phone Pastor Holmes and make sure that's all right with him."

She picked up the telephone, and as she did so the two men turned toward each other. It was the first time Dave had looked the other man in the face, and he could hardly suppress an exclamation. As he gazed into the man's eyes, he saw another pair of orbs, gleaming and malevolent, as if superimposed over those of the man; Dave knew instantly he was looking into the eyes of a demon. They were vile beyond description, and two powerful feelings emanated from them, Dave couldn't say which was predominant: the utter hatred they felt for him, or the complete fear of him. As Dave stared at the man, another idea immediately made sense: this person was there with the express intention of keeping him from talking with Pastor Holmes.

Jackie cleared the new arrangement with Pastor Holmes and asked Dave to wait in the vestibule; she herself took the man to an elevator which went up to the second floor where the pastor's office was located. Dave sat and read; occasionally he glanced at his watch, and eventually it neared the half-hour. Ordinarily he might have left, but two things kept him seated there: the first was the prescient knowledge he had of the pastor, the other was the understanding there was something hidden and sinister at work, intended to prevent him meeting the man of God.

Eventually the other visitor came down the stairs and walked out the front door, seeming perfectly normal. As soon as he left, Jackie put her head around the door and gave directions to go up to the pastor. Dave thanked her and started walking across the vestibule towards the stairs. And then another shocking event occurred.

Dave felt suddenly as if his whole body was grasped physically by an immense force; he knew that it was evil, and was astounded at its strength. The sensation was as if an impossibly powerful magnet was pulling him from behind, so, although he was walking forward with every muscle pressed into service, his body was nevertheless being slowly and surely pulled backward. The image of Michael Jackson doing the moonwalk[21] flashed into his mind as he continued pulling against this strange power; then, as he realized he was losing the battle, he finally turned and shouted:

"*Let go of me!*"

At that precise moment two elderly ladies came through a door from a back corner of the church. They were both startled and stared at Dave.

"Not you," he said, "him," pointing in the direction he had been pulled. He couldn't see the thing, whatever it was, yet he had no doubt it was still there; nevertheless, it had completely loosed its hold. The elderly ladies continued to look at him in disbelief as he walked across the vestibule and up the stairs into Pastor Holmes' office. The first words that tumbled out of his mouth were:

"You've got something evil downstairs that does not want me talking to you."

"I beg your pardon?"

He could see the pastor was not sure what he was saying, and decided to let it go. Soon he was seated in a comfortable chair opposite the man of God; on the desk between the two men reposed a large black Bible, its leather worn from frequent handling. Pastor Holmes repeated his former question:

"So you have visions?" he asked.

"Yes," replied Dave, "but I don't know where they are coming from, and that is what is worrying me."

"Well, we will test the visions, to see if they are from God or from Satan."

"How do you do that?"

"We test them against scripture," replied the pastor, gesturing to the Bible. "Would you like to tell me what you have been seeing?"

Dave was soon recounting in the ears of an engaged, sympathetic and discerning listener the details of the vision which recurred most frequently. He described the barren landscape of the desert, and the miracle of the rebirth which took place as the rain cloud formed and the life-giving waters were poured out, so the wilderness became lush and verdant. He concluded, and sat waiting with some trepidation, hoping the pastor might be able to explain from where such images came.

Pastor Holmes sat silently for a moment or two, then picked up the Bible and turned with sure hands to a certain passage. "I want you to listen to this," he said, "It's from the 35th chapter of the book of Isaiah. He began reading aloud, and the musical words flowed out:

> *The wilderness and the wasteland shall be glad for them*
> *And the desert shall rejoice and blossom as the rose;*
> *It shall blossom abundantly and rejoice,*
> *Even with joy and singing …*
> *Then the eyes of the blind shall be opened,*
> *And the ears of the deaf be unstopped.*
> *Then the lame shall leap like a deer*
> *And the tongue of the dumb sing.*
> *For waters shall burst forth in the wilderness,*
> *And streams in the desert.*
> *The parched ground shall become a pool,*
> *And the thirsty land springs of water* (Isaiah 35:1-2,5-7).[22]

As he read, the tears were pricking at Dave's eyes, and he felt an overwhelming sense of relief. He realized that it was his own vision, for it described so perfectly what he had been seeing. He also felt reassured that this gift was indeed from God, and that he was given this ability, not for himself, but for those to whom he ministered, and they in turn would relay these truths to others.

Pastor Holmes closed the Bible and sat looking at Dave. "My friend," he said, "this is God speaking to you."

CHAPTER 29

I Will Write Your Name in The Sky

AFTER HIS ENCOUNTER with Pastor Holmes, Dave understood two things clearly. First and foremost, he realized that God Himself had entered his life in a dramatic and wonderful way. He was being brought, through an inconceivable grace and mercy, into a spiritual realm where the love of God was made freely available to him through Jesus Christ. At the same time, the deep things of God were also being revealed to him by that same Lord, in whom are *"all the treasures of wisdom and knowledge,"* through the illuminating power of the Holy Spirit. It was a place where deep spiritual thirst was satisfied, where the life of Christ could now become in him *"rivers of living water, springing up to everlasting life"* (see Colossians 2:3; John 7:38; John 4:14).

However, the other realization was more disturbing. Dave was brought face to face with the fact that there was an active spiritual force which was out to hinder and ultimately ruin everything that was good, in his life, and in the lives of others. This understanding would grow as Dave continued to minister to addicts, and to comprehend more fully the nature of the powers of darkness that were operating to bring these young people into bondage. His experiences with them would highlight the words that Jesus spoke in the Gospel of John concerning the devil: *"The thief does not come except to steal and to kill and destroy."* Yet that same verse continued with great words of comfort: *"I have come that they may have life, and that they might have it more abundantly"* (John 10:10).

At their meeting, Pastor Holmes offered to mentor Dave and to take an active part in nurturing his faith, so every day the two men would meet for an hour or so and delve together into the Bible. In this way, Dave's knowledge of the scriptures grew quickly; he especially loved reading in the book of the prophet Isaiah which Pastor Holmes had first quoted to him. Isaiah's mastery of language, the richness of his vocabulary and magnificence of his poetry are used with consummate skill to portray the breadth of his prophetic vision. This ranged from the revelation of God's glory in the Temple, to the depiction of the suffering and exaltation of a mysterious Servant Figure, and culminated in the picture of new heavens and a new earth.

Dave and Pastor Holmes would also lift Lara in prayer, as well as the other young people battling their addictions. Dave would later speak of his gracious mentor as "the epitome of humility, one of the most wonderful men of God I have had the privilege of meeting." And now a new episode was about to take place, which would bring him into a deeper relationship with God than he had ever imagined. This transformative event had the simplest of beginnings.

It was some months after he had met Lara, and only shortly after he had encountered Pastor Holmes, when Dave needed to drive one of his daughters to Duncan to take part in a school function. The town was situated about an hour's drive north of Victoria, and the two headed out of the capital on Highway 1, climbing first over the mountain ridge of the Malahat, and passing through its dense woods and rocky outcroppings. As they drove, they enjoyed spectacular glimpses of the Saanich Inlet far below, scattered with charming fir-crowned islands, then opening into a wider gulf, blue and gleaming, stretching away to the east. Far in the distance, the snow-crowned Mount Baker on the United States mainland floated in insubstantial majesty. The landscape became rural, dotted with small farming villages, and eventually they drove over the Silver Bridge which led into Duncan.

Dave dropped his daughter off at her venue, parked the car close to the center of town, and soon found the local Tim Horton's where he ordered a coffee. Duncan is much smaller than Victoria, and the main downtown area was roped off for the performance in which his daughter was taking part. Most of the people must have gathered there, as things seemed fairly quiet to him. Dave took his cup of coffee and decided to spend some time walking about.

And then, as he wandered through the peaceful streets of Duncan on that hushed afternoon, he heard God speaking to him.

It was a masculine Voice that he was hearing in the depths of his consciousness, a Voice filled with warmth and comprehension, gently leading him into a depth of communication he had never before experienced. Dave was aware with a heightened clarity that he was speaking to God Himself, and yet he was relaxed; all fear seemed gone, together with any concept of a deity who was frightening or threatening—for this was the Voice of Absolute Love. Time seemed to come to a standstill as the two conversed together. The Voice was asking him questions, and as He did so Dave understood always the answer he was supposed to give.

"What is your name?" asked the Voice.

Dave knew that he should reply with his full name: "Thomas David Richardson," he said.

"And what are you called?"

"Dave." He had never been called by his first name, Thomas.

"Who changed your name?" the Voice continued.

"Well, my mother told me my father did, shortly after I was born."

The Voice said, "Yes, I did," and Dave knew exactly what He meant. Now he wanted to know about his father, who died when he was only four.

"Is my father there with you now?" he asked.

"Yes, David, both of us are here," came the infinitely comforting answer. "Do you know why I changed your name, David?" the Voice persisted.

Dave shook his head. It was one question to which he would gain the answer only after some time had elapsed: the meaning of the Hebrew name given to him, that of Israel's greatest king.

They continued to talk, and as they did so Dave was not afraid to ask this Person questions. And then the Voice spoke to him words which would forever change his way of understanding the events which would subsequently occur to him: "David, *Beloved*, nothing in your life has been, or ever will be, coincidence."

And when He said that, it was as if the floodgates of knowledge opened up: everything–the universe, space, time and matter–seemed to take on a new meaning, and to be completely linked together in an intricate whole; at the same time, Dave knew that every millisecond was important to God, the most minute events of everyday life, and that nothing was beyond His control or His love. And then they talked together of another matter dear to Dave's heart, about Lara, and God made some promises concerning her. Dave then knew the time was drawing near that he should have to go and pick up his daughter.

"Can I talk about these things?" he asked. "Is there anything I am not supposed to mention of what You have shown me, and how will I know?"

"David, *Beloved*," came the answer, "If you remember it, you may talk about it. I have given you this wisdom for a purpose."

"How wise are you?" asked Dave impulsively. He sensed God's smile.

"David, I Am Wisdom."

Dave thought for a minute. "What about humor?" he asked.

"David, I Am Humor."

And Dave knew with a fresh access of complete comprehension that every positive force in the universe belonged completely to God, and came from Him.

As he went and picked up his daughter, as he drove her home, his mind and heart were full of what he had heard and experienced. Later that same day he went to meet with Lara; the sun was still shining, and she was walking a friend's dog in the park. They sat together on a wooden bench to talk.

"Lara," said Dave, "I had a talk with God today."

She rolled her eyes and said, very sarcastically, "Oh, really, and what did *God* have to say?"

"He has a two-part message for you," Dave continued, unperturbed. "The first part is that, although your family has cast you out, saying you're evil, the day will come when the situation will be reversed. In fact, the time will come when you will be the centerpiece of your family; they will look up to you, and you will be a pillar of strength for them."

"You're crazy," she said, shaking her head in disbelief. She was still a heroin addict, and everyone in her family had disowned her. "You know the situation with my folks, and that's impossible."

"It will happen," he said quietly.

She gave him a passive-aggressive look that indicated she disavowed completely what he had shared. Almost caustically she asked, "And what was the second part of what God had to say?"

"He said to tell you to watch the sky."

"Watch the sky?" she repeated, puzzled. "What for?"

"He said to tell you that, when you're free, He's going to write your name in the sky."

"What!" she said, startled.

"It will happen," said Dave again.

"Yeah, sure," she said scornfully. And there they left it for the time.

But the promises shone in Dave's mind like two lustrous pearls set against black velvet, sustaining him in the difficult days that lay ahead.

CHAPTER 30

The Quarter Million Contract

IT WAS NOT only for Lara's sake that the Voice had come to Dave on that amazing afternoon in Duncan. As he looked back over his own life, he was beginning to see God's hand of protection over him, unseen yet powerful; even when he was in the depths of alienation and despair that Presence had never forsaken him. Certain incidents from his past now also appeared to him in a new light, particularly those involving his police career. On many occasions he was in situations of extreme danger, and had nevertheless emerged unscathed. He mulled over these events.

To begin with, there was the matter of his nickname at Police Headquarters–Casper the Ghost–with which his colleagues acknowledged his uncanny ability to seemingly remain invisible in perilous situations. And there was a further strange occurrence. Not just once, but on two occasions, a fellow officer stood in for him when Dave was unable to come in to work. Both times, that officer had ended up being shot at and wounded; in the second incident he only narrowly escaped death. Understandably, he told Dave to look for someone else if he needed a replacement in the future.

There was another event which vividly suggested God's guardianship during those years. Dave was on patrol duty one warm summer evening, when he heard around ten pm that another officer, named Bill, needed some cover. He had driven through the parking lot of the Red Lion Beer Parlor and began running license numbers to see if there were any stolen vehicles, or any with warrants out for arrest. The station radioed back: Bill had a "hit" on one of the license plates belonging to a Volkswagen "bug"; the registered owner was wanted for breach of the Wives and Children Maintenance Act. His name was John W., he was from the mainland, and the station also informed Bill he had no prior criminal record.

Dave pulled into the parking lot of the Red Lion and greeted Bill; they talked together and agreed the offense in question was not a major one, so it seemed hardly worth their while to wait around in the parking area for what might be several hours. Just as they decided to leave, a man emerged from the beer parlor, walked over to the Volkswagen, and got in. He was immaculately dressed in beige slacks and sweater, and was clean-cut and good-looking–Dave remembered thinking he looked like a university professor. Now, however, the two officers were in a quandary, for having seen the person for whom a warrant was made out they were legally obliged to arrest him. Hence, they walked together to the car.

The man was sitting behind the driver's wheel; Dave glanced into the back seat and noticed a number of green garbage bags which were packed full. He asked the man for his driver's license; he handed it over and confirmed he was the person named in the warrant. The policemen were not on any kind of high alert because they knew the offender had no previous record.

"Sorry, sir," said Bill, "We have to take you in; you know there's a warrant out for your arrest."

"I know," the man acknowledged, "It's because of my estranged wife, right? She gets upset if I don't make payments."

"That's correct," affirmed Bill. "And, as I said, we'll need to take you into custody."

The man answered congenially, "Of course, I understand that." He added, "Would it be okay with you if I followed you into the police station in my car?" Dave and Bill looked at one another. The man continued, "I don't want to leave it here, everything I own is in the back seat, all my clothes and possessions; some-one could break in and steal them." And he gestured to the beer parlor he had just left as he spoke.

Now, to allow this was strictly against the rules, but as the police station was only three or four blocks away, as the man's request seemed so reasonable, and in addition because he looked so completely respectable, Bill felt constrained to accede. "Yeah," he said, "That'll be okay."

As soon as he said that, the word "*no*" seemed to be breathed into Dave's mind with utmost resonance and clarity; at the same time, a wave of complete horror washed through his body with so much force he felt he would almost faint with fear. Instantly, the word erupted from his mouth.

"*No!*" he shouted in loud, emphatic tones; and the man switched his head to look at him, startled.

"What?" said Bill in surprise, but Dave was not listening.

"Get your hands where I can see them–now!" he said to the man.

"What's the matter?"

"Now! Get your hands where I can see them," and Dave put hand on his gun to emphasize the point. Bill was looking at him in disbelief, but Dave opened the car door. "Move slowly, get out," he ordered. The man obeyed, and Dave turned to Bill, "Handcuff him and search him."

Bill gave Dave a long look, but handcuffed the man and put him in the back of his police car. Then he turned again to his colleague. "What do you think you're doing?" he asked, with a note of accusation.

"I have no idea," answered Dave, shaking his head. Usually he was the first one to give a guy a break, yet he was still feeling the after-effects of the wave of fear that had washed through him.

"You can't behave like that with an ordinary citizen," Bill remonstrated.

"I know, but there's something's wrong here. You watch him, I'm going to search his car."

He opened the door and leaned in. The car was an early model of Volkswagen, with two bucket seats at the front and the handbrake located between them. A sweater had been neatly laid over the brake, and Dave reached over and lifted it up. Beneath was a sawed-off 22 rifle, perhaps sixteen inches long; it was cocked and ready to fire.

Bill looked at Dave, thunderstruck.

"How could you possibly know it was there?"

"I didn't ... "

The two officers promptly arrested the man and charged him with possession of a sawed-off weapon. Because of its deadly power and concealability, it is a criminal offense to own such a firearm in Canada, punishable by anything up to five years in a federal penitentiary. If a person is caught with it loaded, the sentence could stretch to ten years. It emerged during the court proceedings that the man had planned to shoot both officers at the first opportunity. The green garbage bags Dave noticed in the back seat were found to be full of stolen property.

Even Dave's informants marveled at his ability to stay alive. Dave worked with a number of such men (and women) throughout his career, especially as he later became involved with some high-level crime investigations, and quite a few of these informants, although lawbreakers themselves, proved remarkably loyal to him. Even when Dave was assigned to another branch of duty, they would still phone in and give him details of a crime, and one day a particular informant came to him, a very tough guy indeed.

"I've been hired to kill you," he told Dave with a straight face. "It's Nico N. He said he'd pay me ten thousand dollars to eliminate you, five now, and the other five once you're dead."

"What are you going to do?" asked Dave.

"Well, I guess I'll just have to kill you," he laughed.

Eventually, the two fabricated a story that the target had proved impossible to take down, and Dave arranged for his informant to keep the five thousand he had already received.

Another informant came to him at a later date, with a similar message. He was a witness to the organized crime murders in Cumberland, Ontario,[23] when a drug dealer and his pregnant common-law wife were killed in a horrific execution-style shooting. This led to one of the most convoluted and costly court cases in Canadian history, focusing all the way through on "drugs, debt and death," as a Crown attorney put it. During the ten-year period Dave worked on the case, he spent a great deal of time and energy trying to keep alive this informant, who had evidence vital to the prosecution. He could not count the number of times his contact phoned in the middle of the night fearing for his life; Dave would sigh, roll out of bed, reach for his gun and head out the door.

At one point the bad guys in Ottawa sent a man named "the Hawk" to Victoria to look for Dave. He used to be a crooked cop, and was working for the mob as a private investigator. Yet Dave had other informants who were working for him out of respect, not because they had charges hanging over their heads, and they let him know the Hawk was coming to town.

Dave said to them, "You can tell the Hawk something for me; he doesn't know what I look like, but I know what he looks like, and I know his every move." Then he told them every motel the Hawk had stayed in during the previous week, and continued, "You tell that bastard that if I see him on the street I'm putting a bullet right between his eyes; I'm waiting for him to make a move, and if he does I'm going to kill him. And I mean it."

"You're talking pretty tough," they said.

"You think I'm tough, you'll find out how tough when you get your corpse back."

The next day the Hawk flew back to Ottawa. It had been a bluff, but Dave was worried the rogue cop would find where he lived with his wife and children.

When the case finally dragged to a conclusion, the informant came to him.

"You know what I found out, Dave? Those guys in Ontario had a contract out to kill you for a quarter of a million dollars!"

"You're kidding!" Stil, Dave knew the reason immediately: he was considered a threat because he was able in some measure to testify to his informant's reliability when the man came to give evidence. Yet he had another reaction as well.

"Wow!" he said, "Imagine that! Back east I'm worth a quarter million dollars, but at home only a lousy ten thousand!"

Despite his bantering comment, Dave's primary emotion was awe at the fact he had somehow managed to evade death through all those years. One day, well after the case was over, he met this same informant at a downtown Tim Horton's café. The two men ordered their coffee, sat down together at a corner table and reminisced about the murder trial.

"You know what, Dave?" said his informant, "in that whole file, lasting ten years, the thing that amazes me most?"

"What?"

"That you came out of it alive."

Even as Dave was coming to realize that God's hand of protection had been over him throughout his police career, he had another vision. In it, he found himself standing on a street corner one evening; it was dark and foggy, but a streetlamp shone through the swirling mist and illuminated the scene. He could see another man was standing about thirty feet away from him, silhouetted against the streetlight. Dave saw that he was an older man, with long hair, wearing an army coat with a big collar that reached down almost to his feet, similar to one Dave's father had when he was in the army in World War Two.

Yet what struck Dave most particularly about this man was his height; he was probably all of seven feet tall, and as he stood there he tapped his feet as if waiting for someone. Every once in a while his hand went into his pocket and he pulled out an old fob watch, flipped it open, looked at it, closed it, and put it back. Dave marveled at the patience of the older man, for whoever he was waiting for didn't seem to be arriving. The "eyelid movie" would then vanish away and recur again later, perhaps a dozen times in all.

One day the vision had a different ending. To Dave's surprise, just when he was expecting the scene to fade away, another person walked in out of the darkness and came up to the older man. Again Dave was struck by the immense height of this waiting figure, as he reached out and put his arms around the shoulders of the newly arrived man. Then the light fell on the face of this newcomer, and as it did so Dave realized with a shock that it was *himself*. And, although Dave was over six feet two inches, the waiting man was now clearly seen to be a good foot taller. With his arm around the shoulder of Dave's *alter ego*, he walked away from the streetlight; the two disappeared together into the fog and the street became empty.

In a blinding flash of realization, Dave understood what it was all about: that throughout all those years God had never stopped waiting and watching for him, and he was overwhelmed with the revelation of His patience and forbearance.

And, now that he had the message, Dave never saw the vision again.

CHAPTER 31

Such Knowledge is Too Wonderful

DAVE'S SCHEDULE, WITHIN a few months of his release from detox, had become unimaginably busy. He felt he was beginning a third career as he devoted himself to helping those with addiction problems, nor did he ever turn off his phone. He would sometimes receive calls in the middle of the night, and go out to help some desperate individual.

Dave was also spending a significant portion of time in emergency wards with people who had overdosed. The staff in the detox unit became confident in him and trusted him; if they had a patient who had to visit a doctor, they would phone him and ask him to drive the person, knowing he would not let them "use" while out. As he developed personal relationships with the staff, occasionally they would call and ask him to talk with a particular person. In this way, although a secular agency, they indicated their awareness that a spiritual issue was involved with which Dave might be able to help.

Many times, Dave would also get advance knowledge about people he was going to meet. In his free moments he would lie on his couch, not praying but listening, opening his ears to what God might be saying to him, and thoughts would occasionally well up in his consciousness, showing him things he knew would ultimately happen in real life.

Dave was aware the gifts he had were unusual, and took this problem to Pastor Holmes. Once again his mentor, who was rapidly becoming a close friend, opened the big book on his table. This time he turned to the New Testament.

"Did you know that in the early church the things you describe were happening to quite a few of the new Christians?" he asked. "They had many gifts which God gave them through the Holy Spirit: words of knowledge, wisdom and prophecy, that could not have been known by human means. The Apostle Paul called these gifts *charismata.*"

"That is amazing," said Dave, "And is God giving these same gifts to the church today?"

"I believe so," the pastor told him. "And they are just as needed now as they were in those first congregations. In fact, Paul described his own ministry to the Corinthians as being 'in demonstration of the Spirit and of power.' He did not just preach brilliant messages, he also confirmed them through the awe-inspiring power–or *dunamis*–of God."

"*Dunamis*?" asked Dave, "as in dynamite?"

"Exactly," replied his mentor. "We can understand this power as, first of all, persuading a person of the truth of one's words, so that God's supernatural light floods the heart and soul, and begins that process of transformation into the image of Jesus." He turned the pages of the New Testament, and quoted:

For it is the God who commanded light to shine out of darkness, who has shone in our hearts to give the light of the knowledge of the glory of God in the face of Jesus Christ (2 Corinthians 4:6).

He continued. "But Paul knew that, to reach the pagans in Corinth, it would also require a demonstration of such power that they would be astonished. So his message was backed up by signs and wonders, and gifts of healing and miracles."

Dave was fascinated by what he was hearing. "I've certainly seen the impact of those words of knowledge and prophecy," he said. "Especially when a person is open to the idea there is a spiritual realm."

"That is why Paul urged us to 'earnestly desire' the best spiritual gifts!"

Dave knew there was another matter, more somber and vexing, that he must broach. "What about demonic oppression?" he asked. "I know it's controversial."

Pastor Holmes looked at him with that searching gaze. "I can see it is troubling you," he answered. "Many find it easy to dismiss the idea of a demonic realm. The scientific outlook of our time encourages us to be skeptical of accounts in the gospels that describe Jesus casting out evil spirits from people. It's suggested those individuals were suffering some kind of physical or psychological illness."

"Perhaps the advent of Jesus, the Light of the World, brought about a tremendous contest with the forces of darkness, and that is why there is so much demonic activity in His ministry?" suggested Dave.

"Yes, indeed," agreed the pastor. "And the belief of the church is that demons are real, and as active today as they were in Jesus' time. They work at the behest of Satan, and their intention is always destructive of the human being."

Dave's mind ran over some of the things he had witnessed in his police career. "And surely many of the acts of human wickedness we see in the world today can't simply be explained as due to rationalistic causes."

"That's true. Especially in this modern era, we've seen evil of such magnitude that we need to take seriously the idea there is a supernatural realm, and to consider the truths revealed in the Bible. It shows us a world where devils and demons aren't just myths, but instead are a terrifying reality–and shows at the same time that God's power is more than sufficient to overcome these forces."

These understandings helped Dave greatly in his ministry to the addicts, and most especially with Lara. He found himself teaching her crucial lessons about people, relationships–and above all love–in answer to her searching questions, and he knew this knowledge was not from himself.

The Holy Spirit was giving Dave other kinds of revelation as well. One time he was with Lara at Alicia's apartment; he had with him his cell phone, and noticed there was a number on the screen he had never seen before. He held out the phone to the girls.

"What's this phone number?" he asked.

"What phone number?" Lara asked, holding out her hand for the phone. She looked at the screen, then her face paled and she turned away.

"What's the matter?" he asked.

"Nothing ... where did you get that number?"

"I didn't get it, it's just on my screen; what is it?"

"That's my drug dealer's number," she confessed in a rush.

Another day, down by the Hole, Dave saw a car come round the corner and his eyes were drawn to the license plate: FXD551. He registered the initial letters with a shock; to another person they would have meant nothing, yet to Dave as a former policeman they were significant indeed. The letters FXD were an abbreviation for the word "fixed," and a "fix" in the language of addicts meant an injection of drugs. Dave didn't know if the number 551 had any special import, but stored it in his memory. It was knowledge which would soon prove invaluable.

The following day, Dave went to Central Baptist for his daily meeting with Bob; they were there until late and as he was leaving the church Lara called him on his cell phone. When she hung up, Dave's eyes fell on the time: 5:51 pm. The following day he noticed that she called him at this time once again, and now he knew what it meant.

He challenged her: "You have used two days in a row."

At first she denied it, but when he told her how he knew she "came clean"; she also became wary of his seeming omniscience.

Dave's counseling sessions with other addicts also continued to be intense. "If only," he thought, "there was some kind of extension cord I could plug from my head to theirs, so they could experience freedom, and save all the pain and effort I had to go through."

Yet, even though he was only now beginning to comprehend the riches in the Bible, he knew this liberty came from God, the Creator of the universe, not some unidentifiable cosmic power. And, as Dave was coming closer to God, he was getting further away from what was taught in AA. He was becoming convinced that God was the answer to addiction problems; as he put it, rather than the twelve-step program of AA, he offered a one-step program: *Jesus Christ*.

Many of these recovering young men and women would begin attending church, and dramatically turn their lives around. Dave held Bible studies for them in his home, and his sense of humor came into play in a way he had never imagined. He would turn to the gospel stories, and say: "Here's Jesus and the gang going to Galilee again!" And they would be hanging on his words.

From the gospels Dave learned that all who were suffering could come to Jesus, that He might manifest His wonderful healing power in their lives. He marveled that he was dealing with a God who was so mighty, who had created this whole astonishing universe, yet who counted the very hairs upon the heads of those who came to Him, and cared even for the fall of a sparrow.

At the end of a long day's ministry he loved to read through the book of Psalms, and in one of these lyrical expressions of worship he found a depiction of God which captivated him completely. Psalm 139, attributed to King David, seemed to him to sum up all he had learned so far in this new spiritual journey he had embarked upon.

> *O LORD, You have searched me and known me.*
> *You know my sitting down and my rising up;*
> *You understand my thought afar off.*
> *You comprehend my path and my lying down,*
> *And are acquainted with all my ways.*
> *For there is not a word on my tongue,*
> *But behold, O LORD, You know it altogether.*
> *You have hedged me behind and before,*
> *And laid Your hand upon me* (vv. 1-5).

The psalmist, in his meditation on his relationship with the Lord, recognizes this as the most fundamental thing in his life and the very ground of his being. Caught up in a sphere of exalted consciousness, he apprehends his whole existence as completely embraced by divine power and knowledge, and continually subject to the searching gaze of Absolute Love. As the psalmist continues to reflect upon the intensity of God's care for him, the limits of his understanding are transcended, and he makes his amazed declaration:

> *Such knowledge is too wonderful for me;*
> *It is high, I cannot attain unto it* (v. 6).

Yet even as the revelation of God's intimate presence and His consummate attention to the smallest details of his existence are unveiled to the poet, it also proves overwhelming to him. Some new questions burst forth from his soul, as he desires to escape the One who bends on him such relentless scrutiny:

> *Where can I go from Your Spirit?*
> *Or where can I flee from Your presence?*
> *If I ascend into heaven, You are there;*
> *If I make my bed in hell, behold, You are there.*
> *If I take the wings of the morning,*
> *And dwell in the uttermost parts of the sea,*
> *Even there Your hand shall lead me,*
> *And Your right hand shall hold me* (vv. 7-10).

Paradoxically, the psalmist's flight from God leads to an even greater awareness of the dominion He wields over the cosmos in all its dimensions, reaching to farthermost east and west, from the heights of heaven to the depths of hell. When the psalmist finds himself in the realm of chaos and evil, where he expected to find only disorder and death, he finds instead the light of the Lord's presence; it is here that he is grasped and held by the hand of this God, who transforms the crushing darkness, and brings him into safety and security:

> *If I say, "Surely the darkness shall cover me,"*
> *Even the night shall be light about me;*
> *Indeed, the darkness shall not hide from You,*

But the night shines as the day;
The darkness and the light are both alike to You (vv. 11-12).

Moreover, God's creative ideas concerning him are utterly limitless, and as the psalmist contemplates this fact he finally comes to a place of rest and assurance, with his heart stilled in wonder:

How precious also are Your thoughts to me, O God!
How great is the sum of them!
If I should count them, they would be more in number than the sand;
When I awake, I am still with You.
Search me, O God, and know my heart;
Try me, and know my thoughts;
And see if there is any wicked way in me,
And lead me in the way everlasting (vv. 17-18,23-24).

Dave read the final lines of the psalm with a quickened spirit; he understood from this wonderful ascription of praise that he was dealing with a Deity who comprehended him, his individuality and singularity, with a completeness that surpassed anything he had known, who had infinite plans of good concerning his past, present and future. Is this what it means to worship God, he wondered, to rest in this love with such assurance of His acceptance, with complete understanding that it is He who desires, and will complete, my restoration into the perfect image He had planned from the beginning …

How delightful it was to draw near to such a God in prayer!

CHAPTER 32
The Christ of Compassion

"A TALL MAN who is a marathon runner." The impression formed distinctly in Dave's mind as he prayed; he knew he would be meeting this person, and it would be soon. The following Sunday he went to Central Baptist Church, taking his mother Harriet with him.

As they entered the meeting hall, he saw there was a visiting preacher on the platform, an exceptionally tall man, with fair hair and an attractive open countenance. Dave's senses became alert. As the sermon progressed, the new speaker mentioned he had been a marathon runner, and indeed he had a look about him that spoke of complete physical fitness. After the service, Dave determined he would find a moment to speak to him; first, however, he made sure his mother was engaged with a congenial group of people at the back of the room. He was about to move forward to the platform when his parent turned to him.

"You know, Dave," she said, "I have a feeling that you should go and talk to the preacher."

"You're right," he told her, "That's just what I'm about to do. I'll be back in a few minutes."

Dave turned and started to make his way to the front. As he threaded through the aisle he bumped into a blonde woman, whose eyes were lit up with excitement in a striking countenance, full of warmth and personality. She clutched Dave's arm and spoke to him, it seemed involuntarily. "Do you know," she said, "I've just seen a woman who is shining! She is *visibly filled* with God's love."

"Who is it?" asked Dave, intrigued.

His unknown acquaintance pointed to a figure at the back of the room, "That woman there, in the blue suit."

Dave gazed in that direction. "That's my mother!" he said.

The two looked at one another in surprise, then Dave continued their conversation. "Well, thank you," he said, and added, "I'm just going up now to meet the pastor."

"That's my husband!" she said.

That was how Dave first met John and Lynne Schaper, a gifted and dedicated couple who had recently come to serve the church in Victoria. John had an exceptional talent for preaching, and as their acquaintance deepened into friendship Dave learned he was one of the finest, most honorable men he had met. Soon he began meeting with John on a regular basis, continuing the mentoring experience he had enjoyed with Pastor Holmes; the two men also prayed together often. Dave especially valued one lesson John taught him: he would begin their time of intercession with the beautiful words: "Lord Jesus, speak to us," and then he would be silent and they would wait.

Dave's prayer life now began to deepen, as he learned to draw nearer to this God, who answered petitions "exceedingly abundantly above all he could ask or think." From the scriptures he learned he could bring all the events of his daily life to Him; he also prayed for those to whom he ministered, as well as their families, because all the relatives of a drug addict were affected radically. Because he felt it was the intercessions of his own family which had brought him through, he would plead with those relatives, "Never cease to pray!" A verse from the book of James was coming to mean a great deal to him: *The effective fervent prayer of a righteous man avails much* (James 5:16).

"We have no righteousness of our own," he would explain, "but we do have the imputed righteousness of the Lord. And therefore when we continue in prayer for those we love, we can see His hand at work. He can take a life which has been ruined and turn it around for good."

Dave felt a special compassion for the mothers of addicts because he knew all his own mother had gone through on his behalf; he also believed the prayers of a woman for her child had a special efficacy. Early in his ministry, he encountered such a woman, in another case where he received what he called a "sign."

As a policeman, Dave was trained to be extremely observant and to note details such as license plate numbers; one day he glimpsed a personalized plate featuring the name Wendy and knew with strangest certainty he would meet a woman with that name. He mentioned this to Andre, who was staying in his apartment at the time, as the two men were making their way for a coffee at Starbucks.

"How do you know?" Andre had learned by this time to have a certain respect for Dave's premonitions.

"I'm not sure; it's an assurance I have in my heart."

"When will it happen?" asked Andre curiously. "After all, sooner or later, you're bound to meet a woman named Wendy!"

"Exactly," replied Dave, "That's how I know it will be soon."

The two men arrived at the café as evening drew on, and took their places in an outside covered section. Throughout the day there had been intermittent rain, which ceased as they waited for their coffee. The clouds above them parted, and Andre gazed up at the sky.

"Oh, look," he said, pointing, "there's Orion's belt."

The distinctive constellation shone against the night sky, and the bright luminaries of the belt were clearly delineated. Dave knew instantly that more was involved.

"That's another sign," he said.

"What?" asked Andre, astonished. "Those stars up there?"

"Think of the name, Andre," Dave said. "It means I'm going to meet a person named Ryan."

Andre merely shook his head in wonder, and the two continued with their counseling session. The next day, Dave was at home when his cell phone rang and a woman's voice spoke at the other end.

"Is this Dave Richardson?"

"Yes, it is."

"I got your name from someone at my church," she continued. "I heard you help people with drug problems?"

"Well, I try," he answered.

"Could you help my son?" she asked. Dave could detect the anguish in her voice. "He's a cocaine addict."

"Well, I can talk to him," Dave said. "Where does he live?"

"In Ontario."

Dave groaned to himself. "Well," he said, "that's kind of far away, and I don't travel. I'm sorry, I don't think I can help you."

As he uttered the words, Dave glanced at the call display and noted his caller's initial was "W."

"Excuse me, ma'am," he said suddenly, "what is your name?"

"Wendy," she said.

"And what is your son's name?"

"Ryan."

"I'll be happy to talk to him," said Dave. "When does he get back?"

She sounded surprised. "How did you know he was returning?"

"It doesn't matter," he said quickly.

"He'll be here in two days," answered Wendy, "to attend a rehabilitation program."

"Well," said Dave, "let me know how it works. And don't forget James 5:16!"

Eventually he hung up the phone, and recounted the conversation to Andre. "Now help me get the couch ready," he said, "we'll be having company. I don't think the rehab center will work out."

Two or three days later Wendy called to say the center was unable to take Ryan, and she had no place where he could stay.

"You can send him over," replied Dave, "The bed's ready!"

That is how Ryan ended up staying several months at Dave's place, together with Andre, during which time both young men overcame the worst aspects of their addiction.

While Dave continued to minister to these young people, his own relationship with Jesus was becoming ever more personal and real. So often, as he read the gospels, he was struck by a phrase that seemed to him to sum up the very character of Christ. When the evangelists described Him ministering in Galilee, they frequently wrote that He "had compassion," whether it was for a leper, a grieving widow, a little girl who had died, or the great crowds who gathered to hear Him teach.

John was able to explain to Dave more fully the significance of the phrase.

The Greek word *splagchnizomai* used by the evangelists to signify "compassion" is actually very unusual. The first part of the word, *splagchna*, is a term denoting "internal organs," suggesting it means to be moved so deeply by something that it is felt *physically*. When Jesus looked upon a suffering individual, it was possible for onlookers to perceive His whole being was caught up in a visceral, emotional response, as when He stood by the grave of Lazarus[24], weeping and "groaning within Himself." He was shaken to the depths by the grief of those surrounding Him, as well as His awareness of the human condition, enmeshed in suffering and death.

It is also remarkable that this word for compassion, *splagchnizomai*, is found only in the gospels. Perhaps (suggested John), it was created by the evangelists themselves when they discovered there was simply no word in the classical Greek language which could describe this incredible sympathy of Christ with the suffering of others. In the Greco-Roman culture of the time, the pervasive idea of God was that he was a deity whose primary characteristic was "apatheia," and thus serenely removed from the struggles and sorrows of human beings, an abstract "First Cause" too lofty to feel sympathy with their plight. It was the Hebrew scriptures alone which introduced the revolutionary idea into the pagan worldview of a supreme Deity who is filled with compassion towards human need and suffering.

It was out of His compassion that God had delivered His people from Egyptian bondage, and when He revealed His character to Moses, in the great declaration of Exodus 34, He set these qualities at the forefront: "*The* LORD *God, merciful and gracious, longsuffering, and abounding in goodness and truth.*" Because this was His character, the prophets also called upon His people *"to do justly, to love mercy, and to walk humbly"* with their God. And when, in the fullness of time, God sent His Son, Jesus, into the world, He came to incarnate that same compassion, and to bring healing and redemption to a broken humanity. His longing, His motivation, was to share our sufferings, and enter into our travail. *"Surely He has borne our griefs and carried our sorrows"* (see Exodus 34:6; Micah 6:8; Isaiah 53:4).

It is little wonder that the message of a crucified Saviour took the Mediterranean world by storm. For the wellspring of His compassion was nothing other than *love*, and the cross of Jesus is also the measure of the love that filled His heart, and the compassion that consumed Him utterly.

Compassion, Dave was coming to understood, also lay at the heart of intercession; it was not merely pity, but a dynamic force of love, that desired to see the addicts brought out from under a yoke of oppression and a mantle of darkness. Most of all, he knew that God had given him an exceptional love for Lara, and it was spilling over for the others whom he counseled. But, he was to learn, he did not as yet have enough love.

CHAPTER 33
All You Have to Do Is Love Her

ONE EVENING, NOT long after these realizations came to him, Dave was at Alicia's apartment across the street from his own; Lara was there and two or three others; as the night wore away everyone left, and Dave was there with the two girls. They were talking and listening to music when Dave suddenly felt a strong compulsion to return home and pray for Lara.

He bade the girls goodnight, went home and sat on his bed, and as he began praying for Lara he found himself remembering a common AA expression: "If you want what we have, and are willing to go to any length to get it, then you are ready to take certain steps." Accordingly, he now found himself praying those words: "Make her willing to want what I have," he said, "and make her willing to go to any length to get it." What he meant was freedom from addiction, the same complete liberty he himself was experiencing.

And then God Himself answered Dave, in an indescribable Voice. And He said:

"Are *you* willing to go to any length to know what *she* has?"

Dave knew that this question was of major significance, as was his answer, and he did not spend a lot of time considering what he should say. He was becoming very emotional; the atmosphere in his room seemed to be becoming weightier with the impact of what was taking place. And so he answered,

"Yes."

The moment Dave uttered that word, everything changed. The walls and ceiling of his room vanished and he entered a different realm in which he felt as if he was a part of everything around him, including the scene now being played out in front of him. While still sitting on his bed, he looked up and saw five figures standing before him, ghostly apparitions composed of transparent white mist; their features were indistinguishable, but Dave was able to make out they were both females and males. The most noticeable thing about the figures was that each had his or her arms crossed across the chest, and it struck him they resembled the Oscar statuettes from the Academy Awards; he heard also their voices conversing, although he was unable to discern what they were saying.

As Dave continued to gaze at the figures, he became aware of something extraordinary, that the sights and sounds of this vision were not coming from outside, but rather were being emitted in some way by his own sense organs. It seemed that Dave's eyes were acting as a projector, casting these images onto a screen in midair in front of him; so also the voices he heard were coming out of his own ears, and peripherally he could see the sounds at both sides of his head, resembling golden brown globes.

And then Dave sensed the impending presence of a great sadness. It occurred to him that the apparitions were looking down on him with great indifference; and as he continued to gaze at them they slowly turned their backs on him with arms still crossed, impassive as the statues they resembled. And that was when Dave knew what was taking place, and could not stop the tears from streaming down his face.

Dave understood with a supernatural awareness that, because he had answered "Yes" to God's question: "Are you willing to know what she has?", he was now becoming subjected to the same pain that Lara had lived through in the depths of her addiction. He had become, as it were, center stage in her emotions, knowing not only what she was thinking but also what she was feeling. Even in Lara's worst hours she had never stopped loving her family, and this incredible depth of devotion which Dave now experienced firsthand became coupled in his mind with the excruciating shame of her life as a drug addict. He fell on his knees on the floor, as he began comprehending to the full the suffering that Lara had endured in being cast out by her nearest kin. He knew that in all his years of carousing his own family had never stopped supporting and loving him. Rejection was a new experience for him, and it was devastating.

As Dave knelt there, he felt God was again speaking to him, saying, "Look!" He raised his eyes, the apparitions dissipated, and now he was seeing something new. Floating down diagonally from above were a number of circles, and Dave realized that he was witnessing Lara's actual emotions. Each was about the size of a dinner plate, with one circumference touching the edge of another; all the spheres were of different colors, but muted and pastel, not bright. Dave also knew what each one signified: there was love and rejection, as well as disappointment, betrayal, loss and hopelessness. As he gazed, it was as if every part of her life was unveiled to him so that he might share every shred of pain she experienced, compressed in that short space of time. He understood both how much she was capable of loving and also how much she hurt, and could not bear to look any longer, it was so emotionally draining.

Then God spoke again in his heart and mind, softly, as if regretting He had put Dave through this ordeal, but it was necessary for him to know and understand Lara's anguish. Then He said, "Now David, that you know what she has, are you willing to make a commitment to help her and to never give up on her?"

And Dave said "Yes" out loud with tears again, completely undone. Yet another thought also occurred to him, and he had to bring it to God. He had been a policeman for many years, and knew that drug addicts were extremely practiced in the art of deception. And so he said:

"There's one thing, though; I was only an alcohol and pill addict and those are substances that are legal, but Lara is a drug addict. How will I know when she is telling me the truth or lying?"

The answer came clearly: "David, *Beloved*, all you have to do is love her, and I will look after everything else."

Dave felt a rush of comfort when he heard these words, for they removed a great deal of responsibility from him; at the same time he resolved he would be looking after Lara with all the love of which he was capable. However, the Voice was continuing.

"But David," He said, "your love will not be sufficient. And so I will show you Mine."

And then it was as if the ceiling in his bedroom caved in on him with the weight of this love, as if it filled the room, so he almost felt as if he were drowning in it. He could not have imagined such an overwhelming sensation, a love so pure and altruistic it meant he would die on the spot for Lara to save her from harm, and he was filled with wonder and surprise at the power of this *agape* force. It was a love which seemed to shine in his heart and mind, mirroring a divine radiance and beauty, yet at the same time Dave realized he himself was not to be the source of that love but merely a channel or conduit. He did not know how long the experience lasted as the measureless ocean of God's love bore down upon him and washed through him; however, in that time outside time he experienced an astounding alteration, passing from the shattered wreckage of Lara's emotional pain to the heights of God's own compassion.

And so, on that night when his room was transformed, Dave came to realize he was born not to live his life for himself but for other people, now he began to truly understand what the "third love" was. In the words of the Apostle John:

"Beloved, let us love one another, for love is of God; and everyone who loves is born of God and knows God … God is love, and he who abides in love abides in God, and God in him … There is no fear in love; but perfect love casts out fear … " (1 John 4:7,16, 18).

CHAPTER 34
The Tape Recorder Trick

NOT LONG AFTER this unforgettable evening Dave had another cause for rejoicing: Lara had agreed to attend a recovery center for women called "Crossroads," located on the mainland in Kelowna, about forty miles south of her hometown of Vernon. Dave had already taken several addicts there, and knew its reputation as a caring and professional center with a high rate of success; he himself planned to accompany Lara there and help her check in. Accordingly, one bright fall morning, they drove together to catch one of the great ferries that plied the strait between Victoria and the mainland. The year was in its declining phase, but western Canada was enjoying an "Indian summer" and it was an idyllic passage. The two voyagers relaxed and enjoyed the stunning views as the vessel floated over the waterways, weaving through the islands that strewed the blue waters like gemstones.

On land again, they drove due east through the hills and valleys of interior British Columbia until they reached their destination at Kelowna, in its beautiful location on Okanagan Lake. They made their way to Crossroads, met the members of staff, and were impressed by the warmth and kindness of their reception. The formalities were completed, yet Dave was still reluctant, for some inexplicable reason, to leave his young protégée. Nevertheless, he said goodbye, promised to come and pick her up at the end of the program, and departed.

Dave spent the night in a small motel and rose early the next morning for the long drive back to the coast; first, however, he went and got the car washed and had a cup of coffee. It then occurred to him he was procrastinating, and at some subliminal level was wondering if he was doing the right thing. Resolutely, he put his foot down on the accelerator and headed west out of Kelowna, over the mountain pass.

The episode that now transpired constituted what Dave considered to be the most amazing event in the whole time of his ministry to Lara; he firmly believes that, but for the happenings of that day, Lara would not have survived.

Dave kept driving for an hour or more; it was a sunny day and normally he would have delighted in the scenery, but the whole way tears were pricking behind his eyes. He knew that the center offered an excellent program and he had left Lara in good hands, yet at the same time he felt as if he were deserting her. He remembered how she had said, "Everyone I have ever loved has left me"; and although she had never said, "Now you are leaving too," he felt as if he was. And then, in a high stretch of ground, an area called the "Connector," the miracle occurred.

This spectacular length of road, with an elevation of about four thousand feet, runs between the Okanagan Valley and the Coquihalla Highway; rugged fir-covered peaks rear on either side, and it affords frequent glimpses of rushing streams and mountain lakes. Dave was driving along this highway and had now about twenty minutes to go before the Connector would intersect with Coquihalla, he would then need to turn left, to the south, to reach Vancouver. Just at that point, his attention was caught and held by one of the mountain tarns he was passing. He was a professional photographer from way back, since attending the courses for his work in ID, and it suddenly occurred to him that he would like to take a picture of the scene.

There was no parking lot adjacent to the lake, but he stopped close by in an area of long grass. Beside him on the passenger seat he had a camera and also a hand tape recorder, which he used as a journal to make notes concerning different individuals to whom he ministered. He reached over to the passenger seat, grasped the strap of the camera, swung it out and stepped from the car, then walked down to the lakeside. However, when he got there, it suddenly dawned on him how little there was of appeal in the scene. The trees were bare and ragged, the water seemed bland and grey, the sky offered none of the clouds which add so much interest to composition in photographs. "What on earth am I doing here?" he asked himself. He took four or five frames and returned to the car, all the while castigating himself for his lack of aesthetic judgment. Then he turned the vehicle around and headed toward the west.

Before long, he reached the intersection of the Connector and the Coquihalla Highway. Right beside the overpass, there was a rest area with a kiosk selling food and mementos where Dave usually stopped, yet on this occasion he was so emotionally overwrought that he drove on. As he turned left on to the Coquihalla he had crossed the top of the mountains and was a long way from Kelowna; all the same, as he turned the wheel, the radio station from that city suddenly sprang to life from under the dashboard. It was playing a song that reminded him of Lara; they had often heard it during the months he had counseled her, so he thought he would record it. He reached for the tape recorder which he had left on the passenger seat, but it didn't seem to be there. A small frown creased his brow, and he decided to pull over and look for it.

Dave knew that the Coquihalla was a divided highway with a median strip, and that once a driver was on it some time could elapse before it was possible to stop or do a U-turn. However, he found a small area right after the intersection where he was able to pull over; he then looked again for the recorder but still couldn't find it. At that point he got out and searched the vehicle thoroughly, the floors, between the seats and under the dash; he even knelt on the ground to explore beneath the chassis. Dave was a "drug cop" in the past and knew what it was to search a car with a fine toothcomb; now he went through it a second time, still without success.

Perplexed, he began to think back, and remembered distinctly he had seen the tape recorder at the lake; it was made of silver chrome and he could hardly miss it. He concluded only one thing could have happened: he snagged the tape recorder on the camera strap when he got out, and it landed in the long grass where he couldn't see it. "So that's where it is," he thought, "back at the lake where I took those ridiculous photos!"

And now Dave was left with a dilemma: whether he should go on to Vancouver, or else go back to the lake and try and retrieve the recorder. What tipped the balance for him was that this was one of the more expensive models and had many of his notes, so he decided he should drive back up to the Connector and search for it. He put everything back in the car, started the engine and eased back onto the Coquihalla, driving south until he found a sign saying, "Last U turn." He took the off ramp which led under the highway and came up the other side so he was now driving in the reverse direction, proceeding again toward the intersection. At that moment, when it was impossible to turn back, his hip started to feel uncomfortable, and he reached down to find out what he was sitting on. He almost drove off the road. It was the tape recorder!

Dave knew now that two things were out of kilter: he was a good photographer who had chosen a bad scene, and a good cop who should not have missed finding the recorder. He also had a real problem on his hands, for he now found himself driving back toward the Connector when he no longer had any reason to do so. He began pondering the situation intensely, wondering for what reason he was retracing his steps, and when he came to the same rest area he had previously passed he decided to stop there and think about it. He got a cup of coffee from the little trailer beside the parking lot, and as he ordered and paid for the beverage he was unable to shake the feeling that something was taking place in a supernatural realm, the meaning of which was just eluding him.

He sat down at one of the small tables and drank his coffee, and as he did so he thought of Lara back in Kelowna, and began to wonder if he was being steered in that direction instead of toward Vancouver. Wishing to further mull over the situation, he decided he needed another cup of coffee, so he rose and made his way back to the trailer; at the same time, all his senses came on full alert. He had noticed in the parking lot a truck and camper with seven or eight people standing around, part of a family group, and then, as he took his coffee, he heard behind him one of the women from this group speaking. "Are you going to come to Vancouver with us, or are you going to go back to Kelowna?" she asked. But, as the sentence fell on Dave's ears, it was as if certain words stood out for him in bold print:

"Are you going to come to Vancouver with us, or are you going to *go back to Kelowna?*"

Instantly Dave knew that this was not an option, but a command, and said aloud: "Okay!"

He returned to his car and drove across the Connector, his heart lighter, although he still did not know the reason for his return. As he was driving he saw in the clear blue sky a magnificent cloud formation in the shape of a dove, with a delicate pink tint. Arriving at Kelowna he went directly to the treatment center, and as he walked in the door found Lara in the reception area. Tears came into her eyes when she saw him.

"What are you doing here?" she asked.

"I have no idea, all I know is that I'm supposed to be here."

"Why?"

"I don't know!"

Before he knew what he was doing, Dave turned to one of the staff members behind the desk, whom he had met the previous evening.

"Would it be alright if I took Lara out for the weekend before the program begins? I can assure you that when I bring her back she will not have used."

"Yes, that's fine," was the response, "As long as you can give us that guarantee."

Lara and Dave now had several free days, and together they drove to Vernon, Lara's hometown. They were both experiencing a sense of elation and freedom. Lara showed Dave her childhood haunts and the places significant to her from schooldays and teen years; he got the impression it was important to her to share something of her past with someone interested and sympathetic. It was a time of really getting to know one another in a new way, and once again Dave felt that infilling of wisdom that enabled him to minister to her at a deep level. He was sensing what an extraordinary young woman she was: she had a hunger for truth that was unlike anything he had encountered. Then, after this brief episode, it was time to take her back to Crossroads.

Dave parked in front of the center, and walked around the car to get Lara's backpack.

"Let's leave it here, just in case," she said.

Dave wasn't sure what she meant. Still, he forgot her statement as soon as they walked in through the door, for in the same instant he entered suddenly another realm, one of supernatural awareness. In this new dimension that was opened to him, he found himself understanding in advance everything which would transpire in the next twenty minutes, and knowing every word which would be spoken; all these seemed to flash past him in fast forward in a single moment of time. Caught up in this state of intense knowledge, he watched as Lara started walking through the reception area to speak to the woman behind the desk. He knew that she would say,

"My name is Lara; I'm here to check in for the four-week program."

He knew the woman would look at her quizzically, check her schedule and not see Lara's name, then say,

"I'll have to get the manager, Mr. Hunter," and then she would walk back through the office, enter the second door on the right, come back out with Mr. Hunter, and that he would say,

"Can we sit down here and talk?", and gesture to the couch and chairs in the reception area.

They would sit down, and he would say, "I am sorry, but there has been a breakdown in communication here between the different programs, and through no fault of your own we've given away your bed." And then he would give the next available date Lara could come back, at the end of November.

As Dave looked on, these conversations did take place exactly as he had foreseen; it was as if he was producing a play and they were obeying his directions. And Dave now watched as the manager, a true gentleman, continued to apologize for the mistake–yet Dave knew that no apology was needed. He realized this whole situation was engineered by God, and for this reason alone: that Lara was not meant to stay at Crossroads. They walked back to the car, Dave imbued with a tremendous happiness in understanding that God had an exact plan for Lara's recovery, and that He Himself was putting it into effect. As they got in the vehicle and turned to the west for the long drive back to Victoria, Dave turned to Lara and said,

"It's time to go home."

He switched on the radio, and the first words they heard came from the Eagles' song called "Taking You Home."

As Dave listened to the lyrics, it confirmed his understanding that he and Lara were somehow adhering, without any volition on their part, to a design put in place on a heavenly level. They drove back to the coast, passing on the way the small kiosk where he had received his instructions to return to Kelowna. Although they didn't stop there, for Dave this unassuming rest area was a place of miracle, where God had truly intervened in an awesome way to save Lara's life. In hindsight, he knew that in Kelowna she would have been overcome by loneliness, and that drugs were far too freely available; had she stayed, it would perhaps have meant her death warrant. And as they continued driving, Lara told him how she had seen the most beautiful cloud formation in the sky, pink, like a dove.

They arrived back at Vancouver and caught the ferry to the Island–it was the beginning of a new adventure. Lara moved into the spare bedroom in Dave's apartment; he enjoyed seeing how happy she looked as she emptied the backpack out of which she had been living for so long. She put away her clothes and decorated the room, adding small touches to make it look beautiful; finally she hung a piece of sheer nylon over the ceiling light with clothes tacks and transformed her small living space. Dave had a little black cat named Joey which he had bought for the times his daughters would visit, and Joey was now always to be found curled on Lara's lap.

Dave knew, however, that in the nature of their habit addicts have a deceptive nature; they feel they have accomplished some small victory when they take something that doesn't belong to them. He therefore told her, "This apartment is now yours as well as mine; there is nothing here that you do not own."

He did not want her to feel she had stolen something, to leave an opening for the guilt which is such a huge factor in relapse, and Dave watched Lara blossom as she now found a place she could call home. She had always been a lovely girl, but now she had a new confidence, and there were always two or three young men dancing attendance on her. Sometimes Dave would have to move out of his apartment for a day or two. He would take his Bible and stay at a motel, giving Lara his phone number and telling her not to share it with anyone. And now his own relationship with God was continuing to grow deeper, in ways he had never foreseen.

PART IV:
THE HAND THAT WRITES THE LOVE
SONG ALSO HOLDS THE GUN

CHAPTER 35
Pity the Moon

DAVE WAS COMING to think increasingly on the wonderful words from the 61st Chapter of Isaiah which Jesus had quoted in the synagogue in Nazareth at the beginning of His ministry:

> *The Spirit of the LORD is upon Me,*
> *Because He has anointed Me*
> *To preach the gospel to the poor;*
> *He has sent Me to heal the brokenhearted,*
> *To proclaim liberty to the captives*
> *And recovery of sight to the blind,*
> *To set at liberty those who are oppressed ...* (Luke 4:18).

He was learning that he was entering into the same work the Man from Nazareth had undertaken–bringing the message of freedom and deliverance to those held bound and captive, imprisoned, as it were, by their addictions. And this meant that he was to become engaged in a spiritual battle, the intensity of which he had never before fathomed.

Dave was no stranger to evil. During his long career in law enforcement he had become extensively acquainted with the excesses of violence and degradation which exist within even a civilized society. He had witnessed numberless crime scenes, including those involving the mutilated bodies of men and women, some only in their first youth, slain in horrific circumstances. He had stood over the naked body of a young girl, killed in a situation of unspeakable cruelty, and looked at the gaping and eloquent wounds which covered her slight form. "Who did this to you?" he had asked through clenched teeth (it was a scene which gave him nightmares for years). He had been called many times to the scene of a suicide, and sought to bring counsel and comfort to the devastated families. He had been confronted by homicide, manslaughter, rape, robbery, assault and a myriad of lesser acts of lawlessness. *Nothing*, he would say with more than a touch of cynicism, could surprise him any more about the human race.

It was not just these events which he, together with countless other police officers, was concerned with combating from day to day. He was also grimly aware that society, although growing in technological sophistication and affluence, was becoming inured to the very real threat posed by a prevalent philosophy. This held that criminals were simply maladjusted individuals who were themselves suffering the effects of a disadvantaged background or other ameliorating cause, and so the pendulum had swung to maintaining the rights of offenders, sometimes even above those of their victims. This often resulted in a palpable miscarriage of justice during the court process. Dave had written one of his poems about this tendency, verses in which his anger could not be hidden:

THE MORNING PAPER

This morning I got out of bed
Rubbed my eyes and shook my head
And read the morning paper.
In the Middle East, it says, there's war
And somewhere else there could be more
A tidal wave has smashed some shore
Taking many lives.
A man got shot sometime last night,
It seems a woman caused the fight
The dead man is survived by someone
But neither has the woman;
A little girl was raped and murdered
They found her body mutilated
For a while the killer will be hated
By newspaper readers infuriated
But before her epitaph has faded
The hangman will find that he has waited
For nothing. The man was not a killer,
Just sick …

Ah, the morning paper!
There are train wrecks, plane wrecks
Burning bodies, broken necks
Mountains crumbling, statesmen fumbling
LSD and nations bungling
Suicides and blinded eyes
Cities burning, alibis
Tax increases, new diseases
Radiation in the breezes
Take a pill if someone sneezes
He might be a communist.
Hatred here, suspicion there
Psychedelics everywhere
Prostitution, destitution
Dissolution, revolution
Institutions and diffusion
Nothing seems to have solution
Possibly the one conclusion:
Everything is mass confusion;
On page ten it says that soon
Man is going to hit the moon!
It seems the earth has no more room
Pity the moon …

And so I put the paper down
Drank my coffee to the grounds
I met the milkman on the walk
We stopped a little bit to talk
"Good morning, sir" he said to me
And yet I have the gravest doubts
That when day's dawn had come about
He'd read the morning paper.

One case in which Dave was involved brought home this truth vividly. He was working alone in his police car, and around ten in the evening received a call on his radio to attend a downtown motel; he was only a block away, and shortly pulled in and walked to the front office. Standing in the lobby with the manager was a young woman, only about nineteen or twenty years old, dark-haired and pretty in a quiet way, but petite and visibly shaken. She told Dave in a trembling voice that she was placed in the motel by the Ministry of Social Services while awaiting housing, and she was presently staying there with her baby. Because the rooms at the motel were built in an L-shaped pattern, she could look out her window and see into the adjoining suite, and there she had glimpsed a man who was staying alone. The man had also noticed her, and some moments ago had come over and banged on her door with his boot.

"I want to talk with you," he said loudly.

"Go away and leave me alone," she replied firmly through the door, glancing anxiously toward the next room where her baby lay sleeping.

"I just want to talk," he insisted in a slurred voice.

The young woman didn't answer, but put out her lights and peered cautiously through the window. She saw the man go back into his suite, and then came the sound of furniture being upended and smashed. At that point, because the motel suite had no telephone, she ran out to the manager, told him what was happening, and he called the police.

After he elicited this information, Dave asked the girl–her name was Elizabeth–to show him her suite. They walked out of the office; she looked across the yard, and gasped in horror.

"Oh, no," she cried, "The light is on in my suite, and my baby is in there!"

Dave didn't want to waste time going to the car to get cover, so he stepped back and told the manager to phone the police and get reinforcements. He then left the girl there and went over to her suite. The door was not locked; he opened it, and slowly stepped in sideways with his hand on the gun at his hip. As he entered he saw the intruder about ten feet away, sitting on a chair and holding a large-bladed knife; immediately as Dave stepped in he dropped the weapon on the floor between his feet. It was a buck knife, sharp-edged and gleaming.

Still keeping the man covered, Dave asked, "What are you doing here?"

"I only wanted to talk with her," he responded.

"What's the knife for?" countered Dave. He wanted to keep him talking until help arrived; he was noting the sheer brute strength of the fellow, as well as the fact he was in an advanced stage of intoxication. Within minutes a fellow officer had entered the room, and they talked the man into going back to his suite. At that point they proceeded to arrest him–and then the fight was on. The trespasser was powerfully built, well over six feet tall, and he was resisting the whole way; however, the two officers eventually got him handcuffed, even though his wrists were abnormally large. Dave received a scar on his own wrist from that encounter.

At the police station, Dave charged the man, Raymond Rafuse, with breaking and entering with intent to commit an indictable offense; he felt the knife was a sure indication that, whatever Rafuse was planning to do in the young woman's room, it would be an act of violence. To his utter chagrin, the Crown prosecution reduced the charge to one which was significantly less serious, that of being unlawfully in a dwelling house. The defendant kept failing to show up for his court case; eventually when he was brought before the bar the case of Crown V Rafuse proceeded. Elizabeth, although terrified, came and testified against him. And then the judge delivered his verdict: *Not Guilty.*

Dave was stunned: the defendant had escaped even the conviction for the lesser offence. The judge gave as the reason for the verdict the fact there was no evidence he was going to do anything unlawful.

"If he was going to attack anyone," asked this legal authority, "then why didn't he attack Richardson?"

"Oh yeah," thought Dave to himself, "Why didn't he attack Richardson, who was six feet two with a gun on his hip?"

He knew that Elizabeth, who was less than five feet tall, with a baby, would have been helpless to resist anything the man had intended, and was appalled by the verdict; he also had the feeling Rafuse was truly dangerous, and tried to convince his superiors to appeal the case. When they would not, he felt so strongly about the matter he took his complaint to the chief prosecutor, but was informed unequivocally that he should drop the issue.

"It's up to you to bring the criminals before the court," he was told, "not to convict."

Dave didn't disagree with that; he nevertheless had an intuitive feeling this man was going to cause injury in the future–but he let it go.

It was perhaps a year later that Elizabeth phoned him and told him she had heard of Rafuse again on the news the previous evening; Dave could detect the nervousness in her voice. He started phoning around, and learned that Rafuse had murdered a woman and her baby in Richmond on the mainland, in a situation which was an exact repeat of the one with Elizabeth and her child. Dave was furious when he heard that, so upset that he talked to one of the investigators and asked him to send pictures of the body; he wanted to show them to the prosecutor and the judge. Once again, however, he was told to desist.

Some years later, after getting out of prison—life imprisonment is twenty years and it is possible to be out in seven—Rafuse was responsible for the worst multiple murder in Calgary. He went on a rampage at a party in a basement suite and shot five people, killing four. Among the dead were a fifteen-year-old boy and his mother; the lone survivor was shot twice in the back before she escaped up the stairs of the apartment. Rafuse received five life sentences—two for first-degree murder, two for second-degree murder, and one for attempted murder. And then, Dave learned later, Rafuse killed a prison guard while in jail.[25]

All this was distressing to Dave, for he felt that, had the prosecution acted initially on his findings, those victims might still be alive. He was dismayed by the naiveté of current assessments of the criminal mind, as well as the moral relativism which was pervading every aspect of his culture. In particular, he felt the condoning of lenient treatment for hardened offenders in the egregious name of compassion could only lead to the undermining of justice in the legal system, as well as a spiraling of violence in society. Even at that time, Dave was cognizant of a force of evil which sprang from the dark recesses of the human psyche, and worked like leaven to spread corruption through every area of life.

Just recently, also, through his meeting with the demonic opposition in Pastor Holmes' office, Dave had become aware of a spiritual power which was personal and utterly malevolent. Now, as he sought guidance in his present ministry, he turned again and again to the gospels. It was clear to him he was dealing with the same entities Jesus had encountered two thousand years ago, when He, with majestic utterance and unequalled authority, had "cast out the spirits with a word." For this He had faced great opposition from the religious authorities of the day, who, jealous of His charismatic power and presence, sought to discredit Him on every occasion.

> "*He casts out demons,*" they said, "*by Beelzebub, the ruler of the demons.*" With perfect incisiveness Jesus exposed the inherently illogical nature of their claim: "*Every kingdom divided against itself is brought to desolation, and a house divided against a house falls ... But if I cast out demons with the finger of God, surely the kingdom of God has come upon you* (see Luke 11:15,16,18).

Those satanic forces that sought to harass and destroy in the time of Jesus were still fearfully alive, and as bent on their task as ever. And this ruin of the human being, in spirit, soul and body, could be brought about through any number of afflictions and diseases, or through various forms of mental and emotional bondage. Dave was coming to understand that addiction was not a psychological nor yet an emotional problem; rather, it was a battle in the spiritual realm. He considered the AA mantra concerning alcohol: "cunning, powerful, and baffling," and saw it in a new light. "That is absurd," he told himself. "Alcohol is just a liquid in a bottle. But it is the demonic opposition which is indeed cunning, powerful, and baffling."

Dave was to learn much more about the nature of the opposition he faced in his ministry to addicts–and also that those dark and destructive forces could be completely routed.

CHAPTER 36
I Caligula

WHEN DAVE WAS working in the police force, he had always liked the night and darkness because it was then the "bad guys" were out. One inky evening he intercepted a passerby in a shadowed back street. "There are only two kinds of people out at this hour," he said, "cops and crooks. I'm a cop—what's your excuse?"

There was another dark side he also learned about during his police career. At one stage he was asked to attend a course on identifying occultic activities, and finding ways to deal with these legally. Dave was aware that Victoria—despite its outwardly sedate appearance—had a reputation as a center for spiritualism and the occult, and decided to take advantage of the opportunity. The sessions were held in Vancouver, and the instructor, Peter, was a sergeant from Chicago who was clearly very knowledgeable in his field. Although some of the officers attending the course were inclined to scoff at the subject matter, he obviously took what he was teaching very seriously indeed.

Dave knew there was no law against involvement in occult practices *per se*, such as membership of covens, Satan worship, or professing to be a witch or warlock. Yet, because these activities frequently led to crimes that included animal cruelty, child abuse, desecration of graveyards, and in extreme cases murder, they could be dealt with under existing laws. The main thrust of the course was to help the officers understand the way in which occultic practices could infiltrate and impact society. This could take place either through the practices in which adherents engaged—some of them unspeakable—or through various mechanisms of mind control. It was emphasized that paramount within the different occultic organizations is secrecy, that initiates can come from the highest echelons of society, and indoctrination can take place over a long period of time, as evidenced by recent cases which had come to light—children hidden and abused for many years in suburban dwellings.

Most particularly, the officers were taught the signs they should watch for to identify occultic activities taking place within a home. If everything within the room of a teenager, for example, featured posters and poems with a negative or sinister connotation, or images of snakes, it would suggest a knowing involvement with dubious practices. Their choice of music could also have a powerful impact on young people, especially on those taking drugs; sometimes the lyrics to which they listened could be construed as encouraging self-harm, even leading to suicide. "One other thing you will see in almost every home that is in the occult," Peter told them, "is drawings of the eye. The symbolism of this is 'we're watching you,' and it is intended to create psychological fear."

He went on to tell of an incident which concerned a female psychologist he had consulted to learn more about the mental damage inflicted through engagement with the occultic masterminds. This woman, Lauren, was working with him at the precinct, when one day a parcel arrived for her, addressed to the police station. Perplexed, she opened it and found inside a small box containing a crystal tear drop such as can be found on a chandelier. They puzzled over it for a while, and it then dawned on Lauren that she had a chandelier in her home with similar crystals. They looked at one another in horrified surmise, then drove to her house; and sure enough, the crystal was missing. The message to Lauren had not been written down, but was very clear: "*We can get to you any time we want.*" And it had the desired result, because from that point she became nervous and evasive.

Dave found the course interesting, and even at the time was aware there was a spiritual element involved, that the "dark arts" could open up a realm beyond human consciousness. He took note as Peter described how young people became drawn into the occult. This was through what he called "dabbling": curiosity, the urge to experiment, or the lure of the forbidden. All these things might compel a teen or young adult to take the first tentative steps into this unknown realm, so that it might start out as a seemingly harmless game. Yet, as the participant became increasingly enmeshed in a world of secrecy and darkness, perhaps engaging in rituals that were blasphemous and barbaric, the ultimate consequences could be horrific. Dave was later to witness this sequence of events firsthand in one of British Columbia's most notorious murder cases.

In the late Eighties, Darren Huenemann[26] was in high school in Saanich; he lived with his mother and stepfather, wealthy and influential people, in an upper middle-class area. His maternal grandmother Doris Leatherbarrow, widowed after the war, had raised enough money to fulfill her dream of owning a dress shop; later she expanded this to a large fashion warehouse with four stores. The young boy grew up with almost constant attention from his mother Sharon and his "beloved gran"; from an early age he learned to be polite and under control. In fact, he was known to be a "perfect gentleman." However, Darren interacted differently with his peers: he didn't engage in physical sport often but was popular due to his financial status. Eventually he became involved with a group of role-players in the controversial game "Dungeons & Dragons,"[27] alleged to blur the boundaries between real life and fantasy, and here he let some of his true feelings loose: the desire to rebel and his suppressed violence.

Darren now went on to plan and direct a play at his school called *Caligula*, with himself playing the title role. In an age which was a byword for its decadence and vice, this Roman emperor of the first century stood out for his unbridled extravagance, pretensions to deity, and a tyrannical cruelty which probably stemmed from insanity. The historian Seneca chronicled some of Caligula's more perverse excesses, from his desire to install his horse Incitatus as a consul, to having a statue of himself erected in the temple at Jerusalem as a god. Darren was clearly obsessed with this character, and seemed to slip seamlessly into the role he had created. He became delusional, and began to speak of ruling small countries.

When his grandmother Doris made out her will in 1989, she left of her four-million-dollar estate to her daughter Sharon, and the other half to Darren. At the same time, Sharon updated her will to include Darren as the sole beneficiary. This seemed to be a turning point for the young man, who persuaded two of his friends, David Muir and Derik Lord, both sixteen years old and both of whom had already dealt in illegal activities, to murder his grandmother and mother. He promised them large rewards: for David a cabin in the woods, a new car and about one hundred thousand dollars; for Derik, that he would become Darren's bodyguard and also receive land and money for weapons. They agreed, and Darren now masterminded a plan, deciding the best time to kill the victims would be when Sharon visited Doris in nearby Tsawwassen on the mainland.

Derik and David entered the house of Doris Leatherbarrow on October 5, 1990, stating they were Darren's friends stopping by. Sharon put two more helpings of dinner into the microwave, and set two extra places at the table. Derik and David then struck the two with their concealed crowbars, and used kitchen knives to slit their throats. They overturned furniture and emptied drawers in an attempt to make it look like a botched break and enter, and made their getaway, taking the ferry back to Vancouver Island where Darren picked them up. He drove his friends home, then returned to his house, ostensibly "to wait for his mother's return."

Because Darren was on the Island on the night of the murder, he had an alibi. The police had other suspects for the crime, including business associates, yet Darren had the motive of financial gain and so they began investigating his circle of friends, including Lord and Muir. According to their version of the story, all three boys were at the Lord family home at 8:30 p.m. that evening, which meant they couldn't have been in Tsawwassen. It was then that Darren hired lawyers for the youths, which fueled the suspicions of the police. The three young men became aware they were suspects and were careful not to speak on their home phones, but the police wire-tapped all the pay phones in their vicinity, and every call the young men made was taped. They then decided to step up the surveillance, and it was at this point that Dave, who was working with CLEU at the time, became involved with the case.

The officers had worked out that one of the two, Lord, was the weak link, most likely to cave in and confess or act in panic. He worked in a department store in Saanich, and the plan was that a policeman nicknamed Spiderman, one of the primary investigators, would go into the store in plain clothes, come up to Lord and "put a fire under him"–intimate the police had evidence and would soon be coming to take him in. Spiderman would then leave, but Dave would also be in the store in plain clothes, watching Lord closely to see what he would do.

The plan went ahead: Spiderman spoke his message in Lord's ear and departed, and Dave observed the result. The young man became visibly nervous, went to a payphone and called Darren, who came down shortly thereafter to pick up his friend. Darren was unaware that his car was also wire-tapped, and that Dave, with two or three other officers, was now in a police car following closely behind them to listen in to and record their conversation.

Everything had so far gone beautifully, and the policemen were hoping that the evidence they needed might now be forthcoming. And then the strangest thing happened. Suddenly the men in the police car heard the bars of a song come floating out: "*She's faced the hardest times you can imagine.*" It was the opening line of "Wildflower"! At first the officers thought it was their own radio. "Turn that thing down!" exclaimed someone. Then, incredulously, they realized the song was being played in the car they were tailing; the young men must have turned up the volume on the radio when it came on, presumably as fans of Dave's ballad! Any conversation the men might have taped was now completely lost.

"You and that song!" expostulated his fellow officers, "You might have helped those guys get away with murder."

They were joking, of course, and it was not long before the young men were brought to trial. The prosecutors headed into court with some significant evidence, including tapes of an anxious spate of phone calls between the boys after police told Muir they had a witness who could place the boy in Tsawwassen at the time of the murders. Muir, Lord and Huenemann were tried for first degree murder, and all three were sentenced to life imprisonment; Huenemann would not have eligibility for parole for twenty-five years. He, the mastermind of the murder, was composed throughout the trial, but when the verdict was pronounced he dropped his mask and cursed the judge, the court, and the world.

Now, in the crucible of his present work, Dave understood with newfound insight the spiritual forces which had driven Darren and his co-conspirators. Yet, through the gospels Dave also learned of the saving work of Jesus Christ, who had shattered the powers of darkness through His cross and resurrection.

As a result, Dave learned, there was one power which was able to utterly rout all attacks from the Enemy of human souls–the Name of Jesus. At the mention of that "Name above all names," all demonic opposition had to yield, and in this way those held captive and enslaved by their addictions could emerge into the light of the freedom that Jesus had purchased for them–at such great cost to Himself.

CHAPTER 37
Be Strong in the Lord and the Power of His Might

THE SOCIETY WITHIN which Dave lived, he was learning, was woefully ignorant of this spiritual dimension, but strangely enough he had little trouble in convincing the addicts that demonic opposition was real. They understood they were locked in a combat with devastatingly powerful spiritual forces, simply because no other explanation could so fit the facts of what they were experiencing. An episode which transpired soon after Lara moved into Dave's apartment, while Alicia was still living across the road, illustrated this vividly.

The area in which Dave lived maintained a reputation as one with a high rate of drug abuse. One day he drove both girls home from a meeting, and as they came within a block of his home he felt a prickling sensation on the back of his neck, and at the same moment a strong presentiment of evil. He could not only feel this malign presence, he could see it. The color of the surroundings–the streets through which he was driving and the very air–had taken on a brownish-gray hue, as if he was looking through a thin sheet of cellophane. His breath became stifled, his heart was beating fast, and as he drove he spoke urgently to the girls:

"There's evil here; can you see it?"

They shook their heads, incomprehension in their eyes.

"There's evil here, in the whole neighborhood–it's like driving into a wall," he said forcefully, "And it's deadly."

The girls' faces expressed only perplexity.

As Dave drove down his street he felt a terrible apprehension, because he knew they were both addicts. When they pulled into the parking space, he said with great emphasis, as if pleading with them, "Be careful–someone can die today."

They got out of his car and Alicia crossed the road to her apartment; Lara and Dave went into his, and she took a book and curled up in an armchair. However, Dave remained restless, and kept crossing to the window to see if the strange taupe color still filtered its eerie light over the surroundings. After forty minutes passed he said abruptly,

"I'm going to check on Alicia." He added sternly, "Don't go out, and don't answer the phone."

Lara nodded her head, looking scared, and Dave left her and went across the street; the presence of evil seemed to him almost palpable. Someone came walking out of the controlled front entrance to Alicia's building, and Dave entered and went up to the second floor. The door was slightly ajar, so he knocked, then pushed the door open and called her name. There was no answer, so he walked into the apartment, and came around the corner to her living room, where a very eloquent scene awaited him.

Alicia was lying slumped on the couch, as was another woman whom Dave had never seen. They both appeared to be dead. The syringes they had used were abandoned on the coffee table in front of them, and the unknown woman actually had a needle still in her arm. She must also have been smoking a cigarette when she overdosed, and her cigarette had fallen onto her sweater and was just at that moment beginning to catch fire. Dave grabbed a cushion and doused the flames; he then tried to rouse them, shaking them and calling Alicia's name, but it seemed tragically certain both had expired. His heart in his mouth, and breathing urgent prayers, he seized Alicia's telephone and called 911.

The operator answered swiftly; Dave gave the address and asked them to send an ambulance for a drug overdose. Within seconds, it seemed, two paramedics were coming through the door and taking in the situation at a glance. They injected the two prostrate women immediately with Narcan, an adrenalin-like substance which could kick-start their hearts. Dave's eyes were fixed on those lifeless forms, and an enormous wave of relief washed over him: both stirred, and began returning to consciousness. He felt a huge gratitude to those paramedics, and was astonished by the speed with which they arrived on the scene; apparently they were driving right by Alicia's building when his call came in.

The two women were taken to the hospital, and some time later Dave talked with Alicia. "Why didn't you listen to me?" he asked. "I warned you there was danger."

"I knew what you said was true," she replied shamefacedly, "but I was thinking it was Lara, not me, who was at risk. Next time I'll really pay attention."

Dave looked at her with mingled sternness and compassion. "Don't let there be a next time, Alicia," he entreated.

On another occasion in which Dave had a premonition of evil, the outcome was not so fortunate. Dave had first met Rhianna in detox; she was a pleasant woman with two teenage daughters, around forty years of age. She continued to struggle with her addiction, and Dave would meet her for coffee or go to her apartment to counsel her, although she seemed to prefer her New Age beliefs. At some point in their acquaintance she had to move from her apartment, and Dave lost touch with her. Then, one day, she phoned him.

"Dave, I've just moved into my new apartment and I think there's something evil in here."

"What do you mean?"

"Well, the phone rang in the middle of the night, and when I answered I heard a man's voice, but he sounded like an animal and growled. It was as if he was half-man, half-beast–it was *awful*."

"Did you remember what I taught you about spiritual warfare?" he asked.

"Yes of course, but I can't find the Bible you gave me. Dave, this thing on the phone is evil and it's really scaring me; would you please come and pray?"

Dave took down Rhianna's address and drove over to the place she was now staying, in a low-rental housing complex of ground floor flats. He parked his car and began to make his way along the sidewalk to Number 10, when a terrible apprehension began to fill his mind, and he suddenly recognized where he was.

"Oh, no," he thought to himself. He knew he had been here before. "Does she live in the same apartment as Mrs. Albertson?"

That was the name of a woman who was a murder victim in a case he had investigated many years previously, when he was working as a detective. She was killed by her daughter, who was seventeen years old at the time. During the investigation it came out that Mrs. Albertson had become a Christian, and as a result had adopted a simpler lifestyle. The daughter, Anna, was steadily pawning her jewels and her silverware, but was afraid this would eventually be discovered.

One day, Mrs. Albertson came home from shopping on her payday, walked through the front door and set her groceries down on the floor, as was her routine. Her daughter came from behind and stabbed her in the back several times, yet it took much longer to kill her mother than she anticipated, and the whole scene was eventually covered in blood: the floor, the walls and even the ceiling. In the process, Anna also got a serious cut requiring surgery, and as the forensic evidence would be sure to turn up the mingled blood groups she came in to the police station and confessed.

All these details came back to Dave with great vividness as he walked in the door, and filled him with dismay. And now he knew that there was indeed a problem with the apartment; now he was taking very seriously what Rhianna had said about the bestial voice. He prayed with her and also spent some time counseling her daughters. After that, he made a point of staying in touch with Rhianna; then one day, when he had not heard from her for some time, called the apartment. One of the daughters answered the phone.

"How is Rhianna?" he asked.

"Didn't you know, Dave? She died of an overdose."

And Dave grieved, knowing Rhianna was among many vulnerable people God had sent to him, to help her experience the abundant life and freedom He offered.

Around the same time this sad event took place, he was also disturbed by a repeat of the earlier vision he had received concerning the mysterious twin towers that were set on fire, and this time there were some frightening new details.

He was lying down at home with his eyes closed, when he found himself transported in a moment of time to a large office suite with a number of desks inside it. Directly in front of him was a big picture window, and as he gazed out he realized the office must be very high up, hundreds of feet in the air, for he could see over to the horizon of the city. As he looked out, he suddenly saw a full-size passenger jet airplane, some distance away, but coming straight toward him in a dreamlike, ultra-slow motion.

As the plane drew closer, he noticed its tail was projecting high into the air, and appearing between the wings seemed to take the form of a cross, which was colored blood-red by the effect of the sunlight behind it. And then the nose of the jet reached the plate glass of the window and shattered it, and the plane was coming through, still in that incredibly slow motion. As it did, the aluminum sheeting started to peel back so that Dave could see the ribs of the framework, while simultaneously flames of fire roared into life about him, together with great, swirling billows of smoke.

At the same moment, Dave became aware that behind him, a little to the left, there were several men conversing about the fantastically impossible scene they were witnessing. The first said, "It's got to be Hollywood"; and then a second voice said, "No, it has to do with the Israelites."

Dave turned to them and said vehemently, "You fools, can't you see we're about to die!"

Then there was a massive explosion, with flames erupting in a huge fireball, but he was still a conscious spectator of the scene, without knowing whether he was alive or had died. Now he found himself over by the window, where another terrible prospect greeted his eyes. As he looked out, he could see people jumping from the skyscraper from great heights, and watched in appalled anguish as they hurtled to their deaths, seeming to fall forever.

Standing there transfixed, with the flames engulfing his surroundings, he suddenly realized with a shock that the building in which he stood was crumbling about him, turning to powder; and even as absorbed this new development he became aware the same thing was happening to a second building off to his left. The whole scene was being completely duplicated, with a second airplane hitting a second tower, followed by an explosion, and before his eyes that building also disintegrated in a great avalanche of soft grey dust.

Dave emerged from this subsequent vision with profound disquiet. He took the account to Bob Holmes, relating it as his mentor listened with minute attention and a grave countenance. At the conclusion the pastor shook his head, ruminating. "It's reminiscent of the scene described by the Apostle Peter in Acts, Chapter Two," he said slowly, *"blood and fire and vapor of smoke … before the coming of the great and awesome day of the LORD."*

"It did remind me of that prophecy," said Dave, and then added, "You know, Bob, I wouldn't be surprised if this is really going to happen."

"But how can a building turn to powder?" asked his mentor, still puzzling over the strange sequence of events.

"I don't know," responded Dave, and there they left it for the time. However, the prophetic insight he was given would be played out on the world stage before much more time had elapsed.

When, later still, he reflected back on this vision and the events that had preceded it, he wondered how he had endured in a ministry which demanded such extremes of emotional and spiritual energy. He was conscious it was only through God's grace and enabling, and the words of a song by The Pretenders, "I'll Stand by You," came to mean a great deal to him. It seemed to represent the Lord's encouragement to him in his darkest hours.

Dave was also becoming convinced that what Paul said in Chapter 6 of Ephesians was true; that this battle was not about drugs at all, but rather it was a life-and-death conflict with the "principalities and powers" which waged war against the bodies and souls of men and women. Now Dave knew firsthand the great apostle was right in his teaching, and he found himself turning repeatedly to the scriptures for counsel and strength for the spiritual struggles in which he was engaged:

Be strong in the Lord and in the power of His might," he read. *"Put on the whole armor of God, that you may be able to stand against the wiles of the devil* (Ephesians 6:1011).

What was this armor of God of which Paul wrote? Dave looked at the list which followed: faith, hope, truth, prayer, righteousness–all things which the world deemed intangible and negligible. Yet Dave was finding out what millions of believers throughout the ages had discovered before him: that these qualities, spiritual and mystical as they undoubtedly were, gave to the one who possessed them a power which was mighty to bring down strongholds of opposition, and enabled that person to walk through his or her life in peace, joy and victory.

CHAPTER 38
If You Give Up On Her, She Will Die

LARA WAS CONTINUALLY relapsing, and each time it happened Dave would be filled with disappointment. Moreover, he would know every time she used; there were the evident physical symptoms, but there were also the "signs" he received concerning her. Above all, the number 551 which he had first seen on the car with the FXD number plate was a key to what was happening.

On one occasion he was driving and listening to the car radio, when his attention was caught and held as two disc jockeys, one male and one female, got into a play argument. They each followed different football teams in Washington State, and the woman made an unkind comment about the team the man supported. The male DJ responded in mock indignation, "That upsets me! Just for that, I'm not going to speak to you until … let me see … 5:51!" At that time it was just after five in the afternoon, and Dave knew straight away what had happened. He phoned Lara, and he was right: Lara admitted she had used, and became afraid of his prescience.

The most dramatic occurrence with the 551 number came when Dave was paying a short visit to friends in North Carolina. He was invited to stay in a cabin in the beautiful mountainous area near Boone, and one evening went with his friends to Hebron Colony, a facility for recovering drug addicts located in the area, to hear the director speak on the treatment they provided. Just before the lecture started, Dave thought he would go to the washroom.

This was located downstairs, and as he went in he discovered it was quite small, with just a sink and one cubicle. A middle-aged man wearing shorts and a short-sleeved shirt walked in behind Dave, and at the same moment his senses were flooded with a kind of supernatural awareness. The paper towel dispenser on the wall beside the sink was empty, and when Dave opened the door to the cubicle the man spoke to him: "Do you mind if I get some toilet paper?" He tore some paper off the roll and explained, "I just got stung by a wasp."

And then, as Dave was watching, he began dabbing his right arm with the tissue, just above the elbow crease. Dave observed him applying pressure to the area, and looked at his watch; it was exactly 5:51 pm Eastern Time, and now he was sure he knew what was going on. He listened to the lecture, talked and had coffee afterwards, then got in the car with his friends to return to the cabin. As he did so, he looked again at his watch–it was 8:51, which meant that on Vancouver Island it would be exactly 5:51.

When they arrived back at the cabin, he asked if he could borrow the phone to call back home; both Lara and Nolan were staying in his apartment. He telephoned his number in Victoria, and waited for Lara to answer.

She picked up the phone: "Hello?"

He said, "Lara, don't lie to me. Tonight at nine minutes to six, either you or Nolan injected drugs, not in the left arm, but in the right, a quarter inch above the elbow crease." Dave knew that both Nolan and Lara were right-handed.

There was silence on the phone for a number of seconds, then she said, "*Where are you?*"

"In North Carolina."

"How could you *possibly* know?" And so Lara confessed all to him: she had injected the drugs for Nolan in his right arm because his left arm was sore from a previous injection, and it was about ten to six when they did so.

Once, it so happened, there were two weeks or so in which he did not get any signs which showed him Lara was using, and he became happy, thinking, "Wow! She's finally got it." They were sitting in the park together on the grass; it was a sunny day and he was in a good mood, laughing and joshing her, when suddenly she spoke loudly:

"Would you knock it off!"

"What?" he asked, surprised.

He was trying to understand why she was angry, but she said again, "Would you please knock it off! You know I've been using, God always shows you, so stop playing this stupid game!"

She was accusing Dave of deceiving her, yet he wasn't upset. It occurred to him that a sense of wrongdoing was now working on Lara's conscience directly. Still, the battle continued. Dave was at home one evening; Lara was out, and he knew she had been using. When she returned to the apartment, she came in and greeted him breezily as if nothing were amiss.

"Hi!" she said.

Dave didn't say, "I know you've been using." Instead, he said quietly, "Lara, take off your clothes."

"What!" she said, looking completely shocked.

He repeated, "Take off all your clothes right now." Then he pointed to the balcony door. "Go and walk out that door and up the street. You're young and beautiful, they'll be lined up to have you!"

Lara's mouth fell open. Her eyes became enormous, filled with misery. Dave said, "That's where you're going—just stop and think about it. You're so close to prostitution."

Tears welled up in her eyes; she knew what he was saying was true, and his words had the desired impact. Nevertheless, Dave's methods were a little unorthodox, to say the least. Some time after that he was invited to speak at a Bible study for young people, mostly teenage girls, and Lara accompanied him. Dave was introduced to the group by their regular pastor, Lee. "This is Dave," he said, "He's a gentle, caring person who counsels drug addicts."

Lara gave a snort, and Lee looked at her in surprise. "What is it, Lara?"

"He's not always that gentle and caring," she said wryly, and recounted the incident. She did add that Dave used those tactics as a last resort, but Dave could see the shock on the faces of those present—most had led comparatively sheltered lives, and this was an eye-opener for them.

Yet that was later.

For the present, Dave was still saddened because Lara was relapsing continually, and he had that "third love" for her that would not let him go. Additionally, he was troubled by a song that seemed to come on the radio each time he thought of her. It was currently a hit for Lara Fabian, called "Givin' Up on You," and the lyrics seemed to tear at his heart.

"Oh no!" he would think whenever it came on the air, and as he remembered the promise he had made to God, to never relinquish the task he was given, to love Lara to the end. One afternoon, as those lyrics came sidling into his room once again, a terrible gloom clamped its icy fingers around his heart, and the despondent thought insinuated itself into his mind:

"I don't know, maybe I should give up on her ..."

Then he heard a gentle Voice saying, "David, no."

Dave looked at the door, but no one was there. Yet the Voice continued, "No matter what you hear, no matter what happens, do not give up on her ... if you give up on her, she will die."

"Okay!" said Dave.

CHAPTER 39

The Galatians 6:9 Principle

IT WAS ALL about perseverance, Dave was learning. And, fortunately, he had a long training in the exercise of this gift during his days as a police officer.

One time, back in the Seventies, Dave was out on the road with his colleague, Rick, when they got a call to go to a local service station. A man had gone to the station and bought two tires with a credit card in the name of JD Winger, but the owner of the station became suspicious, checked the card, and discovered it was stolen. Dave and Rick obtained a description of the man's vehicle, and tracked it out to Central Saanich near Butchart Gardens. They found the perpetrator staying in a cheap rooming house with his Mexican girlfriend. He confessed his real name was Michael Timmins; he was polite and persuasive, but the officers determined they had enough to arrest him.

There was one other thing that bothered Dave. As the man was bidding farewell to his girlfriend, Dave thought he heard her call the man "Chris." His ears pricked up.

"If your name is Michael, why does she call you Chris?" he asked.

"Oh, no, she called me 'Grease'," he said quickly. "My nickname is 'Grease,' but with her Mexican accent it just sounded like Chris."

Dave filed the incident away in his mind. He and Rick took the man to the station, and because he had no fixed address they kept him overnight. Dave lodged the charge for his court appearance on the following day, and added a note in bold: "Attention, prosecutor–do not release this man until we get his fingerprints back." Dave was almost certain the offender was not who he claimed to be.

By the time Dave put in the charge it was quite late, and consequently he was not on duty for the man's court appearance the following morning. When he came in for his afternoon shift he discovered the fingerprints had come back–and his hunch was correct. The man they apprehended was an American citizen by the name of Thomas James Seeker; he had twenty different aliases, and was wanted in a number of states. Dave was elated he had asked the man to be held–and then discovered the court had swallowed the lies this true con artist had told, and set him free.

Needless to say, Dave was quite upset. He and Rick went out to the rundown hotel where they had first apprehended Seeker; they then drove all over Saanich looking for him in various hangouts, without success. Yet Dave was determined to track him down. It was not so much that a heinous offence was committed; the charge was simply that of fraudulent use of a credit card. Rather, it was the fact that the offender had "put one over" the Canadian legal system–it was this that Dave could neither forget nor forgive.

Seeker had given an address located some way out of town, an isolated area in the hills near Butchart Gardens. It was so secluded it was impossible to drive there in a police vehicle, but Dave had a motorcycle, and some days off. He decided he would seize the opportunity to check out the address the man had given.

Dave had visited Butchart Gardens on many occasions; it was a major tourist attraction in Victoria, sometimes called "the eighth wonder of the world" because of the spectacular garden areas, laid out with meticulous artistry. All the beauty of the Island seems concentrated in the display of green lawns and the myriad hues of richly flowering plants and trees, together with the distant vistas of blue Gulf waters. Whenever Dave had previously visited the Gardens it had usually been to take visitors whom he knew would delight in the scenery, but that had always been in summer. Now, as he traveled out in that direction on his motorcycle to find his man, it was winter–and it had begun to snow.

Dave located the address Seeker had given, a small cabin surrounded by tall trees that appeared uninhabited. He parked his bike out of sight in the woods and climbed up on a high side of road to gain an unimpeded view of the property. Some leafy bushes provided him with cover, and he lay down beneath them and trained his binoculars on the small house opposite. The snow began to come down in great flurries, and as some protection against the weather he found a tarpaulin with which he covered himself. So he settled down to watch and wait, keeping his lonely vigil throughout two days and two nights ... but no one came, nor was there any sign of life or movement, either to or from the cabin.

After the second day, Dave knew his man would probably not come to the house; he returned to work and had a warrant put out for his arrest, under both his real name and his twenty aliases. One of these, of course, was the name of the owner of the credit card, a man from Vancouver, and he kept getting arrested mistakenly until Dave arranged for a letter to be given to him from the Attorney-General's department. There were other problems with maintaining the record on Seeker. Every six months the computer automatically requested that unused files be deleted, and the director of records, a man named Les, would come to Dave twice a year, as regularly as clockwork. When asked if he still wanted Seeker's file kept open, Dave always said yes.

The years rolled by. The service station at which the fraud took place was demolished and a new business arose in its place. Any witnesses to the crime had long since dispersed. After seven or eight years, Les finally asked, "Why won't you let it go, Dave?"

Dave shook his head. "It's the principle of the thing, Les. I'm just not giving up on this one." And Les left the file open.

One day Dave was on the road, and got a call to come to the station; he needed to contact an RCMP detachment in northern British Columbia.

"Hey," he heard when he phoned the number, "We have a guy here we arrested on a charge, and he produced ID in the name of one of the aliases you entered on the computer."

"Is it an indictable offence?" asked Dave, his senses alert.

"Yep–do you want us to take his fingerprints?"

"I sure do. Let us know as soon as you have any information."

The Mountie called back shortly. "It's your guy!" he said. "But do you still want him after all this time?"

"You bet!" said Dave. "Ship him down here!"

It was a day or two later, and Dave received a call telling him the man he requested to have sent down was now in custody. He went to the police station and entered the prison area; Seeker was the only one in the cells at that time. The prisoner looked at the officer through the bars, and Dave could see that Seeker recognized him.

"Nice to see you again," he said to the offender.

"Nice to see you, too," responded Seeker, without a trace of malice–he was always a perfect gentleman in their encounters.

Dave then said, "Before we get down to the official stuff, I've got to tell you something." He paused. "You're awfully good at what you do."

The prisoner's smile glinted through the bars. "Well," he drawled, "apparently not as good as you are at what you do!"

Dave acknowledged the tribute with a brief nod of his head, and then got down to business. "We've maintained your file and we're charging you. It's my duty to warn you ..." and he gave Seeker his rights. There was no way he was going to let his prisoner know that he no longer had witnesses, with the result that the following morning Seeker went to court and pleaded guilty.

And his sentence? He was deported back to the United States. So, for all Dave knew, Seeker could still be running around using a hundred different aliases. But he didn't care–it was the principle of the thing!

Another case that stayed in Dave's mind concerned a break-in at a drug store. The pharmacy was set away from the road in a big open field, and in order to effect their entry the robbers had taken a large rock and thrown it through the front glass door, which shattered on impact. They had run in, seized whatever drugs they could lay their hands on, and made their escape. Dave was working in Ident at the time and was called to the scene the same night. He could see where a car had driven through soft dirt up to the pharmacy, so he photographed the tracks, and also the rock which was lying on the floor where the thieves had thrown it through the glass. It was jagged with sharp edges, and as he took the photographs Dave was reflecting. He decided to take the rock back to the station with him.

He was thinking the boulder must have been carried close to the chest, so it might be possible to find some shreds of fabric and obtain a lead on a garment. The bottom of the rock also interested him; it was covered in soil, so he thought it had probably been pulled from a garden bed. He went back in daylight and checked the backyards in the vicinity of the drug store, but found no kind of indentation that would suggest its removal. The stone was sixteen inches across and weighed about thirty pounds; the thieves could surely not have walked down the street with it. Now Dave was certain they had brought the rock with them in the vehicle they had driven, for which he had the tire treads.

The following day Dave heard that two known drug addicts were arrested while driving in downtown Victoria with a large haul of prescription drugs. He arranged to have their car towed back to the police station and went to examine it, together with his boss, Norm. The first thing that struck him was how filthy the car was. He then turned his gaze upon the dirt and pebbles which littered the floor of the passenger seat, and noticed a small chip that seemed a different shape from the other debris; it was long and narrow with a sharp point. He reached down and picked it up.

"I wonder if this chip came from the big rock," he said to Norm.

"What!" exclaimed his boss.

"Maybe when they put the rock on the floor this piece broke off. I might see if I can match it."

Norm shook his head dubiously. "I don't want you to waste time on this, Dave. I'll give you fifteen minutes."

Dave took the chip, and started examining the rock minutely, poring over the jagged edges. And then–he couldn't believe his eyes–he found a tiny nick where a piece of the rock had recently broken off, and it seemed exactly the size and shape of the sliver he had found. He took the small pick he used for examining prints under a magnifying glass, and inserted the chip into the nick. It fitted like a glove.

He called Norm, gave him the magnifying glass, and said, "I want you to watch this closely."

"What?" Norm took the glass and looked at the rock in the place Dave indicated.

The fit of the sliver in its home base was so perfect Dave had trouble finding it again. "Are you watching?" he said to Norm.

"Yeah, I'm watching–what am I watching?"

Dave took the fingerprint pick and lifted one end of the little chip slightly in the air as Norm was gazing through the glass, just so he could see, and set it back down.

Norm put down the glass, stood up and looked at his watch. "This is not good," he said, "I gave you fifteen minutes and it took you twenty!" Then he laughed. "Dave," he said, "this is incredible!"

When Dave went to court and told the story of finding the chip, he had photographs of the rock without the chip, taken from different angles, then re-photographed with the chip nestling in place, using a technique called macrophotography which made the evidence as strong as fingerprints.

When Dave presented these findings, the defense lawyer at first had sneered: "Do you really expect this court to believe you went to all this trouble, and found that chip as you say?" He was implying that Dave had broken off the piece himself.

"My boss, Norm, was with me when I found the chip," Dave answered coolly. "He watched me pick it up and put it in a vial, and can verify what I say."

It was this fact which proved convincing to the court. At the end of the presentation of evidence, as Dave was being excused, the judge added a statement. "In all my days on the bench," he said, "I rarely see a case of perseverance like this."

Now Dave was learning about perseverance in a new realm, the realm of faith, and it was far more challenging. He was coming to cling repeatedly to a promise from Paul's Letter to the Galatians, Chapter 6, verse 9: *"And let us not grow weary while doing good, for in due season we shall reap if we do not give up."*

It was as if God was engraving that truth on his very soul–and now he was also beginning to see miracles.

CHAPTER 40
The God of Miracles

DAVE WAS NO stranger to miracles during his police career. He well recalled a case concerning a break-in at a drug store, which had led to an accusation of attempted homicide being leveled against a fellow police officer. Dave was again in Ident at the time; he got called to the scene in the middle of the night, and learned what happened.

The two "perps" were after drugs, and because they believed the pharmacy they targeted would have an alarm they decided to break in to the dry cleaners next door and then effect an entrance through the inside wall. One of the robbers, Jim, tried to pry open the front door of the dry cleaners, but the door wouldn't give and the wooden handle of his file bent out of shape. They made their way to the back of the store where there was an alleyway, forced a window and got inside. A lone policeman named Alan was on duty that night, checking property in the lane, and came across the break-in almost immediately. The criminals inside, Jim and his accomplice, were about to force their way through the inner wall when Alan appeared behind them with his gun in his hand.

"Don't move!" he said.

Jim turned swiftly. He had the bent file in his hand, and in the darkness Alan thought it was a gun. He dropped to his knee and fired a shot in the air above the robber; it didn't seem to deter him and Alan fired again, this time hitting Jim in the shoulder. The wound was not a major one, but after the robbers were taken in Jim made a serious allegation against the policeman: he claimed he was kneeling down, and Alan intended to execute him.

Now the matter was over to Dave, who knew Alan personally and was aware the officer was gentle and softhearted, a pacifist who would always err on the side of leniency. Dave knew also that Jim's charge was a ploy to shift culpability–but he had to prove it.

In the daylight, Dave examined the crime scene carefully. He found the jimmy marks on the front door of the dry cleaner, which perfectly matched the ridges of the file, then went inside to look at the scene of the shooting. He knew that if Alan meant to execute Jim he had to be shooting downward, but couldn't find any evidence of a bullet striking the floor. He then shifted his gaze to a false wall placed in between the back and front sections of the dry cleaner. It was as thin as cardboard, and when Dave examined it he found a small hole in it, about the size of a bullet. He moved forward to check the front glass wall of the dry cleaner and found a second hole, the same size as the first, and higher up.

Dave knew he could vindicate Alan if he could prove these were bullet holes and they were on an upward trajectory. He went again to the back door and lined up the hole from the false wall to the front wall; and then, as he stood calculating intently the direction of the putative bullet, his eyes traveled past the front wall and fixed themselves on a telephone wire across the street. An incredible hope sprang into his mind: it looked as if the holes lined up exactly at that wire.

"I wonder," he thought to himself, "Could the bullet possibly have clipped it?"

He took his photography kit, ran outside and looked up at the wire; it was a good twenty feet above his head. He knew the chances were astronomical and he was clutching at straws. "And how am I possibly going to get up there and check?" he asked himself.

At that precise moment came the thunder of wheels and he looked around. A truck was coming toward him, and loaded upon it was a large cherry picker and boom. The officer didn't hesitate for a second. He flagged down the truck and showed the driver his badge.

"Would you mind giving me a few minutes of your time, and taking me up in your cherry picker?" he asked. "I'm trying to find evidence about a shooting last night."

The driver was only too willing to oblige. Dave got in the bucket, and the driver lifted him slowly until he was high in the air and standing beside the wire. He began examining each section of the wire minutely; as he completed each segment he would wave to the driver, who slowly inched his truck forward. Then, with an exultant leap of his heart, he saw a nick on the wire–and it was freshly made.

"Stop!" he called to the driver. "I've got it!"

Dave photographed the nick; he noted also that the bullet had hit the bottom of the wire, which meant it must have entered its downward trajectory. He turned his gaze to the side of the street opposite the store and saw a gravel parking lot, then gestured to the truck driver to bring him down. On the ground, he thanked the man profusely.

"You have helped me prove a policeman is innocent," he said.

Then he got down on hands and knees and after half an hour of searching found the gray bullet nestling in the gray gravel. It was the final confirmation he needed when the case came to court: Alan was duly vindicated, and Jim went to jail. To Dave, it was particularly noteworthy that guilt and innocence were proved in the same case.

As he now looked back on this episode, Dave could see the spiritual realities involved: the intervention of a God of justice who did not want to see a blameless man condemned. He knew also that the way in which Alan's innocence was demonstrated was nothing short of a miracle. And now that he was involved with his ministry to addicts, Dave began to realize he was seeing occurrences which were so remarkable they could only be designated the same way. One incident in particular seemed to demonstrate to him God's amazing favor toward him as he carried out his work with these troubled persons.

Dave continued to have young people battling various problems living in his apartment for short periods of time, and at one stage had a young man named Nick, from Ontario, staying there. He seemed to be continually down and out, and frequently asked Dave for financial assistance, but the former policeman was beginning to feel uncomfortable about the situation. As he was driving down the road, and pondering Nick's latest request, he found his eyes drawn to a sign displayed prominently outside a motel: *Why Pay More?* He knew instantly this was a message telling him not to lavish any more funds on the youth, and that he should ask Nick to leave.

Unbeknownst to Dave, however, before he vacated the apartment Nick had found his checkbook and stolen one of his checks. Not so long afterwards, Dave received a phone call from his bank, a different branch from his own, asking if he could come in and talk with them. At this meeting, he found out a young person had come into the branch with a check in the amount of five hundred dollars, made out in Dave's name. The lady teller described the individual, and Dave realized who it was: Nick!

"That's quite a way to repay the hospitality he received," he thought ruefully.

The woman explained to him what happened next.

"Usually," she said, "we don't phone a competitive bank to verify a check, but something made me do it this time. When I told this young man I was going to verify it, he grabbed the check, said 'Never mind,' and took off."

Dave thought that was probably the end of the story, but the bank clerk was continuing. "I would have forgotten about it," she said, "except for what happened the following day."

He listened attentively.

"The next morning it so happened I had to go to a different branch, out in Colwood. They had someone phone in sick, and because I was a reserve teller I was sent out to that branch just for the day. In fact, it was the only time I had ever been there. Now Colwood, as you know, is a long way out of town."

Dave nodded.

"Well, no sooner did we open up than this same young fellow came up to me with the same check and tried to cash it. He didn't remember me, but I remembered him, so this time I grabbed the check and he took off like lightning. So, fortunately, we're able to return it to you."

Dave took the check the lady teller handed to him, and looked at his signature forged in bold letters at the bottom. He was sincerely thankful for her acumen, which had prevented the fraudulent transaction, and expressed this to her.

Yet she was looking at him curiously, and shook her head in wonder. "Do you know," she said, "the odds of that happening are a million to one." Then she added, "Someone must really be looking after you!"

"Yes, I know," thought Dave, "and I know who it is!"

As he continued in his ministry, it was as if his eyes were opened to see God's hand at work in the smallest details of his life. Everyday events now seemed to be infused with a kind of indwelling significance which elated him; the words of a song called "Ordinary Miracle" by Sarah McLachlan, the Canadian songstress with the exquisite voice, seemed to express these feelings perfectly.

Still more, Dave began to perceive in the world about him the presence of an all-pervasive wisdom and power. He felt as though he had been granted new faculties to apprehend the wonder of the vast creation that surrounded him, the earth with its manifold treasures, and the celestial bodies traveling high in the heavens with such meticulous precision. "*Lift up your eyes on high*,"[28] the prophet Isaiah had been instructed,

> *And see who has created these things,*
> *Who brings out their host by number;*
> *He calls them all by name,*
> *By the greatness of His might*
> *And the strength of His power;*
> *Not one is missing* (Isaiah 40:26).

It was as if Dave's heart was being opened to an incandescent truth: it was the love at the heart of the universe which moved the sun, moon and stars; nay more, which condescended to enter the lives of men and women with such matchless grace and efficacy. He knew this was a God of miracles, as in the days of old, a God of "signs and wonders."

CHAPTER 41
The Great Exchange

LARA WAS NOW beginning to make some progress on the road to recovery, and although still living at Dave's place felt it was time to become more independent. Because she had training and some experience as a hairdresser, Dave drove her to a number of salons around the city to leave her resume, and one day they called in at a salon in Cordova Bay on the north side of Victoria.

The young woman took in her documents, and when she re-emerged she was hopeful and excited. She told Dave the owner had sounded positive about her resume and seemed to be thinking of hiring her. She also felt good about the place because of the beautiful location on the shores of the sea–and it was far away from the downtown area and the whole drug scene.

As they drove back toward the apartment later in the day the salon owner called her on Dave's cellphone; Lara's eyes lit up and she answered. And then she sat silently listening, and the tears began to fill her eyes and spill down her cheeks. Eventually she put down the phone and began sobbing.

Dave pulled over. "What's the matter, Lara?" he asked. "What did he say?"

"He called one of my references back in the Interior," she named a woman for whom she had worked, "and she gave me a bad report, told him I was a drug addict." She dissolved into tears again.

Dave sat silent for a minute, and then he said, "Listen, Lara, it doesn't matter what he says, or what this woman says, God is going to look out for you. He knows you're trying. This is going to work out, and you have to have faith that it will."

She nodded her head, and began to calm down. They prayed together, then continued driving, when the cellphone rang again. It was the salon owner.

"I've been thinking about it," he said, "and everyone deserves a second chance. You're hired!"

So Lara began working at the salon in Cordova Bay; Dave would drive her there each day, or she would take a bus. He also made an appointment to have his hair cut by her–he didn't care if she did a good job, just wanted to encourage her–but she was a wonderful hairdresser. Another person who went to have his hair trimmed by her was Pastor Holmes, who made the trip to the salon despite the handicap of his wheelchair and cane; he would have done anything to help her. For Lara had started going to Central Baptist Church, and his wife, Jean, had also started to mentor her.

One Sunday morning, Dave and Lara were at church together, listening to Pastor Holmes preaching, when Dave glanced over at Lara and noticed tears in her eyes.

"Wow," he thought to himself, "that's beautiful; she's really listening."

After church they went out and got in the car, and he asked, "Are you okay? That was really a great message; I was amazed it got to you so emotionally."

She turned her face away from him. "It wasn't that," she said dully.

"What's the matter?" he asked, perplexed.

She turned to him suddenly and spoke vehemently. "Do you have any idea," she asked, "how much it hurts me to go to church and want to learn about Jesus, when all I can think about is how badly I want to get out of there and score heroin?"

Dave was stunned by the devastating honesty of her answer. And then a kind of exultant assurance filled his heart. "She's going to make it," he thought. "She's too truthful to do otherwise."

It was a beautiful day in late fall; they stopped in the park on the way home and sat at one of the benches to talk. Dave was visited with a sudden inspiration. He took two coins out of his pocket, a dime and a Canadian two-dollar coin called a "toonie." He held them up before her.

"Which one is worth more?"

Lara knew a lesson was coming and smiled. She never resisted his object talks; she knew they were given out of love. "The toonie," she said.

She was sitting on the opposite side of the park bench, and Dave was holding the coins beside each other so they were at exactly the same distance from her. Then he started moving the dime closer to her, and at the same time moved the toonie closer to himself.

"Tell me when you see them as exactly the same size." He continued to move the coins so her perspective would be changed.

"Okay, stop," she said. The dime was very close to her, the toonie out of reach.

"Now tell me which one is worth more," he said.

She shook her head, puzzled.

"The one that's close to you," he said. "The one can you reach. Take what is attainable, don't try for what is beyond your grasp at this point."

Dave saw the light come on in her eyes and continued to drive home the lesson. "There's a battle going on in your life, take it one step at a time. The day will come when you'll be able to reach further."

It was a truth that Dave himself held onto, as Lara and others to whom he ministered continued to relapse. He accepted this as part of the process: "Relapse is the road to recovery" was one of his favorite sayings.

And then, one evening, Lara and Dave were at home at his apartment. Lara was quiet, and as Dave glanced at her he could see she was pale and in distress.

"What's wrong?" he asked.

"It's my back, I have a cramp in my back."

Dave knew instantly what it was: withdrawal from heroin is not only psychological, but rather causes very real, very agonizing physical pain. He put his hand on Lara's back in the place she indicated, left of her spine. He could feel where the muscles had knotted together in a hard lump and tried to massage it away, but she told him it was only getting worse, and began crying with distress.

Dave started praying under his breath. "Please take the pain from her," he begged, "she can't stand it. She's so petite, please take it away." And then he felt a new, powerful emotion arising within him–anger. He was angry with God for letting her suffer, angry because the pain refused to diminish. He stood up abruptly, left Lara in the sitting room and went and lay down on his bed. After a few moments a resolve settled in his mind, and he prayed out loud.

"Okay," he said, "if you won't take the pain from her, then give it to me! I can stand it, but she can't, she's too fragile. *Please*," he put all his heart and soul into his prayer, "I just can't bear to see her suffer like that any more."

He continued praying for her, lying there in his room, and within about ten minutes started to feel a sensation of discomfort in his back, exactly where Lara's cramp was. At first he thought it was his imagination, but it increased, and he started rubbing the area. Then Lara came and stood in the doorway.

"Finally!" she said, "The pain is going."

He said, "Yes, I know. And I know where it's going."

"What?"

"*I've* got it."

The searing sensation Dave's back lasted until after midnight, and when it finally subsided he fell into an exhausted sleep.

It was not until some time later that Dave understood what had taken place on a spiritual level during that strange evening. He had always taught that addiction is not a disease; rather, it is a sin, which he had learned from Paul's warning to the new converts in the notorious city of Corinth[29]. Accordingly, he thought to himself, if a person's physical affliction is the result of transgression, there needs also to be some kind of reparation–an *atonement*, to use the great theological term. So, while he was asking "Take the pain away," nothing happened, but as soon as he said, "Give me the pain, she can't stand it"–*that* was when it started to diminish.

The picture of Christ in the gospels had become very dear to Dave, and he loved to contemplate the way He went about to bring healing to all who were suffering in body, soul or spirit. This Heavenly Physician had entered our world to bring life in its fullest, most abundant sense, and to restore to the utmost what sin had corrupted. Many centuries earlier the prophet Isaiah had foretold the coming of a Messiah, and understood the purpose of His incarnation: that "*the chastisement for our peace was upon him; and by his stripes we are healed*" (53:5). In Jesus this prophecy was fulfilled, and in Him this great promise had come to pass.

And as Dave continued to ponder what had taken place that evening, he came to realize that it was a perfect illustration of what had taken place at Calvary two thousand years earlier. When Christ endured His sacrificial death there, and poured out His life in love for Lara, for himself, for all people, it had won for them vast, unmerited benefits. Gradually, the great truth of the atoning work of Jesus Christ became unfolded to him: it was upon the cross that the perfect Son of God, as our Substitute, had taken upon Himself the sins and suffering of the whole world, so that we, the transgressors, might receive as a free gift His healing, righteousness, and peace. The Great Exchange effected there is described in the words of the Apostle Paul:

> He made Him who knew no sin to be sin for us, that we might become the righteousness of God in Him (2 Corinthians 5:21).

CHAPTER 42
It's No Secret What God Can Do

THE UNUSUAL EVENTS which took place in his ministry to Lara and others brought Dave these wonderful new illuminations of the riches to be found in the scriptures. He also continued his mentoring sessions with John Schaper, the gifted preacher who had been born in Holland.

John had come with his family at an early age to live in Canada, and when he grew up he became a Christian and attended seminary. Later he worked extensively with evangelical ministries around the world, including the Billy Graham Organization, and when he came to reside in Victoria had met his wife, Lynne. John's surname in Dutch meant "shepherd," and as Dave learned more of the character and integrity of this man, and listened to the brilliance of his preaching, he became convinced that here was a pastor with a sincere heart for God and His flock.

Eventually John and Lynne began pastoring a church in Victoria, which they called "Arbutus Christian Fellowship" after the beautiful hardwood tree with its characteristic red bark. This tree, which flourished extensively in the streets and gardens of Victoria, possessed a wonderful symbolism to the church founders. As an evergreen it never loses its leaves, even in the coldest of winters, whilst in summer its perfumed white blossoms are followed by clusters of red berries on which birds and deer can feed. Arbutus trees are also extremely resilient, sometimes living many hundreds of years, and display their fullest splendor while clinging to rocky crags overlooking the oceans of the Pacific Northwest.

As Dave participated in the life of this vibrant fellowship, his ministry also began to flourish in new directions. A passage in the book of Isaiah seemed to speak to him again:

> *Enlarge the place of your tent,*
> *And let them stretch out the curtains of your dwellings;*
> *Do not spare;*

Lengthen your cords,
And strengthen your stakes,
For you shall expand to the right and to the left (Isaiah 54:2,3).

This enlargement was given additional impetus when Lara taught him how to use emails and he decided to buy a computer; he little dreamed what that small move was going to accomplish. He had always encouraged the addicts he was counseling to come to church with him, and when members of the congregation met Lara and the others, and learned of their struggles, their hearts would go out to them and they would want to pray for them. Dave would phone the congregants and give painstaking details concerning each situation over the phone. One day someone made a suggestion: "Why don't you send out these prayer requests by email?" Within six months of this prompting, Dave had an internet prayer network that spread over the world.

Seemingly under its own momentum, it had just exploded. Somehow–Dave never learned how–Kevin Corbin, a dedicated believer from Edmonton who sent out a daily inspirational called "Gleanings from the Word," read by many thousands of Christians, started receiving his messages. He in turn took Dave's prayer requests and sent them out; there was also a wonderful, caring woman named Jennie Lee, in Florida, who placed them on her television and internet prayer system. Before long, Dave was receiving emails from people all over the globe, asking about the men and women he was working with.

Dave's gift for writing was now put to an entirely new use. He would take the stories of each of the addicts, and describe them as vividly as possible–explain how one was accused falsely of stealing, another had ended up on the street, the way in which still another had suffered a relapse. In this way, his correspondents became really caught up in the lives of those for whom they prayed; often they could hardly wait for the next installment–"It's like a soap opera!" thought Dave. He also found himself receiving cards and parcels sent from faraway lands, boxes of knitted blankets, clothes and other items. They would contain simple messages: "Please give this to So-and-So, from a Christian who is praying."

Often Dave never met the addicts for whom he requested prayer. Just occasionally, though, he would learn of the lives changed through this hidden ministry. At one time a woman who was a missionary in the Dominican Republic sent him an email, explaining she had a brother named Mike Kaye who was a heroin addict and lived in B.C. She asked Dave to put him on the prayer network, and whether he could suggest a recovery center. He highly recommended Teen Challenge, just outside Vancouver, and heard that Mike had agreed to go.

Some time later, he visited a church in Abbotsford on the mainland for the baptism of a young woman he had counseled. There was quite a crowd there, and during the reception a young man came up to him. He was handsome and clean-cut, wearing a suit.

"Excuse me, you're Dave Richardson?"

"Yes," Dave answered, extending his hand.

The young man shook it warmly. "I'm Mike Kaye," he said, "It's wonderful to finally meet you."

"It's better to finally meet you," answered Dave, who was always genuinely overwhelmed when he saw the God's work of grace in the lives of former addicts.

"I want to let you know that I'm going out as a missionary to help my sister."

It was especially rewarding for Dave when a life was turned around so greatly that the young person would decide to devote his or her life to Christian ministry. Yet when they came to him, saying they also wanted to bring healing to lives ruined by drug abuse, he was careful to caution them.

"Are you sure?" he would ask wryly. He had learned that the ministry was not just to a single person; a far greater commitment was involved. The whole family was affected by the substance abuser–spouse, kids, pets–and that meant his work of counseling included baby-sitting their children while they were in detox, walking their dogs, comforting devastated parents, being polite to cranky relatives, sitting for hours in hospital wards …

"It means you've got to love everything about them," he would say.

There was one individual about whom Dave felt differently. David M. was living under a bridge with a tarpaulin as his only shelter when Dave first met him; he was heavily addicted, and washing windows for money to supply his habit. He was fifty-four at the time but looked ten years older, was skin and bone, with no teeth, and virtually at death's door. One day, after Dave had finished counseling some addicts in the detox unit, David had come up to him and said,

"Excuse me, I couldn't help overhearing your conversation–you're saying that Jesus Christ can set you free from all this misery?"

Dave looked at the wreck of humanity before him and his heart went out to him. "Yes, He can," he said gently.

"Would you come back and talk to me about it?"

"I surely will," said Dave. The chorus from an old hit song from the Fifties came into his mind: "It Is No Secret What God Can Do," sung by Pat Boone.

"The Lord has helped me and countless others," he said to David. "And what He's done for others, He'll do for you."

He saw an answering gleam of hope in the sunken eyes looking at him. Dave started visiting this new protégé on a regular basis and felt a sense of genuine sincerity in the man. After David came out of detox he and Dave prayed together, and three weeks later he was baptized–he was the first individual Dave counseled who had no relapses. On his own initiative David then undertook a course on counseling for addiction and started helping at the Salvation Army. He ended up buying a used BMW, got his own apartment, and came out from under Dave's wing. This, of course, is what Dave always desired for those with whom he worked.

Today David is a fine-looking man, brimming with health and strength, working with a counseling center in Victoria and helping scores of men battle the same problems he himself once faced.

Lara also was playing a part in helping other addicts turn their lives around. She was proving a great success in the hairdressing salon through the appeal of her sparkling personality, and her warm, sympathetic manner also invited the clients' confidences. One day she was cutting the hair of an older gentleman and he let fall he had a problem: his son was an addict and he wasn't sure how to help him.

Lara paused in her ministrations. "Well," she said, "I have a friend who helps addicts–he helped me too."

"Do you think I could get in touch with him?"

"I'm sure he'd be happy to help you."

That was how Dave came in contact with a man named Bryson, whom he discovered to be both gentle and a gentleman, and began ministering to his son Martin. It became another long struggle, that ended with Martin turning his life around; Bryson and his wife Maureen were themselves so thankful and inspired by this turn of events that they themselves started going to Arbutus Fellowship. It was through this couple that Dave also learned something of how his ministry by email was continuing to expand.

Bryson and Maureen had gone to Hawaii on holiday, and while there they found a church where they attended the Sunday morning service. At the meeting, one of the elders announced the pastor was ill and there would be no sermon; he suggested instead that different people could share a testimony as they felt led. Bryson was a reserved individual, but felt he should speak. He got to his feet and told the story of his son's addiction, of meeting a young woman in a hair salon, which had led to his contacting her friend who worked with drug addicts, of the turnaround in Martin's life, and his own return to faith in God. After the service a man came up to him.

"Did you say you're from Victoria?" he asked.

"That's right."

"I'm on a prayer network that was referred to me, and I pray for this fellow in Victoria who works for addicts; his name is Dave Richardson."

"What!" said Bryson, who hadn't mentioned any names in his testimony. "That's who I'm talking about!"

When he shared this story upon his return to Canada, Dave was greatly encouraged. Those emails he was writing in the middle of the night, sending out prayer requests for different individuals–now he had an idea just how far they were reaching. "Yes, it's worth it," he thought to himself, "Don't give up!"

There was another realization as well, one which humbled him. Bryson's story made him understand his ministry was null and void without the prayer which was all the time undergirding it. He knew the people who interceded faithfully at Central Baptist Church, Arbutus Fellowship, and indeed through-out the globe, were many of them older and retired; although restricted in their movements they were serving in a way that was bearing rich fruit. "This is an-other beautiful thing," Dave thought to himself, "I'm actually the smallest part of the whole ministry!"

One evening, he was reading in the book of the prophet Jeremiah, and his eye was caught by a verse that seemed to stand out to him, in Chapter 33 and Verse 3. The numbers struck him as significant; perhaps, he thought, they sym-bolized the Trinity of Father, Son and Spirit who worked together in such mar-velous harmony to bring redemption and healing in a person's life. In any event, it was a marvelous promise:

> *"Call to me, and I will answer you, and show you great and mighty things, which you do not know"* (Jeremiah 33:3).[30]

"It's true," Dave reflected, as he looked back over the time of his ministry. "You've revealed to me so many wonderful things, of which I had no knowledge before. And You have done so many great things in the lives of so many."

.

CHAPTER 43

The 333 Principle

AS THE MONTHS of his ministry stretched into years, Dave ended up counseling several hundred addicts, many of whom came to faith. Yet there was an "inner circle" to whom he continued to devote most of his attention; they were all addicts concerning whom he had received a "sign" confirming he was meant to work with them. This was a double-edged sword; on the one hand, it meant this particular man or woman would end up coming to faith–but it also indicated a battle was ahead. They were tough cases; however, Dave had a supernatural determination concerning them, as well as a special love for them.

First there was Andre and Murdo, former cocaine addicts, whom he had counseled right from the beginning. Dave could see a unique attractiveness in each of these young men, and could discern their spiritual potential. Andre ended up staying in Dave's apartment for several months and made a great deal of progress, although he was not yet completely "out of the woods." Dave stayed in touch with him after he went to Calgary to take up a job, and at one stage sent him an email suggesting he take an "Alpha" program, a course exploring the meaning of life and the Christian faith through a series of informal discussions.

The following day he got a phone call from Andre, who was still in a state of astonishment. He told Dave what had happened.

"Hey, Dave," he began, "do you still have that attachment to the number 3?"

"Yes, "Dave replied, not sure where this was leading. "Why?"

"Well, yesterday I went downtown here in Calgary to go to an internet café–I don't have a computer in my apartment. When I went online, I saw your email suggesting I find a church and take the Alpha program."

"Yes, I really felt that it would be of benefit for you …" Dave was beginning.

"Listen," Andre interrupted. "I didn't take it seriously when I saw your suggestion–just sort of thought 'Oh yeah' in my mind. So I signed off and walked out the front door of the café." He paused.

"Yes?"

"Straight away, a man walked up to me with a pamphlet in his hand and said, 'Here, this is for you.' He put it in my hand, and when I looked at it, Dave, do you know what it said?"

"What?"

"'*Take the Alpha Program, starting shortly, at Bethany Chapel, 3333 Richardson Way, Calgary*.' I'm not kidding, Dave, I jumped–I thought I was going to get hit by lightning!"

Dave laughed, but he was also astounded. God had done many miraculous things, yet he never got entirely used to them.

Then there were Ryan and Nolan, personable and deeply searching individuals, whom Dave came to count as close friends, as well as Alicia, a tall and lovely young woman, who in turn introduced Dave to another who became part of the "inner circle."

"I have a friend who is a cocaine addict," she said to him one day, "and Dave, I really believe you should talk with her."

"What's the name of your friend?"

"Melanie."

"Okay, have her give me a call."

Dave still preferred it if the person with the drug problem would call him on their own initiative; it demonstrated a genuine desire to seek help. But Melanie didn't call, and one day Alicia contacted Dave again. She spoke urgently.

"Listen, Dave, my friend Mel is talking of committing suicide. Please won't you call her?"

"What's her number?

Alicia gave the number and he called immediately.

"It's Dave Richardson," he said when Melanie answered.

She sounded distraught. "It's too late, I'm going to kill myself."

"I'm coming over," he said, "Don't do anything till I come," he pleaded.

"By the time you come, I'll be dead."

"I'm on my way."

Dave hung up, the specter of imminent death gripping him. He knew of the "party packs" of variety pills which addicts kept on hand for those times when they might feel overwhelmed by their situation. It was imperative that Melanie be kept occupied until he arrived, so he phoned a local pastor he knew named Scott, explained the situation, and asked him to call Melanie and keep her talking. The pastor sounded dubious.

"I don't know much about drugs," he said.

"You know about God … that's all you need to know!"

Dave gave Scott the number, jumped in his car and sped over to Melanie's place close to Willows Beach. He pulled in the driveway and knocked on her door; when she answered she was still talking to the pastor. At one stage during their conversation, Dave heard Melanie mention how much she loved the song "Light the Fire Again," and when the call ended he continued where Scott had left off.

"God is going to work a miracle in your life," he said, "He is going to reveal Himself to you."

He talked with and prayed with her, until he felt he could safely leave. "Now 'psalm down,'" he said to her in farewell, and turned the radio to a Christian station so she could hear some comforting music. The song playing was "Light the Fire Again."

That was the beginning of a long journey together. Melanie suffered from agoraphobia, and Dave went over to her place late at night, when no one was around, and coaxed her to take a few steps outside. Each evening he convinced her to walk a little further, until finally he persuaded her to go with him to Macdonald's and get a hamburger. She went home feeling as if she had conquered the world.

"Now you do it yourself," he said to her, and this beautiful young woman gradually rebuilt her life. She had embarked on a journey that Dave wished for all his counselees: to develop a character filled with goodness, kindness and love.

Yet in the midst of his busy life of counseling, his primary focus remained on his ministry to Lara, and he was happy that she herself was now comprehending God's power at work in her life–and even taking part in leading others to find help in Him.

One day at home, Dave was leafing through the phone book when he saw a number which struck him; it was the address of a dwelling on Richmond Road, and the number was identical to the last digits of his bank account. He was so sure the number had a special significance that he showed it to Lara. Within a few days, she wanted to go to Camosun College to look up a program; Dave drove her there, and noticed he was within a block of the address he had seen. When Lara had completed her registration, he drove with her past the dwelling located at that number and pointed it out to her.

"There's the house that was in the phone book," he said.

Lara gazed at the place Dave indicated; it was a good area and a nice home, but otherwise unremarkable. "What is it with that house?"

"Lara, I'm going to meet someone who lives there; he will be a heroin addict and he will come to faith in Christ."

"How do you know?"

"I just know," he replied.

Quite some time later, Lara was at work at the salon in Cordova Bay, cutting the hair of a teenage girl. She sensed the young person was upset, and asked concernedly, "Are you alright?"

Her client started crying, "No," she said, "I don't know what to do about my dad; he got into drugs and is addicted to heroin."

"I have a friend who helps people with problems like that," Lara told her, "and he helped me too."

"Would he help my father?" she asked.

"I'm sure he would; I'll ask him right away."

Dave told Lara to give the daughter his phone number, and within a day or two her father, Ken, phoned him.

"I understand you assist people with drug problems?" he asked.

"I try to."

"I'm addicted to heroin," he continued, "Do you think you can you help me?"

"Well, let's get together and talk."

"I don't have a car."

"I have a car and can pick you up; where do you live?"

"I live up near Camosun College."

"You live at ..." Dave gave the address he had seen some time earlier in the phone book.

There was silence. Then he said, "How could you possibly know that? I've only been here a few days!"

"How long have you been addicted to heroin?" Dave responded.

"Nine months."

"I've known I was going to meet you before you started using heroin."

This very fact helped Ken understand that whatever Dave was telling him was likely to be true; the two men met a number of times, and Ken was delivered from his addiction.

Yet the very successes he was having in his ministry caused Dave to search his heart. He didn't want to think it was his own power or goodness that turned around these lives, and a brief encounter led to some intense questioning of his own inner motivations. He had accompanied Lara to an NA meeting, and after it was over became engaged in conversation with a younger man named Ian, telling him a little of his work with Lara and the progress she had made.

"Well," Ian commented, "I can see why you would help Lara, she's gorgeous! I'd be willing to help her myself–anyone would."

The casual remark arrowed its way into Dave's heart. "Would I be doing this for her if she wasn't so attractive?" he asked himself. He wanted so much to make sure his motives were pure.

One or two evenings later, Dave was at the hospital, as one of the people to whom he was ministering had taken an overdose. There was another person in the emergency waiting room, a woman of about thirty-five years of age. She was painfully thin, and wearing a singlet top which exposed the ugly tracks snaking up and down her inner arms. Many of her teeth were missing, and she had the blemished skin that is an indicator of drug use; her hair hung in stringy locks around her gaunt face, and she offered the impression she had not bathed in weeks. Altogether, she was an object either to be pitied or scorned. Yet she must somehow have known about Dave, and came up to him.

"You're Dave Richardson?" she asked. Dave replied in the affirmative. "You help people with addiction problems?" she continued.

"I try to," he replied, looking into the pitiful eyes that stared at him out of the ravaged countenance.

"Would you help me?" she asked. "I'm addicted and I can't quit."

Dave felt a sudden wave of compassion for this wrecked specimen of humanity flow through him; it was all he could do to choke back tears. "I would be honored to help you," he said, and gave her his card.

He never did hear from this nameless woman, and came to realize the incident was sent as a reassurance to him: that he was not ministering from self-serving motives, but through God's own love that had been sent into his heart. With new eyes he looked at the example set before him in Jesus, a Saviour who never shrank from any who came to Him, but who met with publicans and harlots with His heart overflowing with mercy. Never did He speak words of condescension from afar, never did He hold back from contact with mortality and disease, but laid His hands upon sickness, even on the rotting flesh of leprosy, and it was made whole.

Dave was coming to understand that God's love could take and restore the most broken and shattered life to blessed usefulness and beauty.

CHAPTER 44
Hannah's Story

EVEN AS DAVE continued to be thankful for the spiritual gifts that had assisted him so greatly in his ministry, he came to another realization: that the *charismata* were to be exercised on behalf of those who were suffering, not from addiction, but from a variety of other causes.

Dave first met Alison through his niece Marcie, Doug's daughter. He was at his brother's place one morning when Marcie received a phone call; she put down the phone and turned to Dave. "That was my friend Alison," she said. "I'm concerned about her, because her husband has been away for a long time, and she is worried about his health. He's a Christian and living in Africa on mission work, but he's sick with a flesh-eating disease. Would you come with me and pray with her?"

Dave knew that Marcie had a beautiful, compassionate nature, and assented readily. He met Alison, prayed with her, and later went a number of times to visit her in her apartment to counsel and encourage her. On these occasions, Alison gradually unfolded to him the story of how she had met her husband. They shared an unusual relationship, to say the least.

Peter was an evangelist from Africa, who had come to Vancouver Island to speak at different churches to raise funds for his ministry and for an orphanage he was running. At one of these meetings he met Alison; he was a good-looking man, and shortly after she made his acquaintance she agreed to marry him. They spent only one night together as husband and wife before he needed to return to his ministry in Africa. She gave him what money she had to help him with funds for the work, even selling her wedding ring, and then he was gone–but Alison had fallen pregnant. She gave birth to a little boy she called William, who at that point was about five years old, and the light of her life.

However, she was by now extremely worried about her husband, whom she had not seen for some time. Apparently he was suffering from a terrible virus and needed quite a lot of money for his medical treatment; Alison was desperately trying to raise extra funds for him, and in doing so had used up all her available credit. Dave was touched by her situation and thought he would try and help; he phoned two close friends, both of whom were wealthy and generous, but as it happened one was tied up financially, and he was unable to contact the other. It then occurred to Dave that he was not supposed to ask them for assistance, and he also started to wonder if this man Peter was genuine, or whether he was using his wife.

One evening not long afterwards Dave was again visiting Alison, and during the conversation mentioned to her a phrase he heard on several occasions throughout the day:

"It's from the TV series *Kung Fu*. The central character has flashbacks to when he was a small boy, and his mentor would speak to him and say, 'Some day you will learn, Grasshopper.' Do you know it?"

"Yes, I remember it," she said.

"Well, I've heard that phrase three times today, all from different sources," he said, "and I know that means something is coming about grasshoppers."

Alison was aware of Dave's special insights, and her brow wrinkled. "I think I might know what that is," she said slowly. "I heard a news item on television, and it mentioned that in Alberta a swarm of grasshoppers had destroyed all the crops in a town."

Dave leaned forward in interest. "I used to live in Alberta," he said, "What was the name of the town?"

"Hannah," she said.

"I know that town," he said, and sat thinking for a moment. "Well, I'm not sure what it means," he said, "but I guess it will become clear."

He spent some time in prayer with Alison, then returned home. It was just a day or two later that he went to pick up Lara at Cordova Bay after she had finished her day of hairdressing. When he dropped in to the salon, she told him she was just doing her last customer.

"I'll go and wait on the beach; come down and I'll give you a ride home," he said.

It was a beautiful sunny afternoon, and while he was waiting he decided to phone Alison, knowing she was still distraught about her husband and his illness. He listened sympathetically as she talked, and then she said something which made him sit up.

"*What* did you say?" he asked.

"I said I feel like Hannah from the Book of Samuel," she repeated.

Dave's mind traveled back immediately to their previous conversation concerning the grasshopper plague in the town in Alberta. Alison didn't get the connection but he did, and he sensed the statement was significant. They continued to talk for an hour on the phone, and when the conversation finished Lara still hadn't showed up. He walked back to the salon but it was closed, and he knew without a trace of doubt she had gone into town to score heroin. Still, he had an inexplicable inner peace; he knew he was meant to have the conversation with Alison, and it was important Lara should not have interrupted it. Nor did he forget about the "Hannah" connection, and reread her story from the book of First Samuel.

Hannah was married to a man named Elkanah, a good man who loved his wife dearly, yet when the reader first encounters her she is sorrowful and cast down because she is unable to have a child. The story goes on to relate that, while she was at Shiloh during the yearly pilgrimage of the family, she was "in bitterness of soul, and prayed to the Lord and wept in anguish." She made a vow that, if the Lord should remember her and grant her a son, she would give him back to the Lord to serve Him all the days of his life. After she had poured out her soul in this intense supplication, Eli the priest spoke to her: "Go in peace, and may the God of Israel grant your petition which you have asked of Him." And Hannah conceived and bore a son whom she named Samuel; he became one of the greatest prophets of Israel.

As he read through the narrative Dave couldn't see the parallel of Alison's situation with that of Hannah, apart from the matter of the extreme grief they shared, because Alison already had a child. Nevertheless, he felt sure its significance would emerge. A few weeks later he was once again at his brother Doug's place and Marcie also was there. She was planning on taking her two small girls to a playground, as well as Alison's little boy, William, who she was looking after. She asked Dave if he would like to join them, and when he drove there he saw around sixty small children romping on the grass, enjoying the beautiful warm morning. Marcie had put out a blanket and was watching the two girls as they played, then saw him arriving.

"Uncle Dave," she said, "do you mind keeping an eye on William for a bit? I'm going to take the girls to the washroom."

She and her daughters vanished in the direction of the restroom, and Dave sat down on the blanket with his Bible beside him. As he gazed at the scene in front of him he felt enveloped in a sense of supernatural awareness, and knew he should be alert. He looked again at the children, and noticed they had all put their lunch boxes and bags in a big circle on the grass away from the play area; as his eyes scanned this pile, his attention was drawn to a thermos on which a boy's name was written in black marking pen. The name was Luke.

No sooner had he noted that, than his gaze shifted a little to the right, and there was William sitting at the top of a slide. His gaze on the young boy, and thinking of the name on the thermos, Dave began praying, "Are you telling me to look in Luke's Gospel?" he asked. "What chapter, Lord?" At the same moment, his gaze sharpened and focused on the little sports jersey that William was wearing; on the front, written in large letters, was the number 22.

Dave knew straight away that he should look at Chapter 22 of Luke, and reached for his Bible, wondering what he would see. He leafed through the pages and found the place where the chapter began. His eye was immediately drawn to the heading of the chapter, which stood out in bold print, and as he looked at it everything suddenly fell into place–Alison's misery, her husband's absence, and all the confusion of the situation. The three words of the heading read simply as follows: "*Peter Disowns Jesus.*" It was the start of the gospel passage which relates how the leader of the disciples, Peter, denied knowing the Lord on the night He was betrayed.

Peter, of course, was the name of Alison's husband, and Dave knew instantly as he looked at the heading that the man's whole story was a sham. He was digesting this new information as Marcie came back and sat beside him; he explained to her what had occurred as she listened wide-eyed. She knew that what he said bore the ring of truth, and her countenance became filled with foreboding.

"How are we going to tell this to Alison?" she asked.

They looked at one another silently, knowing it was not an easy task that confronted them.

Alison came over to Marcie's place that afternoon after she had finished work to pick up her son. "Alison, we have to talk," said Marcie, and the three went outside and found a picnic table. "I want to tell you something that happened today," continued Marcie after they were seated, and went on to relate everything that had transpired that morning.

Alison began crying as she told the story, and was shaking her head in disbelief. "It's true, Alison," said Marcie gently. "I was there and I saw it all happen."

Dave interrupted suddenly. "What was William doing wearing that shirt, the one with the number 22?"

Alison looked at him in surprise. "How could you know that–that it wasn't William's shirt?"

"I don't know," he said, "I just knew."

"I'd washed his shirt but the dryer wouldn't work, so I had to borrow that shirt from my neighbor," she said slowly.

Dave could see that, although she was professing not to accept what they were saying, the reality was beginning to sink in. Dave himself was happy that he didn't have to say directly to Alison, "Your husband is a charlatan"; rather they were able to narrate the events of the morning and let her draw her own conclusions. He also felt strongly that in the whole sorry situation there were several rays of hope.

The first concerned her husband, Peter. "There is something that is important in this from Luke 22," he said to her urgently. "The chapter heading states that 'Peter disowns Jesus,' yet you know that eventually, after he repents, Peter is reinstated and becomes one of the greatest of the apostles. So pray for Peter, your husband, that he returns to his faith."

Alison, her head bowed, nodded wordlessly. Dave looked at her, remembering how she had said she felt just like Hannah, sobbing and crying.

"Another thing," he said, "and this is probably the most important part." He reached out and took her hand gently, and she raised her head to look into his eyes. "Alison," he continued, "you're a type of Hannah, and your son William is a type of Samuel. Just as God blessed Hannah with a pregnancy, so He blessed you. William is the Lord's gift to you, and you need to dedicate him to God just as Hannah dedicated Samuel."

Alison's eyes were fixed upon him as she listened, and even in their depth of misery Dave thought he saw a spark of hope. "Just concentrate on that," he said.

He opened his Bible and found Hannah's song of thanksgiving, the lyrical ascription of praise composed by this remarkable mother in Israel, who had so early comprehended the character of the God her people worshiped. In words that were both passionate and prophetic she extolled His strength and greatness, His complete sovereignty over the world, and His power to alter any situation, no matter how desperate. Dave knew that in these inspired phrases God was providing a message to comfort and reassure His daughter Alison, and that in the future He would strengthen her to meet the challenges of her situation.

No one is holy like the LORD,
For there is none besides You,
Nor is there any rock like our God ...
The LORD kills and makes alive;
He brings down to the grave and brings up.
The LORD makes poor and makes rich;
He brings low and lifts up.
He raises the poor from the dust
And lifts the beggar from the ash heap,
To set them among princes
And make them inherit the throne of glory.
For the pillars of the earth are the LORD's,
And He has set the world upon them (1 Samuel 2:2,6-8).

AND THEN, THERE was Carla.

One evening, Dave was at a Bible study and one of the participants, who knew Dave was involved in work with addicts, took him aside and produced a photograph from a local paper. It showed a young girl sitting on a bridge, being talked out of suicide by the police.

"I know this girl, she really needs prayer."

"Who is she?"

"Her name is Carla."

"Yes, I'll pray."

Following this incident, Dave was at the detox clinic, and after he finished speaking with one of his counselees a young First Nations woman came up to him.

"Excuse me," she said, "I overheard what you were saying, and I was wondering if you might be able to talk with me?"

"Sure, I can come back and talk ... what's your name?"

"Carla."

Dave always had a special empathy with the First Nations people, ever since his days at primary school, a little place called Craigflower down by the Gorge. A good percentage of the students at the school came from the reserve located just across the bridge, so he grew up with them side by side. He knew he was as welcome in their homes as they were in his, and loved the warmth shown in their families. Only one thing bothered him, and that was when they played Cowboys and Indians.

"How come I never get to be an Indian?" he would ask.

"Because you're not one, of course!" they would chorus.

As he grew older, and hockey and baseball became substituted for childhood games, Dave continued to value his relationship with these early friends. Also, as he grew to manhood, he became aware of the distinctive culture and tumultuous history of the First Nations people.

As recently as two hundred years ago, the northwest coast of North America was one of the least explored places on the planet. The geography of the land presented many formidable natural barriers to European explorers: to the east the soaring Rocky Mountains, and to the west the vast Pacific. Prior to the advent of the Europeans, the area was home to many different tribes. On Vancouver Island, the Indian way of life was based on the generous bounty of the earth, while their spirituality lay fundamentally in reverence for the natural world. This land of misty forests, awe-inspiring mountains, sparkling rivers and lakes held the fulfillment of every physical and spiritual need, and the inherent sacredness of earth and sky lived in the souls of every member of their race. As such, the Indigenous tribes were charged with the responsibility of being caretakers of the land. In the words of Chief Sealth (also known as Seattle):

> *Every part of this earth is sacred to my people. Every shining pine needle, every sandy shore, every mist in the dark woods, every clearing, and humming insect is holy in the memory and experience of my people.*

Yet this hidden world was about to be drastically altered.

In 1778, Captain James Cook, in search of the legendary Northwest passage, set foot on Nootka Island on the northwest coast of Vancouver Island; the Spanish also arrived and set up a base. Shortly thereafter, adventurous explorers and fur traders were heading west across the Rockies, blazing a trail through an unexplored pass long known to the First Nations people. Struggles by various European powers for control of the territory and its lucrative resources followed, while the commercial ventures caused the Indigenous peoples to abandon their traditional homesites in favor of settlements close to the forts. The newcomers also introduced muskets, alcohol and smallpox, all of which had a devastating effect on the native peoples.

The Hudson's Bay Company built Fort Victoria in 1843, and in 1858 gold was discovered inland in the Fraser Canyon and the Cariboo region. Prospectors flocked to Victoria, the only ocean port and outfitting center on their way to the gold fields. In response to this discovery the British Government quickly created the mainland colony of British Columbia with Victoria as the capital. In the following years, as the powerful cadre of merchant adventurers turned their attention from gold to coal, then moved to lumber and other natural resources, the prosperity of the new colony burgeoned. Inevitably, land ownership conflicts also followed.

There was a fundamental misunderstanding in the early dialogues between the Native American peoples and the Europeans who sought to purchase their land. Long before the first settlers arrived, the Indian tribes had developed sophisticated legal systems that incorporated treaties, delineated rights and specified ways to resolve disputes. None, however, had any institution like the "land title" of the Europeans. The earth and the fruits of it belonged to all, and as such they had no tradition of "alienating," or relinquishing rights to the land. In the words of Chief Sealth[31]:

> *The earth does not belong to man; man belongs to the earth. This we know. All things are connected like the blood which unites one family. You may think now that you own Him as you wish to own our land; but you cannot. He is the God of man, and His compassion is equal for the red man and the white. This earth is precious to Him, and to harm the earth is to heap contempt on its Creator.*

Treaty after treaty now relocated the Indians, and frequently corrupt means were used to compel them to forfeit their territory. Lacking the technology and weapons of the Europeans, the Indians were eventually forced to subsist in a total area only a fraction of that which they had once occupied. In British Columbia itself, while few treaties were signed, the First Nations were confined to small, scattered reserves, where they had only restricted access to the timber, mineral or water resources around which the new economies were being constructed. For many years also, the government also developed policies aimed at eliminating the diverse languages and customs of the tribes.

However, despite the huge impact of the European arrival, this dynamic culture eventually reasserted itself. In 2005, the Government of British Columbia and the First Nations Leadership Council entered a new relationship founded on respect, reconciliation and recognition of Aboriginal title and rights. Today there are approximately 200,000 native people in B.C., and the province has the greatest diversity of First Nations cultures in Canada. The amalgam of their traditions with those of the West can be seen throughout Vancouver Island, with its unique combination of spectacular wilderness, European sophistication, and evidence of the vibrant First Nations way of life, especially noticeable in their impressive artwork and wood carvings.

Nevertheless, this period in the history of the First Nations people in Canada involved a cataclysmic upheaval of their society and way of life that has affected them to the present day. Native peoples in Canada suffer from high rates of unemployment, poverty and breakdown of family relationships, as well as other adverse socioeconomic circumstances, factors which in turn often lead to substance addiction and suicide. As Dave began ministering to Carla, he began to learn firsthand about those problems. He in turn shared with her his conviction that her problem was not primarily with drugs and alcohol, but involved a spiritual dimension. She listened to his words and was persuaded to become a Christian, then finally was well enough to leave the detox unit.

Yet Carla's days of struggle were far from over. She was naturally high spirited, and the episodes with drug-taking had only increased this volatile element in her personality. She assumed, as did many, the minute she came to faith all temptation to use drugs would be gone, and she could simply resume her life as it was before. In fact, she had embarked on a long battle—and Dave was there to share it with her.

He was taking Carla to church, to New Life and Arbutus Fellowship, and as she got to know the people there she gradually built a network of support. Dave also got to meet Carla's family: her mother Odette, and her sisters and brothers; Carla also had two charming small children, Timmy and Juliette. Dave counted his friendship with this extended clan of First Nations people a great privilege. He told Odette, who was a tower of strength for her sons and daughters throughout their various challenges, "If you ever want someone to talk to, I'm here," and they would go to Tim Horton's and have coffee and just share.

Still, Dave's ministry with Carla was proving something of a saga. He arranged for her to go to Lydia Home on the mainland, an excellent facility for recovering female addicts; she was there for three months, and at the end of that time Dave went over to her graduation with Odette and other family members. Coming back on the ferry, they saw the most magnificent sunset. The sapphire sky had paled toward evening, and as the sun sank lower a rich golden light suffused the heavens, turning the Gulf waters below to molten fire. Then, as the sun dropped below the horizon, the dazzling light softened into pastel hues, adorning the great vault of the sky and painting the snow-tipped mountains behind with splendor. The little group watched in awe, and as the first stars began to blaze in the clear sky, it seemed to Dave a tangible reiteration of God's promises.

Yet although Carla was clean for a time, she then relapsed heavily into the world of drugs, and was drawn inexorably into a tough and vicious circle. Dave didn't see her for a long while, but eventually she called and they met together in a park to talk.

"Carla," he said, "I think you need another time in a recovery center, something more comprehensive. Teen Challenge on the mainland is a wonderful facility; I know the director, and can get you in if you decide to go."

She thought for a few minutes and replied slowly. "You know my stepfather says that my addiction will go away if I just have the right medication."

This led to a serious heart-to-heart conversation about her life, and how much there might be left–or not left–of it. Dave laid out her options: "You can listen to your stepfather," he said, "and go on medication–and I respect his opinion. Or you can accept this is a spiritual battle, that your whole life needs to change, and go to Teen Challenge. However, it has to be your decision." Dave knew that if he talked her into going, and it failed, she would have reason to blame him.

Carla was very quiet in that hour of sharing, weighing her options. "I want to think about it," she finally said.

"That's a good thing to do, I'll leave you here," said Dave.

He walked up the hill away from her, then stopped and looked back, and never forgot that sight. Carla was sitting in the midst of a huge field, a tiny figure who looked completely alone; she seemed to him at that moment somehow to embody the strugglings and sufferings of her people. He prayed she would make the right decision and waited for her at her home. After an hour she came back and said,

"I'm going."

Dave took her over to Teen Challenge in the Fraser Valley, a home in a beautiful setting, and visited her while she was there, taking Odette and Timmy; they also went for her baptism in Abbotsford. It was an emotional moment, and Carla's life seemed transformed after her long haul, but in fact, it was just an interlude. She did well for a while, then had a major relapse and went back heavily to drugs. Once again she phoned Dave needing help, and again he met her in the park. She was wearing tight, revealing clothes, on crystal meth, and her head was spinning like a top; she was absolutely terrified of shadows, of darkness, of everything.

"This time I'm going to die, Dave," she said.

He got her back into another program on the mainland, and again she seemed to be doing well. While she was there, however, her uncle died. He had been a member of the Ahousaht Band, and the funeral was to take place at the reserve, located on a small island off the west coast of Vancouver Island. Carla very much wanted to attend the funeral, but at that stage could still not be left alone, so Dave picked her up at the ferry at Nanaimo, and they drove together across the Island to Tofino. Together they marveled at the scenery on the west coast, justly famed for its wild untamed beauty. Surging blue waves are held back by perfect white beaches, and further framed by towering pines, tipped golden in the sunlight. And behind all, the majestic snow-capped mountains which dominate the northern end of the Island.

The two travelers set off from the harbor in a small speedboat; it was a forty-minute ride to the reserve, and once there it seemed to Dave he was stepping into a different place and time. Beside the dock and in the harbor were sunken boats, the roads were unpaved, and the homes ill-maintained. He discovered that about five hundred people lived on the island, many of them related, all part of the Ahousaht Band. Quite a number of people had come for the funeral of Carla's uncle, for he was a man of honor in the native community, and all the houses were full. Dave slept on the floor of Carla's grandmother's house and attended the memorial service the next day; the whole time he was observing the scene with an intensity of insight, consciously aware of the spiritual battle which had enmeshed the First Nations people.

He watched the faces of the men and women about him, reflecting the innate dignity and pride of their race, yet also revealing lines of suffering carved in the mahogany of their countenances. Few expressions were hawk-like or fierce; rather, this people seemed subdued and chastened and many, he knew, were escaping their problems with alcohol and drugs. His heart seemed full to bursting with the compassion he felt for them. The contrast between the almost mystical allure of the landscape through which he had traveled, and the present living conditions of the people who had once roamed this land in such nobility and freedom, depressed him profoundly.

It was difficult to tear Carla away from her family and friends, but she returned to Lydia Home once again, and this time seemed truly to have turned her life around. Then she met a good man, also called David, and they planned to get married and build their family together. Once again Carla was filled with laughter and her own special joie de vivre; after the wedding she started to build her life afresh and to manifest a radiant new womanhood.

Around this time, Carla's family called Dave and asked him to come over for the evening. The room was full of Carla's First Nations relatives; Dave was the only European there. And then her Uncle Carl stood up and formally thanked him in the presence of all who were there.

"We want to let you know how grateful we are for everything you've done for Carla," he said, and held out a gift.

Dave took the artifact Carl presented to him. It was a native paddle, about five feet in length, carved from a single piece of maple wood and beautifully finished. He knew that through this gift he was being given an honorary place in their family, and was overwhelmed. As he gazed at the paddle and gave his thanks, his mind flew back to the detox unit at the beginning of his journey, when he had seen the First Nations man in the waiting room and told Jan he had come to learn to carve totem poles. He knew just how far God had brought him, and was filled with gratitude.

And there was another wonderful event awaiting Dave in the days ahead.

PART V:

IT WAS ALL OUT OF LOVE

CHAPTER 46

The Theme of Lara's Story: *Agape*

DAVE ALMOST HELD his breath as the scene unfolded before his eyes, as if it were fragile as a dream that vanishes with dawn, as if the merest shimmer of air might shatter the delicate tableau he was witnessing. And yet what was taking place was something firm and definite; it was occurring in a spiritual realm, but the results would be revealed in the natural and physical.

It was an ordinary morning in Victoria. Outside the skies were drawn and gray, for winter was approaching, but the scene transpiring in Bob Holmes' small office seemed light-filled to Dave. The elderly pastor was there, the black, leather-bound Bible in his right hand. Dave's brother Don, who was visiting his hometown, was also present. There was Dave himself, and the fourth person in the room was Lara. Her head was bowed, and she was listening to Bob as he was speaking about God's gift of Jesus, of the Saviour's death upon the cross, of His resurrection, of the greatness of His love for her. And now Bob was speaking to her directly.

"Lara, do you want to accept Jesus Christ as your own Lord and Saviour?"

"Yes, I do," came the soft reply.

"Do you repent of your sins, and trust in the power of His cross and blood to cleanse you from all unrighteousness?"

She nodded. Bob laid his hands gently on Lara's head and prayed for her, the other two men joining in. It was a sacred moment and the culmination of a long journey, and Dave's heart was full as they drove back to his apartment.

That night he was soundly asleep, when something woke him with a start. He opened his eyes and saw a figure standing beside his bed, and at the same time heard a whisper. He could hardly make out the words, "Help me." He reached over to the bedside light and turned it on, and there was Lara standing there in her nightclothes, tears coming down her face, trembling, clearly too terrified to speak aloud.

"Help me," she breathed again, and now he was waking up, asking her what was wrong, but she had turned around and walked out of the room. Dave got up and followed, and found her sitting in the kitchen; she had both feet up on the chair, her arms wrapped round her knees and was shaking and crying. She looked so small and fragile that he was filled with pity and a terrible apprehension.

"What's happened, Lara?" he asked.

"I was in bed," she told him between sobs, "and all of a sudden I felt a presence in the room and knew I wasn't alone, and when I looked I saw a dark shape in the corner, and it was moving."

"Could you see what it was?" he asked.

"It was like a black shadow, and it would turn and then disappear, as if it was two dimensional. I didn't know if I was awake or asleep, but I got out of bed and was going to go to you for help. And then when I got to the doorway of my room …" She broke off and started crying again.

"This thing–this demon–it was there, Dave, it had taken the shape of a person, and somehow he had *made himself look like you.* Just like you, except he was shorter and heavier, he was trying to make you look ugly. And I was so confused. And then he, it, spoke to me, and even his voice was like yours, but not quite."

"What did it say?"

"It said, '*He* can't help you now.' And I knew he was referring to Jesus, and also to you. And I was terrified, I was never so afraid in my life." She hugged her knees, her slender frame still shaking.

"What happened then?" he asked.

"Then I wanted to try and escape, but when I looked at the door into the hallway, I could see it was nailed shut. And then it–he–told me that I was his and belonged to him for eternity, and he took a knife and slashed it across my stomach. Oh, God …"

Lara paused and went on, speaking slowly, as if reliving the horror. "And Dave, I watched him reach inside me and pull something out–and I saw it was a baby I was carrying …"

Dave exclaimed involuntarily and she went on. "And he said, 'This is what you get for the way you've been living, all you've done, all the swear words you've been using.' And then he reminded me of all the bad things I had done, and all I could think about was getting to you for help, but he reminded me that he *was* you."

Dave continued to listen quietly. He understood how she had felt absolutely cornered, with the door to the hallway nailed shut, and terrified of himself because he was suddenly the enemy. He patted her shoulder, and her trembling subsided a little. "What happened then?" he prompted her again.

"And then when he saw I didn't believe him, he started trying to convince me that you were evil and that I couldn't trust you. He was very persuasive … and then I had to take a chance." She paused, and went on, "And I said to him, 'No, Dave is *not like that*. Dave is *love*.'"

Dave felt a rush of relief and thankfulness.

"And then I looked, and the door was open again. So I made my way into your room, but when I spoke to you my voice wouldn't work, all I could get out was 'Help me,' and I thought I couldn't make you hear me. Then when you woke up and turned on the light, I was afraid you were going to attack me." The tears flowed again.

"Listen, Lara," he said to her urgently, "This is the devil, retaliating because you've turned to Christ. He's trying to accuse you of all your former sins, and make you feel unforgiven. The truth is, you've had a major victory here, you had the courage to stand against him."

He continued reassuring her in this vein for some time, and she gradually calmed down until peace reigned again in their household.

Dave knew that Lara did achieve a major breakthrough in the spiritual realm that night as she held steadfastly in faith to what she believed to be the truth. After that traumatic evening she went from strength to strength, and shortly thereafter was baptized, together with Andre and Nolan. As she was submerged in the waters and came up again, radiant in her newfound faith, Dave was filled with thanksgiving. He was proud of his little flock, knowing everything they had been through.

Dave himself was baptized at almost the same time by his brother Don, who was still visiting Victoria. What stayed in his mind long after the ceremony was over was the picture of Lara, seated in the front row. Before undergoing the rite, Dave had spoken briefly to the people gathered in the church. "I want to thank someone here today," he said, "who has been an example of strength to me—and that person is Lara." Dave saw the ready tears spring to her eyes at the unexpected tribute. "It's her strength that has given me strength, and helped bring me to this day," he added.

It was true Dave saw in Lara a depth of character she didn't know she had. She had been, as it were, the catalyst for his own path toward finding God; in fact, his journey and hers were intertwined and inseparable, as if it was designed that way. Dave knew also that their pilgrimage together was drawing to its predetermined end.

Right at the beginning of their relationship, he had drawn for her a diagram of a circle with a number of stick figures inside. He pointed to them. "These are your family members, Lara," he said. And then he drew two more figures, this time outside the sphere. "And this is you and me, outside the circle," he continued. "You've been cast out, but one day …" he drew a line from the figures outside to the middle of the circle, "you'll be the centerpiece of your family." He paused and looked at her, then drew another line, back outside the sphere. "I'll bring you back in—and then I leave the circle."

Dave knew this time was drawing closer. Nevertheless, he also remembered how Lara had said that everyone she loved had left her, and understood this was a major issue for her. Not long after his baptism, they were walking together in Mount Douglas Park, and Lara was fighting a mood of sadness. "Everyone I've ever loved has gone away, and you will too," she said.

"No, I won't," he said.

"Yes, you will."

They were passing a large tree, and he stopped and concealed himself behind the trunk; Lara kept walking with her head bowed. After she continued about twenty feet, she realized he was no longer beside her.

"Dave, where are you?" He didn't reply. "Dave, what are you doing!" She retraced her steps and saw him behind the tree.

"How did you know I was here?" he asked.

"I just knew, because you had been there."

"Lara," he said, "I'll always be there for you. And so will the Lord, even though you can't see Him. He's promised that He will never leave you nor forsake you. So remember the tree!"

And Lara smiled …

For Dave, it all came back to the message of First Corinthians 13, the great love chapter. The story of Lara, from beginning to end, was completely about love: the absence of love and the need for love, and Dave knew that everything he had done for her was as a result of the outpouring of God's own *agape* for Lara, the wonderful, abounding love from the heart of the Father.

Another momentous event transpired around the same time as this conversation. At a Bible study in John Schaper's house a young man was present by the name of Jason; he was tall and handsome, with an open and honest countenance and a gentle manner. Dave liked him instantly.

"He might be the one for Lara!" he thought. "I'll do the introductions—and Lord, if this is from You, You do the rest!"

CHAPTER 47

A Free and Gentle Flower, Growing Wild

DAVE CONSIDERED HIMSELF blessed to have grown up in the Fifties and Sixties, an era when incomparable popular ballads filled the airwaves. Even as a child, he loved the unabashed romanticism of the lyrics then being composed, and as a young man was swept away by the passionate idealism of songs such as "Twilight Time" by the Platters. As he grew older, he realized the lyrics of that era might be thought over-sentimental. Still he felt that, if such were the case, the pendulum had swung much too far in the other direction.

At one stage he was asked to give a course in songwriting, and, although he didn't really believe this was something that could be taught, there were certain guidelines he could impart. He emphasized it was important to avoid "flowery" language, and instead to use simple words that could be put together creatively. Particular examples were the songs of Jim Webb, such as "McArthur Park" and "By the Time I Get to Phoenix." The lines of Kris Kristofferson's "Loving Her Was Easier" were brilliant, but Dave stressed that Kristofferson was one of the few writers who could get away with such complexity. The songs he delighted in most were those he wished that he himself had written; "Fields of Gold" by Sting was a particular favorite.

He thought it interesting that his own song "Wildflower," although a love ballad, did not actually mention the word "love" at all. The phrases he wrote were simple, disguising their emotional depth, but in the central part, the "bridge" of the song, the poet's own feelings concerning this "free and gentle flower" of whom he writes are made manifest. It was her unique qualities of longsuffering and kindness which made her so precious in his sight and inspired his longing for her; it was as if his eyes alone could perceive her loveliness of character, as a thing apart from her physical beauty, and he could only marvel at the fragility which concealed such inner strength:

And if by chance that I should hold her
Let me hold her for a time
But if allowed just one possession
I would pick her from the garden
To be mine.

Dave continued to be overwhelmed by the continuing success of his composition. Over six decades "Wildflower" had become one of the most performed songs in Canadian popular music, sung at weddings, funerals, graduations and the Olympics. It has been recorded in every imaginable genre by more than one hundred artists, including Johnny Mathis, Hank Crawford, The O'Jays, The New Birth, Blake Shelton, The Neville Brothers, and Lisa Fischer. It's been sampled by Tupac Shakur, Kanye West, Jamie Foxx and many others. In 1990, it was honored with a BMI Millionaire Award, joining the small percentage of hit songs that receive more than one million radio plays in the United States.

The simple poem written by a Canadian policeman as a homage to his nurse girlfriend has also become beloved around the world. It was the only English song on Cantonese superstar Sandy Lam's classic CD "Wildflower," and sung by Arnel Pineda as the title and theme song for a 200-episode docudrama in the Philippines. The 1990s TV series "New York Undercover" featured "Wildflower" (although the producers didn't know the song was written by a cop), as did the 2018 Tupac Shakur biopic "Unsolved." The song is treasured in its home country as well. In 1988, "Wildflower" received a PROCAN Crystal Award for radio performances in Canada, and in 2011 the song and its writers were inducted into the Canadian Song Writers Hall of Fame.

Dave's song seems to have an appeal which transcends its time and setting, and especially to have a power to comfort persons in situations of emotional and spiritual distress. For this reason, "Wildflower" has served as the soundtrack for a US Army video counseling female veterans with PTSD, as accompaniment to a service for victims of the Columbine tragedy, and as inspiration in a book about recovery from childhood sexual abuse. Performed by British jazz luminary Liane Carroll, it is featured in "Humanité–The Beloved Community," Kirk Whalum's musical documentary promoting global harmony.

Many have tried to account for the lasting influence of the song. Perhaps, it is suggested, it is the tenderness and compassion expressed in the lyrics that causes to them resonate with women of all ages and backgrounds. David Foster's analysis is more penetrating. He discerned it was the melding of the two opposing sides of Dave's character, both the tough law enforcement officer and the poet, which enabled him to compose such beautiful and haunting words. There were few who could write a lyric that "burned into"[32] one as deeply as did "Wildflower," he averred, stating his belief that in this song Dave had accomplished the near impossible. And, concluded Foster, he had done this purely out of his love for writing and not for any other reason—another aspect of his character which made him stand out from others.

At this point in his life, having witnessed the amazing impact of the ballad on so many lives, Dave came to a new understanding: he felt it was God Himself who inspired the song, and he had simply held the pen while the words flowed from above. Now in the final days of his ministry to Lara, he was realizing that the compassion expressed in the lyrics was extended also to her, that she was the one who had faced "the hardest times you could imagine," whose "eyes had fought back the tears" on so many occasions, but was granted strength to overcome and turn her life around. Lara was *par example* the "free and gentle flower, growing wild," and God Himself was the witness to her sufferings, and had sent Dave to help her.

After her baptism, Dave was seeing Lara become transformed. Her spiritual debts were forgiven, and with his guidance she became free of her financial debts also. Her hairdressing career flourished, and Lara herself grew in beauty and vitality; all the joy of living was returning to her. Most remarkably, the disfiguring "tracks" which marred her inner arms vanished away, seemingly overnight. And, all the time, her relationship with Jason was flourishing.

One song more than all others seemed to Dave to recapitulate his battle for Lara's life, and for many others he counseled over those years. It was a poem he had written back in his police days, entitled "The Pen and The Gun," expressing the two sides of his character which supplied the impetus for his actions throughout his whole life. The chorus went as follows:

> *I dream a shadow fallen on the street,*
> *And the last words he said were written in red*
> *As he handed me his pen and his gun, saying*
> *Take one and run; there are words and there are deeds to be done,*
> *A choice of two lives to be living, with time enough only for one;*
> *The hand that writes the love song also holds the gun,*
> *And strangely enough*
> *It's all out of love …*

The song, written so early in his career, seemed an anticipation of the days when Dave would be battling, not against the "bad guys" as in the days when he wore a uniform, but against the more hidden and sinister enemies of the souls of men and women. Even more that that, it revealed the mysterious kinship he had come to feel with one of the greatest figures in the Hebrew scriptures.

CHAPTER 48

The Lost Chord

AS DAVE CONTINUED To study the Bible, he was time and again drawn to the rich deposit of stories that clustered around his own namesake, David. This most famous ruler of Israel, in his many roles–fighter, lover, friend, husband, king and father–was endlessly fascinating. In the King's adventures, misfortunes and triumphs, Dave seemed to see reflected as in a glass his own history.

In particular, as one who had fought against crime and injustice all his life, he could identify King David the warrior, who had faced evil in many guises, and taken up arms against it. His foes included the giant Goliath, whom he slew in that famous encounter, and the tormented figure of Saul, who descended into madness in his jealousy toward the young hero whom the people loved. Numerous were David's other enemies, and many and fierce the battles he fought; even when he was old, his son Absalom rebelled against him in an ultimate act of betrayal. There was little David did not know about what was in the hearts of men.

Yet the King of Israel was poet as well as warrior, and Dave could also trace his likeness to the one who, for the range and beauty of his compositions, was named "the sweet psalmist of Israel." All the chords of David's harp seemed wrung from him in extremes of either distress or joy, so his songs scaled the heights and sounded the depths of human emotion. Even as he unveiled his inmost heart before God in his psalms, while proclaiming his steadfast trust in the Lord's goodness, those myriad experiences in his life were transmuted to words–*living* words, capturing the essence of worship. As such, his psalms have spoken with unparalleled power to lovers of God throughout the three thousand years since they were first set down.

The Canadian poet Leonard Cohen at one stage wrote an inspired song called "Hallelujah," in which he paid tribute to King David's genius, and suggested there was a "secret chord" David played that was pleasing to the Lord. And as he listened to the words of Cohen's song, this present-day David found himself pondering what it was that made the King of Israel the archetypal poet and music-maker. What was this "secret chord" the former David had discovered?

Dave knew well the truth Shakespeare had immortalized: that music was the food of love. Now he knew that God was Himself Love and the Originator of every impulse of love within the human breast; also, that He had created the universe out of love. There is recorded in the book of Job the remembrance of a former time when *the morning stars sang together, And all the sons of God shouted for joy* (38:7). Music was built into the heart of the creation, and all the elements were called upon to praise the Lord, so the original song has of joy has always been sounding throughout the universe. The earth itself, the realm of nature, the great luminous orbs above and the shimmering stars of light, all moving in their appointed spheres, are permeated with this celestial music–a response to the love which has brought all things into being, which far transcends any earthly sound.

The situation in the world today is that this original perfect harmony has been disrupted through the entrance of sin and suffering, and the consequent subjection of creation to "the bondage of corruption" (Romans 8:21). Yet deep in the souls of men and women still glimmers a faint memory, of a time when the original lords of the earth were endowed with a peace, power and joy that has since fled. In the hearts of people everywhere is an inarticulate yearning for wholeness, freedom, for life in its fullness, for that "one lost chord divine."[33] Because, as Cohen expressed it in his song, so often what we have learned of love has only brought forth "a cold and broken hallelujah. "

However, there is a way back–and King David had discovered it.

There was a great disaster in David's life, a terrible fall from grace, and Cohen's song goes on to speak about his affair with the lovely Bathsheba. After that fateful moment when he saw her bathing on the roof, God's king was caught up in an entanglement involving adultery, treachery and murder. When finally confronted with his transgression he was overcome with remorse, and out of that devastating experience composed the exquisite Psalm 51, which enlarges our understanding of God's grace in a manner never previously conceived.

The psalm opens with David's appeal to the sheer magnitude of God's goodness, and continues as he takes full ownership of his sin, using a wide range of Hebrew terms, and revealing the terrible pain this consciousness is causing him:

> *Have mercy upon me, O God,*
> *According to Your lovingkindness;*
> *According to the multitude of Your tender mercies,*

Blot out my transgressions.
Wash me thoroughly from my iniquity,
And cleanse me from my sin.
For I acknowledge my transgressions,
And my sin is always before me (vv. 1-3)

The law condemned David, as did his own conscience. The result was such anguish as to put all his nature "out of joint," as if his very bones were crushed. In his longing for forgiveness, the king utters a number of daring petitions, pushing his conception of God's mercy into a dazzling infinity. He used four verbs to describe his sin, but now utilizes more than twenty metaphors to proclaim his belief in God's power to so completely wash away his guilt that he becomes "whiter than snow." In this way, he anticipates the new covenant a thousand years before the time of Christ:

Behold, You desire truth in the inward parts,
And in the hidden part You will make me to know wisdom.
Purge me with hyssop, and I shall be clean;
Wash me, and I shall be whiter than snow.
Make me hear joy and gladness,
That the bones You have broken may rejoice.
Hide Your face from my sins,
And blot out all my iniquities (vv. 6-9).

The king then prays to be created anew, utilizing the same verb, *bara*, which describes God's original work of creation in Genesis, affirming that God's recreation of his life is of a kind that can only be compared with the divine handiwork at the foundation of the world:

Create in me a clean heart, O God,
And renew a steadfast spirit within me.
Do not cast me away from Your presence,
And do not take Your Holy Spirit from me (vv. 10-11).

Yet now the psalmist extends his petitions even further; he wants not merely peace of mind, but the exultant joy experienced by those who find themselves dwelling once again in the light of God's presence. Nor is this reinstatement for

271

himself alone; it is instead that he might lead others to find the same grace and favor:

> *Restore to me the joy of Your salvation,*
> *And uphold me by Your generous Spirit.*
> *Then I will teach transgressors Your ways,*
> *And sinners shall be converted to You* (vv. 12-13).

There is surely no greater example of the vastness of God's mercy, and the exchange of scarlet sin into snow-white purity, than the subsequent marriage of David and Bathsheba, from which followed the birth of Solomon, the peaceful king.

Since he had come back to the Lord, Dave himself had turned many times to Psalm 51. He felt the king of Israel had never been delineated more clearly than in his songs of penitence–those confessions of the sin which caused a separation from the Lord and brought such sorrow into his life. The king never sought to hide or cover his "bloodguiltiness," and to Dave it was this above all that made him the "man after God's own heart." Although Israel's greatest ruler, he humbled himself under the hand of God in the hope that this relationship, more precious to him than anything else in life, might be restored.

And as Dave looked back over his own life in light of the scriptures, he came to understand the depth of the abyss from which he himself was drawn, and into which his sins were now cast, through a mercy unfathomable in its extent.

King David had found the key to true worship and made free of it to many others. Yet Dave understood more clearly than his great namesake that it was God's love in Jesus Christ that had brought him into a place of acceptance and renewal. Now he also, together with countless numbers of the redeemed, was enabled through the indwelling Spirit to hear again strains of the everlasting song of love, bringing intimations of the world beyond. One day, he knew, according to John's vision in the Book of Revelation, the whole of creation would resound with the Song of the Lamb around the throne of Deity, rising transcendent through the heavenly spheres, until every creature in heaven, and on earth, and under the earth, could be heard singing and saying,

> *Blessing and honor and glory and power*
> *Be to Him who sits on the throne,*
> *And to the Lamb, forever and ever!* (Revelation 5:13).

CHAPTER 49

Love Never Fails

IT WAS A late summer afternoon, just over a year since Dave had told Lara of the promises he had received concerning her on that amazing afternoon in Duncan. He was driving Lara to attend a meeting; it was a perfect day and the sky was cloudless, as if painted a deep cerulean. They were driving eastwards, and the sun was behind them as they turned off the highway onto MacKenzie Avenue, and as Dave drove he felt Lara suddenly stiffen in the seat beside him. His initial thought was she was afraid they were going to hit a small animal, and he looked at her swiftly in enquiry. Conscious of his gaze upon her, she pointed wordlessly up through the windshield with her finger, and Dave looked in that direction.

There in front of them, fairly low in the sky and floating above the tree line, were four small white clouds, distinct against the vivid blue background. They were completely separate, perfectly symmetrical and spaced exactly, as if someone had taken a white marking pen and printed four letters in capitals, spelling out the name:

LARA

Almost without conscious volition, Dave hit the brakes, somehow found the indicator, and pulled over to the side of the road. Together they gazed speechlessly at the astonishing sight before them, until Lara finally managed to articulate some words:

"I think I'm trippin' out!" she said.

And then, in a voice filled with wonder, she added, "Is that my name in the sky?"

Dave could only marvel to himself, "Lord, You're so faithful to Your promise." He had tears in his eyes as he gazed at the letters.

They watched them for several minutes, sitting there silently. And then, all the small clouds seemed to slowly spread apart and dissolve, until there was only a wisp left in the sky, and that too vanished. Lara was visibly moved and shaken.

She turned to Dave and spoke in low tones, which were nevertheless filled with conviction.

"If I ever doubt God again," she said, "I'll remember the day He wrote my name in the sky."

Dave continued to be amazed, and also thankful that he had seen the sight with her; he knew if she had been alone when she saw the vision, and later told him, he might have wondered if she was telling him out of gratitude, to make him happy. It demonstrated to him that God, the God he preached and whom he believed was the Deliverer of those caught in addiction, was a God of miracles. Lara would have a testimony of His love and power she could never forget, and that would also bear witness to others.

There was another promise which the Lord had made concerning Lara, on that timeless afternoon in Duncan, which was also fulfilled in its course. Before many months passed, the day of Lara's wedding to Jason had come. All the immediate members of Lara's family arrived for the ceremony at Cornerstone Church, as well as congregants of ACF and Central Baptist who had prayed for Lara during her struggle; members of Dave's own family were present as well.

Lara arrived at the church looking exquisite in her white bridal gown, her face glowing, and her dark eyes dancing with happiness. Dave could not find the words to describe how lovely she appeared as she walked down the aisle to join her husband-to-be at the altar. He moved over to the lectern to read the scriptures chosen for the marriage liturgy. As he did so, he became filled with emotion, remembering the first time he and Lara read these words together from First Corinthians 13 at the beginning of their shared journey, when she had declared she was an atheist: *"Love suffers long and is patient … love never fails."*

Pastor John addressed the couple in words which rang with warmth and encouragement; he had discerned the spiritual challenges the couple faced, and the momentous nature of their commitment to each other. First, however, he made one of his little remarks designed to set them at their ease.

"Lara," he said, "I noticed as you came up the aisle you looked a little nervous. Just fix your gaze on the altar, and remember these words, 'I'll altar hymn, I'll altar hymn.'"

And after that the ceremony was a blur for Dave, filled as he was with gratitude for this wonderful outcome, and conscious that a spirit of rejoicing was permeating the hearts of all present.

At the reception, Lara's parents came up to speak to Dave. Her father had tears welling in his eyes. "Thank you for not listening to us when we advised you her case was hopeless," he said in fervent tones. "Thank you for never giving up on her ... If it weren't for you, this wouldn't be happening," added Lara's mother, "She wouldn't be alive."

Yet in the midst of the great happiness, there was also a tincture of sorrow; something was beginning, but something else was ending. When he and Lara had a moment to speak, he said to her, "Lara, it's time for me to leave the circle." He had led her back into the center of her family and she was now the focus of their admiration, just as God had promised. Now it was time for him to step away. She knew instantly what he meant, and gave him a hug, saying with her heart in her voice, "Thank you so much for everything."

Later Dave stood a little apart with his mother, watching Lara with her new husband during the reception. "What a transformation!" she said to him.

Dave nodded his agreement. "She is completely changed, everything about her is beautiful. It's like watching one of those old romantic movies with a happy ending."

"And that is due so much to your own faithfulness in being there for her, day and night, over all this time," said his mother. Then she added, "Dave, do you remember when we were talking about you and your three brothers, and about your different characters?"

"Yes, I do, when we were downtown at the Harbor, just before I started the ministry."

"And I told you then I knew what your special gift was?"

"I remember."

"I want to tell you what you have, Dave–it's a very special gift–that of *a compassionate heart.* It is this which has led you into this work, and brought such a change in so many lives."

Dave acknowledged the tribute with a smile, but at the same time he shook his head. He knew that, whatever compassion he possessed, it was just a faint reflection of that in the heart of Jesus Christ, who had laid down His life for Lara, for himself, and for the whole world. He understood also that, even though God had fulfilled His pledges to Lara in such faithfulness, there were other assurances yet to be brought to pass in their time. In the words of the Apostle Peter, He has given to us *exceedingly great and precious promises ...*

> *That the genuineness of your faith, being much more precious than gold that perishes, though it is tested by fire, may be found to praise, honor, and glory at the revelation of Jesus Christ"* (1 Peter 1:7).

CHAPTER 50
A Voice of the Wings

IN HIS OWN life, Dave was becoming intensely aware of the fleeting nature of time, and that, in the words of the Apostle John, *"the world is passing away along with its desires, but whoever does the will of God abides forever"* (1 John 2:17, ESV). He expressed a similar idea in one of his lyrics, suggesting also his belief that the gift of song has a power to endure when all else has been taken:

A VOICE OF THE WINGS

Listen to the cry from high above
As silent feathers rush toward the sun
In vain, the messenger of heaven's love
Scans the earth to see what has been done.

And her voice is the lilt of the last
Of the world that is passing she sings
Now nothing is left to be heard
But the song on a voice of the wings
She was the first, she is the last
And God alone holds fast
To the song on a voice of the wings.

The last of symphonies the earth will hear
The only traveler left to search the sky
The last of tiny ships to sail the sea
The only song, the skylark's distant cry.
With nowhere in the world for her to go

She rests her wings on some forgotten wind
A feather floats to the stillness left below
The final gift that she will ever send.

For her voice is the lilt of the last
Of the world that is passing she sings
Now nothing is left to be heard
But the song on a voice of the wings
She was the first, she is the last
And God alone holds fast
To the song on a voice of the wings.

Some other poems Dave wrote around the same time gave utterance to a new hope that was springing in his heart, concerning the joy that might be experienced during this brief sojourn on earth:

SOMEONE IS WAITING

It never really matters how it ends,
There'll be those lonely nights awake
That bring back memories and mistakes
That you never realize—'til it's too late.

And there'll be calls from all your friends
Who never know quite what to say,
You tell them everything's okay,
But they have to say they're sorry, anyway.

But there's something you're missing in all of the pain,
Something you're missing that you might have gained ...

Someone is waiting,
Someone is waiting for someone just like you—
Who understands what you are going through,
Someone who's been there too;
And with every reason to live,
And with so much love to give,
That someone is waiting for you,
Someone is waiting—for you.

So it never really matters how it ends,
It's only love until it's gone—
So don't look back, just carry on
Until that someone who was waiting for you—
Comes along.

HEAR AND SEE

Hear my song, and come to me,
Leave me not alone,
For my song is a song of love
A love that I want for my own.
A treasured love, of which I dream
That all the poets have known,
Hear my song and come to me
Leave me not alone.

See my dreams, and you'll see why
The nights are cold and long,
For my dreams are dreams of you
And a love that's true and strong;
But nights are dark and lonely,
Long hours that are hard to face,
See my dreams and you'll understand
There are hopes I cannot erase.

Hear my thoughts, and you'll know why
I long to hear your voice,
No matter what is done or said,
This only is my choice;
Take my love, for love is all
I have to give or take,
Take my heart and take it now,
How long, dear, must I wait?

And if perchance you want me not
Then all my dreams are vain,

And I'll not need to dream again
My sun shall drown in rain;
But if your love is for me alone
Then please, please tell me so,
For if I don't hear words of love
Then I shall turn and go.

This is my dream, my every hope
That your love shall be mine,
Blend in perfection in our lives
And as in poems, a perfect rhyme.

So hear my song and come to me,
Let love take up the throne
Remember what the poets said,
That you're my flesh and bone,
Listen to the words I sing
Uttered for you, my own,
For my song is a song of love
For you, and you alone.

That story, of how these hopes were fulfilled, is for another time. Dave was yet to travel to Israel, where he would commence a whole new ministry as a lay pastor. There also he met his future wife, Lesley, and shared with her some of the amazing events that had occurred throughout his life, as a testimony to God's love, His power to do wonderful things in the lives of those who come to Him, and His longing to draw all peoples to Himself.

EPILOGUE

SADLY, DAVE PASSED away in 2019, and the church hall where his Celebration of Life was held in Victoria was crammed with the friends he had made in the different spheres of his life: the worlds of law enforcement, music, and the church. David Foster also traveled from Los Angeles, and in his eulogy spoke some heartfelt words:

I've always been annoyed when I attend a memorial and the speaker gets up and talks about themselves. Well, apologies in advance, but I have to do that for just a moment or two. I met our dear Dave when I was playing piano at the Forge; I was eighteen, he was a few years older. Night after night he would come, sit and totally immerse himself in our music. I would soon come to befriend him, and learn that Dave Richardson was a gentle soul who loved, and I mean loved, music.

I told my mother about this wonderful policeman who loved music and was hanging out with us, and she said to me, "You know, I think he's working undercover and just wants to bust all the musicians that might be doing drugs." Of course, as the months went by, she learned that she was very wrong, and he became a dear friend to my entire family.

My relationship with Dave in those early days was really a love affair—we had a bromance before the word was invented. Night after night after night we would go to Paul's Restaurant and eat chips and gravy and talk about music—we couldn't get enough. And then we would hang out at his place until the sun came up and play records—all night, every night—teaching each other about certain singers or groups, analyzing songs, song structure, guitar solos, harmonies, lyrics, all things music. At this point I just figured he was a cop by day and a music lover by night.

And then, one night, he sprang it on me: "Hey, you know, I'm a songwriter too!" I'm thinking to myself, "Oh God, how am I going to get out of this; this guy has to suck. He's a cop that loves music, not a musician that loves being a cop; I'm qualified, he's not." Well, it goes on the list of "When you're wrong, be wrong big."

He was, as we all now know, a masterful wordsmith. He said things that we were all feeling, but he said it on paper in a way that it had never been said before. The pen was his gun—not his police holster—and he was a deadly shot.

These beautiful lyrics pouring out of him—it was almost like they came through him, not from him. The story of him writing one of the greatest love songs ever is well documented, so I won't go into detail, except to say that the song "Wildflower" helped my career as much as it did his. I will forever be in his debt for that; it was just the jumpstart that I needed.

Dave had a beautiful way of treating everyone with kindness, and more importantly, equality. I guess you couldn't really write those beautiful lyrics time and time again and not be a person that understood sympathy and empathy and the human condition to its fullest. He never walked towards the spotlight, probably because his light from within shined so brightly. He was soft but not weak, he was calm but not complacent, he was quiet but he could always be heard.

I never felt judged by Dave. I certainly have done some things in my life that I'm sure he didn't approve of, but I never, and I mean never, felt his disapproval. That's pretty remarkable over a friendship of some fifty years. And he had a wicked sense of humor. In those early years, he thought it would be really funny if one night he had one of his on-duty Saanich cops follow me home from the Forge and pull me over. And they did, and they handcuffed me and put me in the back of the police car, and I was scared out of my mind: What had I done? Where were they taking me? And then I hear over the radio a roar of laughter from the police station with Dave leading the charge, laughing his ass off. On reflection, I wish he were here to do that to me one more time.

I guess the ultimate turn of events, again well documented, was Dave's decision to go to Jerusalem and, as he put it, do God's work—the ultimate sacrifice. But it made him so happy, and he and Lesley built a life on giving instead of taking—hard for some of us to understand, but it made perfect sense to Dave Richardson.

I had never been to Israel but last summer I traveled there and got to spend time with Dave in his element in Jerusalem. He was so happy there, and full of purpose and doing such great work. I feel so lucky that I was able to make that trip last year and see Dave in all of his glory—doing what he loved doing. In all honesty, it made me feel a bit inadequate, but that wasn't Dave's intention; I think he loved that he could host me on his home turf and his own terms. It was, to say the least, very enlightening. I felt so proud of everything that he had accomplished at that moment …

But we will let Dave have the final word.

Around the same time as Dave's ministry to Lara drew to its conclusion, a major literary competition was held in Victoria, in conjunction with an art exhibit. A First Nations artist had drawn a picture of an eagle with a flint its claw, and the task was to write a poem or essay as a response to the picture. Dave did not learn of the competition until the day before entries were closed, but when he sat down to write a poem, which he called "The Beneficiary," it was once again as if the words flowed from heaven, and took him just a little longer than it had taken to write "Wildflower."

His poem went on to win first prize in the competition. When he arrived at the award ceremony he discovered five hundred people present, and that he was expected to come on stage and give a recital. Fortunately, he found in his suit pocket a rough handwritten copy, and after he read it received a standing ovation. Later, Jim Vining set the poem to music, bringing the words and melody together in an exquisite harmony.

In the poem, Dave expressed some of his ideas about God's wisdom and love, the secrets of creation and the beginning of all things. It is a profound meditation that reveals the depth of his intellectual and spiritual life, and illuminates for us some of the eternal mysteries that encompass us as we journey through our lives under the overarching presence and love of God:

THE BENEFICIARY

Will I ever be entitled to the knowledge that you hold?
For I thirst and I am starving in my mind,
And though I am secure within the future of my soul,
There are histories my heart has yet to find.

How did it all begin, from the void you live within?
Through eternities where none but you exist,
From an endless parallel You joined the lines of Cause and Will,
Creating life from out of the abyss.

You alone have been where time itself cannot survive,
And I long to see beyond the edge of space,
I'd like to look at Heaven through the vision in your eyes,
Or look upon the wisdom on your face.

When did you decide that it was time to cut the key,
That unlocked all the darkness to the light?
Did you breathe upon some spark floating through infinity,
To set the skies on fire in the night?

There are birds with eyes of fire lighting diamonds in the sky,
As the blaze above continues to expand,
With ever changing hues in reds and greens and blues,
In perfection from the Artist's gentle hand.

I am mortal. Life will end, but I shall live to live again,
If I am favored whatsoever in your sight,
Give me time enough to live to enjoy the gifts you give,
And finally, let me shine within your light.

Let my shadow fly through your vast and endless sky,
That I might see the future and the past,
And when this captive life is through, I will come to realize
That my spirit and my soul are free at last.

ENDNOTES

PROLOGUE

1 B.J. (Bonnie Jean) Cook was David Foster's first wife and the mother of his first child, Amy. An article by Adrian Chamberlain that appeared in the *Times Colonist* pays tribute to her talent. In it, David also acknowledged the debt he owed to his ex-wife for her help in facilitating his career. See: "B.J. Cook: Life of a Rock Survivor." Olografix. October 23, 2007 (www.olografix.org/knees/dfnet2/?p=302#astash.OaBOT2QT.dtbs)

2 The beautiful, sustained song the skylark pours out after soaring high into the sky has long inspired musicians and poets. Perhaps the most celebrated of these works is the exquisite classical piece "The Lark Ascending" by Ralph Vaughan-Williams, first performed in 1920. Although English settlers tried to introduce the bird into North America, they succeeded only on southern Vancouver Island, where Foster lived while growing up.

CHAPTER 1: A MILLION MILES OF DAYDREAMS

3 The largest and oldest corporation in Canada, established in England in 1670 to seek a Northwest passage to the Pacific, and subsequently engaging in the fur trade. Eventually the enterprise came to operate on vast areas of Canada and the northwestern United States, and still remains one of the largest marketing entities in the world. For fascinating details of its history, see: https://canadiangeographic.ca/articles/the-untold-story-of-the-hudsons-bay-company/

4 One of the oldest continuously published music magazines in the United States. It began publishing in 1942, was issued monthly, and featured the lyrics to many popular songs of the time. In the 1970s its focus changed to hard rock, and it finally ceased publication in 2008.

5 In Canada this weather phenomenon is most common in southern Alberta. The winds originate on the Pacific coast, climb the Rockies, then warm significantly as they drop down the eastern slopes, bringing astonishing temperature changes of up to twenty degrees, and giving Albertans a short respite from winter's icy grip.

CHAPTER 3: NATURAL BEAUTY, UNNATURAL EVIL

6 Macbeth's famous soliloquy in Act I, Scene 3 comes after the witches have prophesied that he will be king of Scotland. His ambition has been fired by this forecast, and his thoughts reveal he is already beginning to contemplate murder. Immediately as he does so, it appears to him that conventional understandings of good and evil are obscured and overthrown. Shakespeare's amazing insight suggests that humanity's corrupted desires are the source of relativistic philosophies.

7 Retrieved from one of Dave's handwritten letters to a friend dating from that period in his life.

CHAPTER 5: DAVID AND DAVID

8 A video recording of Shani Wallace singing "Reaching Far Too High" can be found at http://www.youtube.com/watch?v=d-CMPV-7yHc.

CHAPTER 7: LIVING THROUGH THE LOVE GENERATION

9 The beach Dave refers to is located on the west coast of southern Vancouver Island, looking across the Juan de Fuca Strait toward Washington State. The surging blue waters of the Pacific and glimpses of marine life such as orcas and seals provide a wild beauty.

CHAPTER 8: GOODBYE TO ALL THAT

10 The name given to the all-powerful dictator who appears in George Orwell's novel *1984*.

11 The 1950s was a golden age for the auto industry in America. The "Big Three," General Motors, Ford and Chrysler, implemented technological and design breakthroughs and produced a dazzling range of new models. Cars became lower, longer, and wider, featured wings and tailpins and shone with chrome. The 1955 Ford Thunderbird was the preferred choice of icons like Frank Sinatra and also the vehicle in which Marilyn Monroe and Arthur Miller drove to their wedding ceremony. Hence America was obsessed by cars in the 1950s, and teenagers like Dave shared the craze.

CHAPTER 17: "MAYBE YOU'RE IN THERE"

12 This rendition of "Maybe You're In There" can be found on Jim Vining's website, together with many of his other beautiful songs, as well as a number of pieces he created in collaboration with Dave. "JimViningMusic" (https://jimviningmusic.com)

CHAPTER 18: THE "MAN'S MAN" OFFICER

13 For Geordon's subsequent career, see "Geordon Rendle," Youth for Christ Canada. Date accessed: August 3, 2023 (https://yfc.ca>team>geordon-rendle)

CHAPTER 19: THE KNIGHT AND THE SHERIFF

14 "Sir Galahad" is a poem by Alfred, Lord Tennyson, published in 1842. It tells the story of Galahad's quest to find the Holy Grail, the mysterious vessel Jesus used at the Last Supper. The opening lines of the poem characterize him as a formidable knight, whose youthful vigor is undergirded by spiritual purity. Many other knights aspire to achieve the vision, but it is to the Christ-like Sir Galahad alone that the sacred chalice is finally disclosed in its glory.

15 Another reference to the movie comes from an unexpected source. In a 2020 book, conservative writer Rod Dreher investigates what gave opponents of regimes in Eastern Europe courage to fight against totalitarianism. Václav Benda and his wife, Kamila, were members of the Czech dissident movement, when in 1979 the Czechoslovak state sentenced Václav to four years in prison. He survived to see the fall of communism in 1989, and his friend Václav Havel become the first president of a free Czechoslovakia. Václav and Kamila are described by their children:

"Our parents were heroes for us. My father was the sheriff from *High Noon* ... Watching *High Noon* really formed our way of fighting against evil. Everyone is asking the sheriff to leave so that the town will have no problems from the bad guys. But the sheriff comes back nevertheless, because his virtue and honor can't allow him to leave. He is looking for assistance, but no one wants to do that. In some way, this was our family's story." Dreher, Rod. *Live Not by Lies* (Penguin Publishing Group, Kindle Edition, 2020), pp. 134-135.

CHAPTER 23: HEROES

16 Prairie College (formerly PBI) is an interdenominational Christian college in Three Hills, Alberta, which recently celebrated its 100-year anniversary. "Prairie's strong mission emphasis caused Prairie graduates to spread around the globe…from war-torn France to the savannas of Africa to the jungles of South America and to remote Asian villages." "Prairie College to Celebrate 100 Years," by Nicolle Ioannidis, June 28, 1922 (https://www.threehillscapital.com/news/10030-prairie-college-to-celebrate-100-years)

17 The words of Don's son, Paul Andrew Richardson, author of *A Certain Risk: Living Your Faith at the Edge* (Zondervan 2010).

CHAPTER 24: MOTHERSONG

18 The first stanza of the 1794 poem by Romantic poet William Blake, "London," a fierce indictment of the evils of the Industrial Revolution. The poet describes the scenes of misery and despair which can be seen in the poorer parts of the city, close to the River Thames. The institutions that wield power have failed to pursue a society based on justice, freedom and godliness; therefore, those in the lower echelons are trapped and enslaved, both physically and spiritually, and their faces bear silent witness to their plight. Even the very River Thames itself is "charter'd," held in bondage and controlled by the merchants and other oppressors.

CHAPTER 26: THE THIRD KIND OF LOVE

19 The Apostle Paul's description of the actions characteristic of love is one of the most famous New Testament passages. The word Paul uses throughout the passage to signify "love" is the Greek word *agape*, which denotes that a whole new understanding of love has dawned upon the world. In the Hebrew Scriptures, the commandments to love God and neighbor were foundational (Deuteronomy 6:5, Leviticus 19:18), and Jesus too puts the command to love at the center of His preaching.

The revelation of God as love became the core of the gospel message, yet the life and sacrificial death of Jesus created a whole new understanding of what that love is: the suffering, self-giving love that is poured out for others, even for those who are unworthy. This is the divine love, which Christians from earliest times called *agape*. The word is not found in classical Greek. Over against the concept of passionate human love, which the ancient Greeks called *eros*, the apostles were compelled to find another word to describe the ideal of altruistic love that emerged in their understanding. *Agape*, therefore, was destined to become the defining characteristic of the followers of Christ, the supreme example of love.

CHAPTER 28: DOING THE MOONWALK

20 From Shakespeare's *Macbeth*, Act V, scene iii.

21 This is the dance move in which a performer glides backward on the stage, even while appearing to walk forward. Jackson did not invent it; dancers stretching back at least to the 1940s entertained audiences with "the backslide"; however, the young pop icon brought his own particular energy to the move. He first broadcast it in May 1983 in the TV special, "Motown 25: Yesterday, Today, Forever," mesmerizing an audience of 47 million. Jackson's surreal step, coasting backward across the stage, became his signature move, and he included the moonwalk in subsequent tours and performances.

22 Isaiah 35 is a powerful poetic promise to the people of Judah, who during the sixth century B.C. were living as exiles in Babylon. Their land had been conquered by the Babylonian army under Nebuchadnezzar, and their temple destroyed, and the only way back was through a desolate wilderness–the *midbar*. Yet the prophet assures the Judahites the barren places on the highway to their homeland will be transformed into a paradise, a source of healing and renewal.

The exiles did return as promised; however, no such transformation of the desert between Babylon and Jerusalem is recorded, which suggests Isaiah is speaking of a future *spiritual* transformation. In Matthew 11:4-5 Jesus referred to the passage as prophesying His miraculous works of healing, and in John 4:14 He promised the gift of "living water" to the Samaritan Woman at the well. There is a deep spiritual thirst in the souls of men and women, and the need for divine power to be poured out, as the life-giving streams poured out in the desert cause it to blossom. This is the essence of the work of Christ.

CHAPTER 30: THE QUARTER MILLION CONTRACT

23 See: "Capital Crimes: 1990 Cumberland murders led to longest, costliest criminal trial(s) in Canadian history," by Bruce Deachman. July 23, 2022 (https://ottawacitizen.com/news/local-news/capital-crimes-1990-cumberland -murders-lead-to-longest-costliest-criminal-trials)

CHAPTER 32: THE CHRIST OF COMPASSION

24 The remarkable story of the raising Lazarus, in which Jesus declares Himself as "the Resurrection and the Life," can be found in Chapter 11 of the Gospel of John, where His strong emotional response to the situation is also depicted.

"CHAPTER 35: PITY THE MOON

25 One of many online articles: "Raymond Russell Rafuse Murdered Four at a 1988 Calgary Party." Christopher di Armani. July 29, 2020 (https://christopherdarmani.com/14870/crime/canadian-mass-murders/raymond-russell-rafuse-murdered-four-injured-one-at-a-Calgary-party)

CHAPTER 36: I CALIGULA

26 One of many online articles: "True Crime Canada: A mother-daughter double homicide still haunts B.C." by Jeremy Hainsworth. December 17, 2022 (https://www.vancouverisawesome.com/highlights/true-crime-canada-a-mother-daughter-double-homicide-still-haunts-B.C.-53065...)

27 This is a role-playing game first published in 1974, which allowed players to create their own characters who then embark upon adventures within a fantasy world. The game has been the subject of numerous controversies, especially during the 1980s, and is alleged to have encouraged Satanism, witchcraft, suicide, and murder. The moral consternation appears to have diminished since that time. From "Dungeons & Dragons Controversies." Wikipedia. Date accessed: July 27, 2023 (https://en.wikipedia.org/wiki/Dungeons_%26_Dragons_controversies)

CHAPTER 40: THE GOD OF MIRACLES

28 An appeal is made to the starry skies as evidence of God's infinite greatness and wisdom. Through His omnipotence He has created these heavenly luminaries, and through His omnipotence He knows their number and all their names. He brings out these armies (the meaning of "hosts"), which keep their rank and order and constantly perform their courses as if under the direction of a mighty general. And when the human raises his eyes to contemplate the sublime harmony and beauty of the heavenly worlds, he is naturally led to the contemplation of eternity.

CHAPTER 41: THE GREAT EXCHANGE

29 In 1 Corinthians, the Apostle Paul deals with a wide range of issues affecting the church he had established in this cosmopolitan Mediterranean city, including immorality, factions, litigation, and participation in pagan rites. His purpose was to exhort the believers there to leave behind their worldly values, and live according to their newly created identity as saints of God, and shining through the remonstrations of the great Apostle to the Gentiles is his tender heart of love toward his new converts.

CHAPTER 42: IT'S NO SECRET WHAT GOD CAN DO

30 In Jeremiah's day these "great and mighty" things were the actions God would undertake in bringing the people of Judah back to their own land after seventy years captivity in Babylon. Yet the words looked beyond these events, to the revelation of spiritual blessings which would later come about, the things God would make known that are unattainable by human discernment. As Paul wrote later: "Eye has not seen, nor ear heard, Nor have entered into the heart of man The things God has prepared for those who love Him. But God has revealed them to us through His Spirit" (1 Corinthians 2:9-10).

CHAPTER 45: CARLA

31 From a speech attributed to Chief Seattle, also known as Sealth (c. 1786-1866), a leader of the Suquamish and Duwamish Native American tribes in what is now Washington State. Endowed with the gift of oratory, he spoke at a meeting called by Governor Isaac Stevens to discuss the surrender or sale of native land; the exact date and location of his speech is debated, but the most common version is that he delivered it on March 11, 1854, to an outdoor gathering in Seattle. Nor is it certain what he actually said, for he spoke in the Lushhootseed language, and his words were then translated into Chinook, and from thence into English.

Nevertheless, his speech in various versions has become famed for its heartfelt declaration of the values of his people, while the village named after him has since grown into a large metropolis known for its beauty and innovation. The quotations of his speech have been taken from Ted Perry's film script for *Home* (produced by the Southern Baptist Radio and Television Commission, 1972). "Ted Perry: Chief Seattle's Speech." University of Washington. Date accessed: August 30, 2023

("https://www,washington.edu/uwired/outreach/cspn/Website/Classroom%20materials/Reading%20the%20region/Texts%20by%20and%20about%20natives)

CHAPTER 47: A FREE AND GENTLE FLOWER, GROWING WILD

32 From a private email written by David Foster to Dave, 2016.

CHAPTER 48: THE LOST CHORD

33 One of the most popular poems of Victorian England was "The Lost Chord" by Adelaide Proctor, published in 1860. It imagines the reflections of a young woman who is improvising on the organ, and inadvertently plays a chord that is so transcendent and beautiful she believes it must have been sent from heaven. She tries to find it again, but fails, and concludes she will only hear it once more in the afterlife:

> *I have sought, but I seek it vainly*
> *That one lost chord divine*
> *Which came from the soul of the organ*
> *And entered into mine*

In 1187 the poem was set to music by Britain's foremost composer, Arthur Sullivan, as he sat at the bedside of his dying brother, and thereafter recorded by many singers, including Enrico Caruso, who sang it at the Metropolitan Opera House in 1912 at a benefit concert for the families of victims of the *Titanic* disaster.

ACKNOWLEDGMENTS

IN 2006, DAVID moved to Israel, to take part in a ministry feeding the poor and homeless in Jerusalem. When he met the woman he would marry in 2009, Lesley, he related to her many of the tales from his days of songwriting and police work, as well as the accounts of his ministry with addicts. She was entranced by his stories and knew they must be set down, and the result is found in the preceding pages. Dave and Lesley have many to thank for their help and encouragement whilst writing this book, including:

- Lara, most especially for her patience and courage as Dave dealt her some tough measures of love;
- And all the others whom Dave counseled, who placed themselves so willingly under his care; it was inspirational to hear the testimonies of so many transformed lives.
- Both our families; most particularly:
- Doug and Marlene, for their truly exceptional warmth and hospitality whenever we visited Victoria;
- Lesley's sisters: Janet, Sarah and Kate, for their unfailing love and support, as well as her other "sisters," Joanna Tait and Nicki Jeffery;
- The late Don Richardson and his wife Carol for their loving family commitment and amazing teaching ministry which has enriched us all;
- And many others, especially:
- David Foster, for his enduring friendship with Dave over so many decades; it was marvelous to share the adventure with him from the beginning;
- Valley Hennell, incomparable friend, wise adviser, and manager of "Wildflower" for so many years;

- Jim Vining, for his creative partnership, and his beautiful and sensitive musical renderings of Dave's poems;
- Geordon Rendle, who honored his "Staff Sergeant" and built such a rewarding relationship with Dave during his years with Saanich Police;
- Pete Schibli, called by Dave "a cross between Marlon Brando and James Dean," and with whom he sailed the beautiful seas around Vancouver Island;
- The late Bob Holmes, who together with his wife Jean was a tower of strength to Dave, and a never-failing source of wisdom;
- Our church family in Victoria, especially John and Lynne Schaper, faithful shepherds of the flock, and the precious folk at Temple Yeshua;
- Our church family in Jerusalem, most particularly David and Carol Pileggi of Christ Church, George Jones, Carrie Franke, Rosalind Hershkovitz, and Irene Bredlow of Mount Zion Fellowship in Galilee;
- Jay and Meridel Rawlings, Canadian-Israelis, who have written a book called *Miracles Among the Nations* which details the remarkable events which took place in their ministry over many decades;
- "The Gang" in Victoria–the late Helen Russell, Bernadette Harding, Boyd and Cora Rempel, and Maggie Simpson–our beloved friends–for all the special times of sharing at Romeo's;
- And all the others who have strengthened us with their prayers, enriched us with their fellowship, and inspired us with so many demonstrations of lovingkindness.

ABOUT LESLEY

Lesley Ann Richardson is originally from Australia, where she grew up and studied English Literature and Theology. Later she moved to Israel, where she worked for several international Christian organizations, and met and married her husband, David Richardson, in Christ Church in Jerusalem's Old City. David was a Canadian with a remarkable life story, which she has set down in the book you hold in your hands. She has also published *Bible Gems from Jerusalem,* an award-winning work on history and theology, and *Creating Beauty from the Abyss*, a biography of Holocaust survivor and artist Sam Herciger. In her writing Lesley desires to focus on *"the Love that moves the sun and all the stars."*

www.lesleyannrichardson.com

aletheiariches@gmail.com

Dear Reader,

If you have enjoyed reading my book, please do leave a review on Amazon or Goodreads. A few kind words would be enough. This would be greatly appreciated.

Alternatively, if you have read my book as a Kindle e-book, you could leave a rating. That is just one simple click, indicating how many stars you think this book deserves.

Thank you very much in advance,

Lesley